Huggable Crochet

Cute and Cuddly Animals from Around the World

Christine Lucas

KRAUSE PUBLICATIONS

Cincinnati, Ohio

www.fwmedia.com

15   14   13   12   11   5   4   3   2   1

DISTRIBUTED IN CANADA BY FRASER DIRECT
100 Armstrong Avenue
Georgetown, ON, Canada L7G 5S4
Tel: (905) 877-4411

DISTRIBUTED IN THE U.K. AND EUROPE BY F&W MEDIA INTERNATIONAL
Brunel House, Newton Abbot, Devon, TQ12 4PU, England
Tel: (+44) 1626 323200
Fax: (+44) 1626 323319
Email: enquiries@fwmedia.com

DISTRIBUTED IN AUSTRALIA BY CAPRICORN LINK
P.O. Box 704, S. Windsor NSW, 2756 Australia
Tel: (02) 4577-3555

SRN: Z9987
ISBN-13: 978-1-4402-1423-3

Edited by Stefanie Laufersweiler
Designed by Corrie Schaffeld
Cover photography by Corrie Schaffeld
Photography by John Carrico, Alias Imaging
Photo styling by Lauren Emmerling
Illustrations by Christine Lucas
Production coordinated by Greg Nock

Dedication

For my husband, who is the personification of all my greatest dreams come true.

Acknowledgments

Thank you to all of the people who worked so hard to help make this book become a reality.

Metric Conversion Chart

To convert	to	multiply by
Inches	Millimeters	25.4
Millimeters	Inches	0.04
Inches	Centimeters	2.54
Centimeters	Inches	0.4
Feet	Centimeters	30.5
Centimeters	Feet	0.03
Yards	Meters	0.9
Meters	Yards	1.1

Contents

Introduction

In this book you'll find crochet patterns for nineteen of the most loveable animals you'll ever create. Unlike others you may have made in the past, these generously sized stuffed animals are truly huggable, measuring from twelve to eighteen inches (thirty to forty-six centimeters) tall.

As you make these projects, I invite you to come on a magical tour of the animal kingdom with me. Inside you'll find animals from all over the world. You are sure to find a cuddly friend that you just can't live without.

Animal lovers of all ages will enjoy these charming creatures. Yours might become the perfect accent piece on the sofa of a themed room. If you have little ones running around, they make the perfect gift for children to snuggle with at night. For this reason, you'll find no choking hazards such as buttons or wire in the patterns.

Each animal appears in two different color palettes—one more realistic, the other whimsical—although they will look adorable in whatever colors you choose. I've created names and background stories for each of the animals here for an extra element of fun. However, the ones you make will be unique and have their own personalities, so give them their own names, backgrounds and maybe even a homemade birth certificate.

I think that crocheting should be fun and relaxing. So, while designing these patterns, I tried to use only the simplest stitches, which are explained and shown step by step. Whether you're eight years old or eighty, there's no better feeling than seeing the smile of a loved one when you give them a handmade gift.

Now, go ahead, take a peek inside—they won't bite!

CHAPTER 1

The Pranksters: Forest Critters

Each ecosystem has its own mischievous inhabitants, but the critters in this forest take mayhem to a whole new level. The squirrel thrives on snatching your food and watching you hunt for it, while the sneaky snake likes to give you a scare. The fun-loving snail and raccoon enjoy playing harmless mind games with their friends. Whatever these tricksters are up to, you can almost always count on them catching you off guard. So, brace yourself and stay sharp as you stroll through their territory!

Sly
the
Snake

Sly the Snake

Sly is the sneakiest of all the pranksters. He loves nothing more than to scare the living daylights out of anyone who crosses his path. Slithering along tree branches until an unsuspecting soul comes along, he then shoots out like a lightning bolt with a hiss. Startled for a second, everyone soon realizes that it's just Sly up to his same old tricks, while he slithers away and has a good, hearty laugh over a prank well played.

YARN

Super bulky (6) yarn in 3 colors; 150 yds (137m) of color **A**, 75 yds (69m) of color **B** and 75 yds (69m) of color **C**

Medium (4) yarn in 1 color; 10 yds (9m) of color **D**

*The project shown on page 7 uses Lion Brand Wool-Ease Thick & Quick (80% acrylic/20% wool, 106 yds [97m], 6 oz [170g]) in Cranberry (**A**), Black (**B**) and Butterscotch (**C**) and Lion Brand Vanna's Choice (acrylic, 170 yds [155m], 3.5 oz [100g]) in Black (**D**).*

HOOKS AND NOTIONS

G/6 (4mm) and H/8 (5mm) crochet hooks • Size 13 darning needle • Polyester fiberfill • Stuffing stick

GAUGE

5 hdc and 4 rows = 2" (5cm) using size H/8 (5mm) hook

FINISHED SIZE

Approx 36" (91cm) long

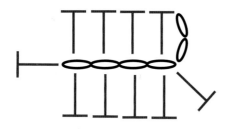

Figure 1 (rings symbolize chain stitches, Ts symbolize single crochet stitches)

Body

Make 1.

Rnd 1 (head end): With H/8 (5mm) hook and A, stuffing as work progresses, ch 6, TW, 1 hdc in 3rd ch from hook and each of next 2 chs, 3 hdc in next ch, working along unused foundation of chs, 1 hdc in each of next 2 chs, 2 hdc in next ch, sl st last hdc to first hdc—10 sts (Fig. 1).

Rnd 2: Ch 2, TW, 1 hdc in each st to end of rnd, sl st last hdc to first hdc—10 sts.

Rnd 3: Ch 2, TW, * 1 hdc in each of next 4 sts, 2 hdc in next st; rep from * one more time to end of rnd, sl st last hdc to first hdc—12 sts.

Rnd 4: Ch 2, TW, * 2 hdc in next st, 1 hdc in each of next 5 sts; rep from * one more time to end of rnd, sl st last hdc to first hdc—14 sts.

Rnd 5: Ch 2, TW, * 1 hdc in each of next 6 sts, 3 hdc in next st; rep from * one more time to end of rnd, drop A, pick up B, sl st last hdc to first hdc—18 sts.

Rnd 6: Ch 2, TW, * 3 hdc in next st, 1 hdc in each of next 8 sts; rep from * one more time to end of rnd, sl st last hdc to first hdc—22 sts.

Rnd 7: Ch 2, TW, 1 hdc in each st to end of rnd, drop B, pick up C, sl st last hdc to first hdc—22 sts.

Rnd 8: Ch 2, * hdc next 2 sts tog, 1 hdc in each of next 9 sts; rep from * one more time to end of rnd, sl st last hdc to first hdc—20 sts.

Rnd 9: Ch 2, TW, * hdc next 2 sts tog, 1 hdc in each of next 8 sts; rep from * one more time to end of rnd, drop C, pick up B, sl st last hdc to first hdc—18 sts.

Rnd 10: Ch 2, TW, 1 hdc in each st to end of rnd, sl st last hdc to first hdc—18 sts.

Rnd 11: Ch 2, TW, 1 hdc in each st to end of rnd, drop B, pick up A, sl st last hdc to first hdc—18 sts.

Rnds 12–18: Ch 2, TW, 1 hdc in each st to end of rnd, sl st last hdc to first hdc—18 sts.

Rnd 19: Ch 2, TW, 1 hdc in each st to end of rnd, drop A, pick up B, sl st last hdc to first hdc—18 sts.

Rnd 20: Ch 2, TW, * 1 hdc in each of next 8 sts, 2 hdc in next st; rep from * one more time to end of rnd, sl st last hdc to first hdc—20 sts.

Rnd 21: Ch 2, TW, 1 hdc in each st to end of rnd, drop B, pick up C, sl st last hdc to first hdc—20 sts.

Rnd 22: Ch 2, TW, 1 hdc in each st to end of rnd, sl st last hdc to first hdc—20 sts.

Rnd 23: Ch 2, TW, 1 hdc in each st to end of rnd, drop C, pick up B, sl st last hdc to first hdc—20 sts.

Rnd 24: Ch 2, TW, 1 hdc in each st to end of rnd, sl st last hdc to first hdc—20 sts.

Rnd 25: Ch 2, TW, * 1 hdc in each of next 9 sts, 2 hdc in next st; rep from * one more time to end of rnd, drop B, pick up A, sl st last hdc to first hdc—22 sts.

Rnds 26-31: Ch 2, TW, 1 hdc in each st to end of rnd, sl st last hdc to first hdc—22 sts.

Rnd 32: Ch 2, TW, * 1 hdc in each of next 10 sts, 2 hdc in next st; rep from * one more time to end of rnd, sl st last hdc to first hdc—24 sts.

Rnd 33: Ch 2, TW, 1 hdc in each st to end of rnd, drop A, pick up B, sl st last hdc to first hdc—24 sts.

Rnd 34: Ch 2, TW, 1 hdc in each st to end of rnd, sl st last hdc to first hdc—24 sts.

Rnd 35: Ch 2, TW, 1 hdc in each st to end of rnd, drop B, pick up C, sl st last hdc to first hdc—24 sts.

Rnd 36: Ch 2, TW, 1 hdc in each st to end of rnd, sl st last hdc to first hdc—24 sts.

Rnd 37: Ch 2, TW, 1 hdc in each st to end of rnd, drop C, pick up B, sl st last hdc to first hdc—24 sts.

Rnd 38: Ch 2, TW, 1 hdc in each st to end of rnd, sl st last hdc to first hdc—24 sts.

Rnd 39: Ch 2, TW, 1 hdc in each st to end of rnd, drop B, pick up A, sl st last hdc to first hdc—24 sts.

Rnds 40-46: Ch 2, TW, 1 hdc in each st to end of rnd, sl st last hdc to first hdc—24 sts.

Rnd 47: Ch 2, TW, 1 hdc in each st to end of rnd, drop A, pick up B, sl st last hdc to first hdc—24 sts.

Rnd 48: Ch 2, TW, 1 hdc in each st to end of rnd, sl st last hdc to first hdc—24 sts.

Rnd 49: Ch 2, TW, 1 hdc in each st to end of rnd, drop B, pick up C, sl st last hdc to first hdc—24 sts.

Rnd 50: Ch 2, TW, 1 hdc in each st to end of rnd, sl st last hdc to first hdc—24 sts.

Rnd 51: Ch 2, TW, 1 hdc in each st to end of rnd, drop C, pick up B, sl st last hdc to first hdc—24 sts.

Rnd 52: Ch 2, TW, 1 hdc in each st to end of rnd, sl st last hdc to first hdc—24 sts.

Rnd 53: Ch 2, TW, 1 hdc in each st to end of rnd, drop B, pick up A, sl st last hdc to first hdc—24 sts.

Rnds 54-60: Ch 2, TW, 1 hdc in each st to end of rnd, sl st last hdc to first hdc—24 sts.

Rnd 61: Ch 2, TW, 1 hdc in each st to end of rnd, drop A, pick up B, sl st last hdc to first hdc—24 sts.

Rnd 62: Ch 2, TW, 1 hdc in each st to end of rnd, sl st last hdc to first hdc—24 sts.

Rnd 63: Ch 2, TW, * 1 hdc in each of next 10 sts, hdc next 2 sts tog; rep from * one more time to end of rnd, drop B, pick up C, sl st last hdc to first hdc—22 sts.

Rnd 64: Ch 2, TW, 1 hdc in each st to end of rnd, sl st last hdc to first hdc—22 sts.

Rnd 65: Ch 2, TW, 1 hdc in each st to end of rnd, drop C, pick up B, sl st last hdc to first hdc—22 sts.

Rnd 66: Ch 2, TW, 1 hdc in each st to end of rnd, sl st last hdc to first hdc—22 sts.

Rnd 67: Ch 2, TW, * 1 hdc in each of next 9 sts, hdc next 2 sts tog; rep from * one more time to end of rnd, drop B, pick up A, sl st last hdc to first hdc—20 sts.

Rnds 68-73: Ch 2, TW, 1 hdc in each st to end of rnd, sl st last hdc to first hdc—20 sts.

Rnd 74: Ch 2, TW, * 1 hdc in each of next 8 sts, hdc next 2 sts tog; rep from * one more time to end of rnd, sl st last hdc to first hdc—18 sts.

Rnd 75: Ch 2, TW, 1 hdc in each st to end of rnd, drop A, pick up B, sl st last hdc to first hdc—18 sts.

Rnd 76: Ch 2, TW, 1 hdc in each st to end of rnd, sl st last hdc to first hdc—18 sts.

Rnd 77: Ch 2, TW, 1 hdc in each st to end of rnd, drop B, pick up C, sl st last hdc to first hdc—18 sts.

Rnd 78: Ch 2, TW, * 1 hdc in each of next 7 sts, hdc next 2 sts tog; rep from * one more time to end of rnd, sl st last hdc to first hdc—16 sts.

Rnd 79: Ch 2, TW, 1 hdc in each st to end of rnd, drop C, pick up B, sl st last hdc to first hdc—16 sts.

Rnd 80: Ch 2, TW, 1 hdc in each st to end of rnd, sl st last hdc to first hdc—16 sts.

Rnd 81: Ch 2, TW, * 1 hdc in each of next 6 sts, hdc next 2 sts tog; rep from * one more time to end of rnd, drop B, pick up A, sl st last hdc to first hdc—14 sts.

Rnds 82–85: Ch 2, TW, 1 hdc in each st to end of rnd, sl st last hdc to first hdc—14 sts.

Rnd 86: Ch 2, TW, 1 hdc in each of next 6 sts, hdc next 2 sts tog, 1 hdc in each of next 6 sts, sl st last hdc to first hdc—13 sts.

Rnd 87: Ch 2, TW, 1 hdc in each st to end of rnd, sl st last hdc to first hdc—13 sts.

Rnd 88: Ch 2, TW, 1 hdc in each of next 4 sts, hdc next 2 sts tog, 1 hdc in each of next 7 sts, sl st last hdc to first hdc—12 sts.

Rnd 89: Ch 2, TW, 1 hdc in each st to end of rnd, tie off A, pick up B, sl st last hdc to first hdc—12 sts.

Rnd 90: Ch 2, TW, 1 hdc in each of next 5 sts, hdc next 2 sts tog, 1 hdc in each of next 5 sts, sl st last hdc to first hdc—11 sts.

Rnd 91: Ch 2, TW, 1 hdc in each st to end of rnd, drop B, pick up C, sl st last hdc to first hdc—11 sts.

Rnd 92: Ch 2, TW, 1 hdc in each of next 4 sts, hdc next 2 sts tog, 1 hdc in each of next 5 sts, sl st last hdc to first hdc—10 sts.

Rnd 93: Ch 2, TW, 1 hdc in each of next 4 sts, hdc next 2 sts tog, 1 hdc in each of next 4 sts, tie off C, pick up B, sl st last hdc to first hdc—9 sts.

Rnd 94: Ch 2, TW, 1 hdc in each of next 3 sts, hdc next 2 sts tog, 1 hdc in each of next 4 sts—8 sts.

Rnd 95: Ch 2, TW, * hdc next 2 sts tog; rep from * three more times, sl st last hdc to first hdc—4 sts. Fasten off, leaving an 8" (20cm) tail. Whip stitch opening closed. Tie off and weave in ends.

Mouth and Eyes

With darning needle and D, embroider mouth and eyes as shown (Fig. 2).

Tongue

Make 1.

Row 1: With G/6 (4mm) hook and D, ch 8, TW, starting with 2nd ch from hook, work 1 sc in each of next 5 chs, ch 2. Fasten off, leaving a 5" (13cm) tail. Whip stitch base of tongue to mouth with forked end facing outward (Fig. 2). Tie off and weave in ends.

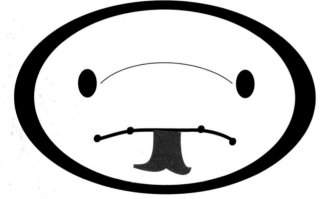

Figure 2 (front view)

Figure 2 (side view)

Stash the Squirrel

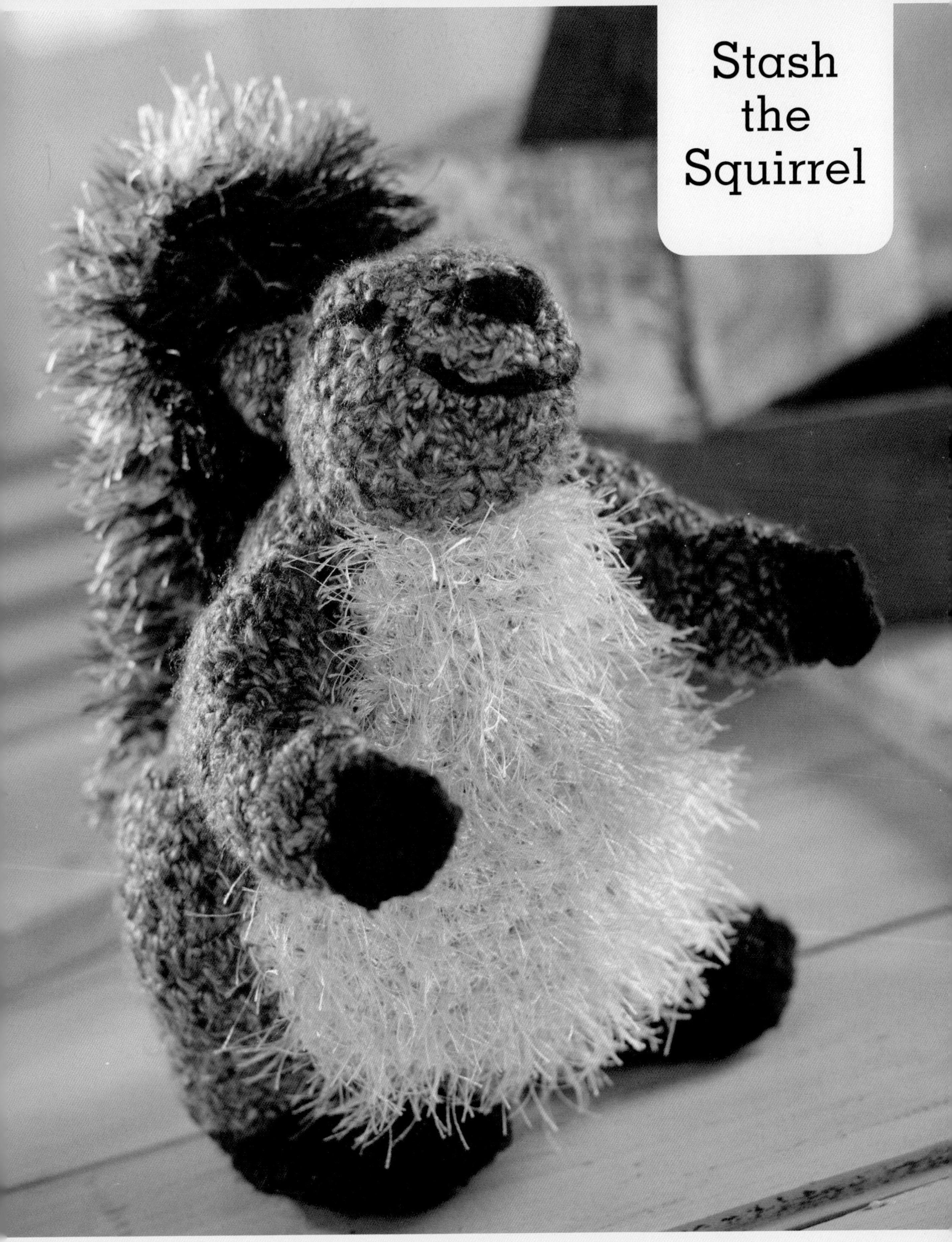

Stash the Squirrel

Squirrels are always finding nuts or trying to hide them. Stash has decided to use these skills to play practical jokes on the rest of the forest creatures. He loves to snatch up their food, hide it, then sit back, relax and watch as everyone scrambles to find their missing meal. Once you crochet one of these mischievous critters to life, be sure to keep an eye on your dinner!

YARN

Bulky (5) yarn in 1 color; 185 yds (169m) of color **A**

Bulky (5) novelty yarn in 3 colors; 95 yds (87m) of color **B**, 95 yds (87m) of color **D** and 95 yds (87m) of color **E**

Medium (4) yarn in 1 color; 6 yds (6m) of color **C**

*The project shown on page 11 uses Lion Brand Homespun (98% acrylic/2% polyester, 185 yds [169m], 6 oz [170g]) in Russet (**A**); Lion Brand Fun Fur (polyester, 64 yds [58m], 1.75 oz [50g]) in Champagne (**B**), Chocolate (**D**) and Black (**E**); and Lion Brand Vanna's Choice (acrylic, 170 yds [155m], 3.5 oz [100g]) in Black (**C**).*

HOOKS AND NOTIONS

H/8 (5mm) crochet hook • Size 13 darning needle • Polyester fiberfill • Stuffing stick

GAUGE

6 hdc and 6 rows = 2" (5cm) using size H/8 (5mm) hook

FINISHED SIZE

Approx 11" (28cm) tall

Head

Make 1.

Row 1: With A, stuffing as work progresses, ch 5, TW, 1 hdc in 3rd ch from hook and each of next 2 chs. Beg working in rnds.

Rnd 1: Ch 2, TW, 1 hdc in each of next 3 sts, 2 hdc in end of Row 1, 1 hdc in each of next 3 sts, 2 hdc in other end of Row 1, sl st last hdc to first hdc—10 sts.

Rnd 2: Ch 2, TW, 1 hdc in each of next 3 sts, 2 hdc in next st, 1 hdc in each of next 4 sts, 2 hdc in next st, 1 hdc in next st, sl st last hdc to first hdc—12 sts.

Rnd 3: Ch 2, TW, 1 hdc in each st to end of rnd, sl st last hdc to first hdc—12 sts.

Rnd 4: Ch 2, TW, * 2 hdc in next st, 1 hdc in next st, 2 hdc in next st, 1 hdc in each of next 3 sts; rep from * one more time to end of rnd, sl st last hdc to first hdc—16 sts.

Rnd 5: Ch 2, TW, * 2 hdc in next st, 1 hdc in each of next 3 sts; rep from * three more times to end of rnd, sl st last hdc to first hdc—20 sts.

Rnd 6: Ch 2, TW, * 1 hdc in each of next 3 sts, 2 hdc in next st, 1 hdc in each of next 5 sts, 2 hdc in next st; rep from * one more time, sl st last hdc to first hdc—24 sts.

Rnds 7-10: Ch 2, TW, 1 hdc in each st to end of rnd, sl st last hdc to first hdc—24 sts.

Rnd 11: Ch 2, TW, * 1 hdc in each of next 4 sts, hdc next 2 sts tog; rep from * three more times to end of rnd, sl st last hdc to first hdc—20 sts.

Rnd 12: Ch 2, TW, * 1 hdc in each of next 3 sts, hdc next 2 sts tog; rep from * three more times to end of rnd, sl st last hdc to first hdc—16 sts.

Rnd 13: Ch 2, TW, * hdc next 2 sts tog; rep from * seven more times to end of rnd, sl st last hdc to first hdc—8 sts. Fasten off, leaving an 8" (20cm) tail. Whip stitch opening closed. Tie off and weave in ends.

Body

Make 1.

Rnd 1: With A, stuffing as work progresses, ch 4, sl st last ch to first ch to make a loop.

Rnd 2: Ch 2, work 8 hdc in center of loop, sl st last hdc to first hdc—8 sts.

Rnd 3: Ch 2, TW, * 1 hdc in next st, 2 hdc in next st; rep from * three more times, sl st last hdc to first hdc—12 sts.

Rnd 4: Ch 2, TW, 2 hdc in each st to end of rnd, sl st last hdc to first hdc—24 sts.

Rnd 5: Ch 2, TW, * 1 hdc in each of next 3 sts, 2 hdc in next st; rep from * five more times to end of rnd, sl st last hdc to first hdc—30 sts.

Rnds 6-11: Ch 2, TW, 1 hdc in each st to end of rnd, sl st last hdc to first hdc—30 sts.

Figure 1 (front view)

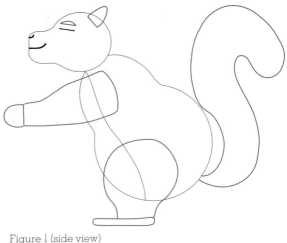

Figure 1 (side view)

Rnd 12: Ch 2, TW, * 1 hdc in next 4 sts, 2 hdc in next st; rep from * five more times to end of rnd, sl st last hdc to first hdc—36 sts.

Rnd 13: Ch 2, TW, * 1 hdc in next 3 sts, 2 hdc in next st; rep from * eight more times to end of rnd, sl st last hdc to first hdc—45 sts.

Rnd 14: Ch 2, TW, * 1 hdc in next 8 sts, 2 hdc in next st; rep from * four more times to end of rnd, sl st last hdc to first hdc—50 sts.

Rnds 15-16: Ch 2, TW, 1 hdc in each st to end of rnd, sl st last hdc to first hdc—50 sts.

Rnd 17: Ch 2, TW, * 1 hdc in next 9 sts, 2 hdc in next st; rep from * four more times to end of rnd, sl st last hdc to first hdc—55 sts.

Rnd 18: Ch 2, TW, * 1 hdc in next 10 sts, 2 hdc in next st; rep from * four more times to end of rnd, sl st last hdc to first hdc—60 sts.

Rnd 19: Ch 2, TW, 1 hdc in each st to end of rnd, sl st last hdc to first hdc—60 sts.

Rnd 20: Ch 2, TW, * 1 hdc in next 4 sts, hdc next 2 sts tog; rep from * nine more times to end of rnd, sl st last hdc to first hdc—50 sts.

Rnd 21: Ch 2, TW, 1 hdc in each st to end of rnd, sl st last hdc to first hdc—50 sts.

Rnd 22: Ch 2, TW, * 1 hdc in next 3 sts, hdc next 2 sts tog; rep from * nine more times to end of rnd, sl st last hdc to first hdc—40 sts.

Rnd 23: Ch 2, TW, * 1 hdc in next 2 sts, hdc next 2 sts tog; rep from * nine more times to end of rnd, sl st last hdc to first hdc—30 sts.

Rnd 24: Ch 2, TW, 1 hdc in each st to end of rnd, sl st last hdc to first hdc—30 sts.

Rnd 25: Ch 2, TW, * 1 hdc in next st, hdc next 2 sts tog; rep from * nine more times to end of rnd, sl st last hdc to first hdc—20 sts.

Rnd 26: Ch 2, TW, * 1 hdc in next 2 sts, hdc next 2 sts tog; rep from * four more times to end of rnd, sl st last hdc to first hdc—15 sts.

Rnd 27: Ch 2, TW, * 1 hdc in next st, hdc next 2 sts tog; rep from * four more times to end of rnd, sl st last hdc to first hdc—10 sts.

Rnd 28: Ch 2, TW, * hdc next 2 sts tog; rep from * four more times to end of rnd, sl st last hdc to first hdc—5 sts. Fasten off. Whip stitch head to body (Fig. 1). Tie off and weave in ends.

Belly

Make 1.

Row 1: With B, ch 16, TW, starting with 3rd ch from hook, 1 hdc in each ch to end of row—14 sts.

Row 2: Ch 2, TW, 2 hdc in next st, 1 hdc in each of next 12 sts, 2 hdc in next st—16 sts.

Row 3: Ch 2, TW, 2 hdc in next st, 1 hdc in each of next 14 sts, 2 hdc in next st—18 sts.

Row 4: Ch 2, TW, 2 hdc in next st, 1 hdc in each of next 16 sts, 2 hdc in next st—20 sts.

Rows 5-11: Ch 2, TW, 1 hdc in each st to end of row—20 sts.

Row 12: Ch 2, TW, hdc next 2 sts tog, 1 hdc in each of next 16 sts, hdc next 2 sts tog—18 sts.

Row 13: Ch 2, TW, hdc next 2 sts tog, 1 hdc in each of next 14 sts, hdc next 2 sts tog—16 sts.

Row 14: Ch 2, TW, hdc next 2 sts tog, 1 hdc in each of next 12 sts, hdc next 2 sts tog—14 sts.

Row 15: Ch 2, TW, hdc next 2 sts tog, 1 hdc in each of next 10 sts, hdc next 2 sts tog—12 sts.

Row 16: Ch 2, TW, hdc next 2 sts tog, 1 hdc in each of next 8 sts, hdc next 2 sts tog—10 sts.

Rows 17–22: Ch 2, TW, 1 hdc in each st to end of row—10 sts.

Row 23: Ch 1, TW, hdc next 2 sts tog, 1 hdc in each of next 6 sts, hdc next 2 sts tog—8 sts.

Row 24 (neck end): Ch 2, TW, 1 hdc in each st to end of rnd—8 sts. Fasten off, leaving a 36" (91cm) tail. Align neck end of belly just under neck. Whip stitch in place, stuffing lightly as work progresses if desired (Fig. 1). Tie off and weave in ends.

Eyes

With darning needle and C, embroider eyes as shown (Fig. 1).

Eyelid

Make 2.

Row 1: With A, leaving a 10" (25cm) tail, ch 6, TW, starting with 2nd ch from hook, sc next 2 chs tog, 1 sc in next ch, sc next 2 chs tog—3 sts. Fasten off. Whip stitch eyelid in place (Fig. 1), stuffing as work progresses. Tie off and weave in ends.

Mouth and Nose

With darning needle and C, embroider mouth and nose as shown (Fig. 1).

Ear

Make 4.

Row 1 (base end): With A, leaving a 12" (30cm) tail, ch 5, TW, starting with 2nd ch from hook, 1 sc in each of next 4 chs—4 sts.

Row 2: Ch 1, TW, sc next 2 sts tog, sc next 2 sts tog—2 sts.

Row 3: Ch 1, TW, 1 sc in each of next 2 sts—2 sts.

Row 4: Ch 1, TW, sc next 2 sts tog—1 st. Fasten off. Align two ear pieces and whip stitch tog, then whip stitch base end of completed ear in place on head (Fig. 1). Tie off and weave in ends.

Arm

Make 4.

Row 1 (base end): With A, leaving a 24" (61cm) tail, ch 9, TW, starting with 3rd ch from hook, 1 hdc in each of next 7 chs—7 sts.

Rows 2–4: Ch 2, TW, 1 hdc in each st to end of row—7 sts.

Row 5: Ch 1, TW, 1 sc in each of next 2 sts, 1 hdc in each of next 2 sts, 1 dc in each of next 3 sts—7 sts.

Row 6: Ch 2, TW, 1 dc in each of next 2 sts, 1 hdc in each of next 2 sts, 1 sc in next st, 1 sl st in next 2 sts—7 sts.

Row 7: Ch 1, TW, sc next 2 sts tog, 1 hdc in each of next 2 sts, 1 dc in each of next 3 sts—6 sts.

Rows 8–9: Ch 2, TW, 1 hdc in each of next 6 sts—6 sts.

Row 10: Ch 2, TW, hdc next 2 sts tog, 1 hdc in each of next 2 sts, hdc next 2 sts tog—4 sts. Tie off A, join C, leaving a 12" (30cm) tail.

Row 11: Ch 1, TW, 2 sc in next st, 1 sc in each of next 2 sts, 2 sc in next st—6 sts.

Row 12: Ch 1, TW, 1 sc in each of next 6 sts—6 sts.

Row 13: Ch 1, TW, sc next 2 sts tog, 1 sc in each of next 2 sts, sc next 2 sts tog—4 sts.

Row 14: Ch 1, TW, 1 sc in each of next 4 sts—4 sts.

Row 15: Ch 1, TW, * sc next 2 sts tog; rep from * one more time—2 sts. Fasten off. Align two arm pieces and whip stitch tog, matching colors (Figs. 2 and 3). Stuff. Whip stitch base end of completed arm to body (Fig. 1). Tie off and weave in ends.

Leg

Make 2.

Row 1 (hip end): With A, leaving a 24" (61cm) tail, ch 6, TW, 2 hdc in 3rd ch from hook, 1 hdc in each of next 2 chs, 2 hdc in next ch—6 sts.

Row 2: Ch 2, TW, 2 hdc in next st, 1 hdc in each of next 4 sts, 2 hdc in next st—8 sts.

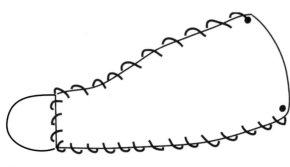

Figure 2

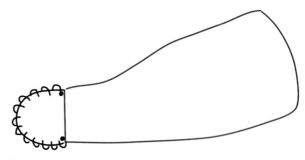

Figure 3

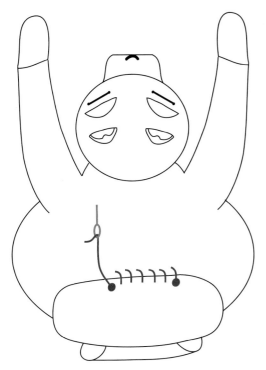

Figure 4

Row 3: Ch 2, TW, 2 hdc in next st, 1 hdc in each of next 6 sts, 2 hdc in next st—10 sts.

Row 4: Ch 2, TW, 1 dc in each of next 3 sts, 1 hdc in each of next 4 sts, 1 sc in each of next 3 sts—10 sts.

Row 5: Ch 1, TW, 1 sc in each of next 2 sts, 1 hdc in each of next 4 sts, 1 dc in each of next 3 sts, 2 dc in next st—11 sts.

Row 6: Ch 2, TW, 1 dc in each of next 3 sts, 1 hdc in each of next 3 sts, 1 sc in next st, 1 sl st in next st—8 sts.

Row 7: Ch 1, TW, 1 sc in next st, 1 hdc in each of next 2 sts, 1 dc in each of next 5 sts—8 sts. Beg working in rnds.

Rnd 1: Ch 2, TW, 1 dc in each of next 3 sts, 1 hdc in next st, 1 sc in next st, 1 sl st in each of next 3 sts, ch 14, sl st last ch to first dc of rnd—22 sts.

Rnd 2: Ch 2, TW, 1 hdc in each st/ch to end of rnd, sl st last hdc to first hdc—22 sts.

Rnd 3: Ch 2, TW, 1 hdc in each st to end of rnd, sl st last hdc to first hdc—22 sts.

Rnd 4 (foot end): Ch 2, TW, 1 hdc in each of next 2 sts, * hdc next 2 sts tog, 1 hdc in each of next 3 sts; rep from * three more times to end of rnd—18 sts. Fasten off, leaving a 24" (61cm) tail. (Note: You may have to turn one leg inside out so you clearly have a right and a left leg.) Whip stitch hip end in place on body (Fig. 1). Tie off and weave in ends. Stuff.

Foot

Make 4.

Row 1: With C, ch 5, TW, starting with 2nd ch from hook, 2 sc in next ch, 1 sc in each of next 2 chs, 2 sc in next ch—6 sts.

Row 2: Ch 1, TW, 2 sc in next st, 1 sc in each of next 4 sts, 2 sc in next st—8 sts.

Rows 3–14: Ch 1, TW, 1 sc in each of next 8 sts—8 sts.

Row 15: Ch 1, TW, sc next 2 sts tog, 1 sc in each of next 4 sts, sc next 2 sts tog—6 sts.

Row 16 (heel end): Ch 1, TW, sc next 2 sts tog, 1 sc in each of next 2 sts, sc next 2 sts tog—4 sts. Fasten off, leaving a 20" (51cm) tail on two of the pieces. Align one piece with a tail to one without a tail and whip stitch around, stuffing as work progresses. Whip stitch completed heel end of foot to leg, using the 24" (61cm) length from the foot end of the leg (Fig. 1). Tie off and weave in ends.

Tail

Make 2.

Row 1 (base end): With D and E held tog, leaving a 20" (51cm) tail, ch 10, TW, starting with 3rd ch from hook, 2 dc in next ch, 1 dc in each of next 6 chs, 2 dc in next ch—10 sts.

Rows 2–5: Ch 2, TW, 1 dc in each st to end of row—10 sts.

Row 6: Ch 2, TW, dc next 2 sts tog, 1 dc in each of next 6 sts, dc next 2 sts tog—8 sts.

Rows 7–10: Ch 2, TW, 1 dc in each st to end of row—8 sts.

Row 11: Ch 2, TW, 2 dc in next st, 1 dc in each of next 6 sts, 2 dc in next st—10 sts.

Row 12: Ch 2, TW, 1 dc in each st to end of row—10 sts.

Row 13: Ch 2, TW, 2 dc in next st, 1 dc in each of next 8 sts, 2 dc in next st—12 sts.

Row 14: Ch 2, TW, 1 dc in each st to end of row—12 sts.

Row 15: Ch 2, TW, dc next 2 sts tog, 1 dc in each of next 8 sts, dc next 2 sts tog—10 sts.

Row 16: Ch 2, TW, dc next 2 sts tog, 1 dc in each of next 6 sts, dc next 2 sts tog—8 sts.

Row 17 (tip of tail): Ch 2, TW, dc next 2 sts tog, 1 dc in each of next 4 sts, dc next 2 sts tog—6 sts. Fasten off. Align pieces and with B, sc edges tog, leaving base end open. Stuff. Using 20" (51cm) yarn tail, whip stitch base end of tail on body (Fig. 1). Measure up approx 5" (13cm) from base of tail and whip stitch back layer of tail to body at this point to hold it up (Fig. 4). Tie off and weave in ends.

Bandit the Raccoon

Bandit the Raccoon

With a name like Bandit and a built-in mask, this furry fella must be a thief, right? Actually, he's just a harmless prankster. He likes to hide behind bushes and lightly tickle the ear of a nearby creature with a long, leafy twig. Thinking that a bug has landed on them, they swat at their ears while Bandit continually pulls back the twig and then goes in for another tickle. He usually gets caught, though, because he can never contain his boisterous laughter.

YARN

Bulky (5) novelty yarn in 3 colors; 555 yds (508m) of color **A**, 555 yds (508m) of color **B** and 56 yds (52m) of color **C**

Super bulky (6) yarn in 1 color; 90 yds (83m) of color **D**

Medium (4) yarn in 1 color; 4 yds (4m) of color **E**

*The project shown on page 16 uses Lion Brand Fun Fur (polyester, 64 yds [58m], 1.75 oz [50g]) in Chocolate (**A**), Black (**B**) and White (**C**); Lion Brand Wool-Ease Thick & Quick (80% acrylic/20% wool, 106 yds [97m], 6 oz [170g]) in Black (**D**); and Lion Brand Vanna's Choice (acrylic, 170 yds [155m], 3.5 oz [100g]) in Toffee (**E**).*

HOOKS AND NOTIONS

G/6 (4mm) crochet hook • Size 13 darning needle • Polyester fiberfill • Stuffing stick

GAUGE

7 hdc and 6 rows = 2" (5cm) in hdc using size G/6 (4mm) hook with colors A and B held tog

FINISHED SIZE

Approx 11" (28cm) tall, 21" (53cm) long

Body

Make 1.

Rnd 1 (hind end): With A and B held tog, stuffing as work progresses, ch 4, sl st last ch to first ch to make a loop.

Rnd 2: Ch 2, TW, work 10 hdc in center of loop, sl st last hdc to first hdc—10 sts.

Rnd 3: Ch 2, TW, 2 hdc in each st to end of rnd, sl st last hdc to first hdc—20 sts.

Rnd 4: Ch 2, TW, 2 hdc in each st to end of rnd, sl st last hdc to first hdc—40 sts.

Rnd 5: Ch 2, TW, * 1 hdc in each of next 4 sts, 2 hdc in next st; rep from * seven more times to end of rnd, sl st last hdc to first hdc—48 sts.

Rnds 6-8: Ch 2, TW, 1 hdc in each st to end of rnd, sl st last hdc to first hdc—48 sts.

Rnd 9: Ch 2, TW, * 1 hdc in each of next 7 sts, 2 hdc in next st; rep from * five more times to end of rnd, sl st last hdc to first hdc—54 sts.

Rnds 10-22: Ch 2, TW, 1 hdc in each st to end of rnd, sl st last hdc to first hdc—54 sts.

Rnd 23: Ch 2, TW, * 1 hdc in each of next 7 sts, hdc next 2 sts tog; rep from * five more times to end of rnd, sl st last hdc to first hdc—48 sts.

Rnd 24: Ch 2, TW, * 1 hdc in each of next 6 sts, hdc next 2 sts tog; rep from * five more times to end of rnd, sl st last hdc to first hdc—42 sts.

Rnds 25-26: Ch 2, TW, 1 hdc in each st to end of rnd, sl st last hdc to first hdc—42 sts.

Rnd 27: Ch 2, TW, * 1 hdc in each of next 4 sts, hdc next 2 sts tog; rep from * six more times to end of rnd, sl st last hdc to first hdc—35 sts.

Rnd 28: Ch 2, TW, * 1 hdc in each of next 3 sts, hdc next 2 sts tog; rep from * six more times to end of rnd, sl st last hdc to first hdc—28 sts.

Rnd 29: Ch 2, TW, * hdc next 2 sts tog; rep from * thirteen more times to end of rnd, sl st last hdc to first hdc—14 sts.

Rnd 30 (head end): Ch 2, TW, * hdc next 2 sts tog; rep from * six more times to end of rnd, sl st last hdc to first hdc—7 sts. Fasten off, leaving a 10" (25cm) tail. Whip stitch opening closed. Tie off and weave in ends.

Head

Make 1.

Row 1: With A and B held tog, ch 8, TW, 2 hdc in 3rd ch from hook, 1 hdc in each of next 4 chs, 2 hdc in next ch—8 sts.

Row 2: Ch 2, TW, 2 hdc in next st, 1 hdc in each of next 6 sts, 2 hdc in next st—10 sts.

Row 3: Ch 2, TW, 2 hdc in each of next 2 sts, 1 hdc in each of next 6 sts, 2 hdc in each of next 2 sts—14 sts.

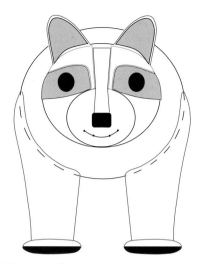

Figure 1 (front view)

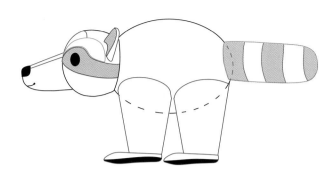

Figure 1 (side view)

Row 4: Ch 2, TW, hdc next 2 sts tog, 1 hdc in each of next 10 sts, hdc last 2 sts tog—12 sts.

Row 5: Ch 2, TW, hdc next 2 sts tog, 1 hdc in each of next 8 sts, hdc next 2 sts tog—10 sts.

Row 6: Ch 2, TW, hdc next 2 sts tog, hdc next 2 sts tog, 1 hdc in each of next 2 sts, hdc next 2 sts tog, hdc next 2 sts tog—6 sts. This is the forehead end of the head. Beg working in rnds, stuffing as work progresses.

Rnd 1: Ch 2, TW, 2 hdc in next st, 1 hdc in each of next 4 sts, 2 hdc in next st, 1 hdc each in the end of Rows 6–1, 2 hdc in next ch of Row 1, 1 hdc in each of next 6 chs, 2 hdc in next ch, 1 hdc each in the end of Rows 1–6, sl st last hdc to first hdc—30 sts.

Rnd 2: Ch 2, TW, * 1 hdc in each of next 5 sts, 2 hdc in next st; rep from * four more times, sl st last hdc to first hdc—35 sts.

Rnds 3–6: Ch 2, TW, 1 hdc in each st to end of rnd, sl st last hdc to first hdc—35 sts.

Rnd 7: Ch 2, TW, * 1 hdc in each of next 5 sts, hdc next 2 sts tog; rep from * four more times to end of rnd, sl st last hdc to first hdc—30 sts.

Rnd 8: Ch 2, TW, * 1 hdc in each of next 4 sts, hdc next 2 sts tog; rep from * four more times to end of rnd, sl st last hdc to first hdc—25 sts.

Rnd 9: Ch 2, TW, * 1 hdc in each of next 3 sts, hdc next 2 sts tog; rep from * four more times to end of rnd, sl st last hdc to first hdc—20 sts.

Rnd 10: Ch 2, TW, * hdc next 2 sts tog; rep from * nine more times to end of rnd, sl st last hdc to first hdc—10 sts. Fasten off, leaving a 10" (25cm) tail to whip stitch opening closed. Tie off and weave in ends. Using a combined 36" (91cm) length of A and B, whip stitch head to body (Fig. 1). Tie off and weave in ends.

Snout

Make 1.

Row 1: With C, ch 6, TW, starting with 3rd ch from hook, work 1 hdc in each of next 4 sts—4 sts.

Rows 2–3: Ch 2, TW, 1 hdc in each of next 4 sts—4 sts. Beg working in rnds, stuffing as work progresses.

Rnd 1: Ch 2, TW, 1 hdc in each of next 4 sts, 1 hdc in the end of Rows 3 and 2, 1 hdc in each of next 4 chs of Row 1, 1 hdc in the end of Rows 2 and 3, sl st last hdc to first hdc—12 sts.

Rnd 2: Ch 2, TW, 1 hdc in each st to end of rnd, sl st last hdc to first hdc—12 sts.

Rnd 3: Ch 2, TW, * 2 hdc in each of next 2 sts, 1 hdc in each of next 4 sts; rep from * one more time to end of rnd, sl st last hdc to first hdc—16 sts.

Rnd 4: Ch 2, TW, 1 hdc in each of next 5 sts, 2 hdc in next st, 1 hdc in each of next 8 sts, 2 hdc in next st, 1 hdc in next st, sl st last hdc to first hdc—18 sts.

Rnd 5: Ch 2, TW, 1 hdc in each st to end of rnd, sl st last hdc to first hdc—18 sts.

Rnd 6: Ch 2, TW, 2 hdc in next st, 1 hdc in each of next 8 sts, 2 hdc in next st, 1 hdc in each of next 8 sts, sl st last hdc to first hdc—20 sts.

Rnd 7: Ch 2, TW, * 1 hdc in each of next 4 sts, 2 hdc in next st; rep from * three more times to end of rnd, sl st last hdc to first hdc—24 sts.

Rnds 8–9: Ch 2, TW, 1 hdc in each st to end of rnd, sl st last hdc to first hdc—24 sts. Fasten off, leaving a 24" (61cm) tail. Stuff. Whip stitch snout to head (Fig. 1). Tie off and weave in ends.

Eye Mask

Make 2.

Row 1: With B, ch 17, TW, starting with 3rd ch from hook, 1 hdc in each of next 14 chs, 2 hdc in next ch—16 sts.

Row 2: Ch 2, TW, 2 hdc in next st, 1 hdc in each of next 15 sts—17 sts.

Row 3: Ch 2, TW, 1 hdc in each st to end of row—17 sts.

Row 4: Ch 2, TW, hdc next 2 sts tog, 1 hdc in each of next 15 sts—16 sts.

Row 5: Ch 2, TW, 1 hdc in each of next 12 sts, * hdc next 2 sts tog; rep from * one more time—14 sts. Fasten off, leaving a 36" (91cm) tail. Whip stitch eye mask to face as shown (Fig. 1). Tie off and weave in ends.

Eye

Make 2.

Rnd 1: With E, ch 3, sl st last ch to first ch to make a loop.

Rnd 2: Ch 2, TW, work 5 hdc in center of loop, sl st last hdc to first hdc—5 sts. Fasten off, leaving a 12" (30cm) tail. Whip stitch eye to center of eye mask (Fig. 1). Tie off and weave in ends.

Nose and Mouth

With darning needle and D, embroider nose and mouth on snout as shown (Fig. 1).

Nose Stripe

Make 1.

Row 1: With A, ch 14, TW, starting with 3rd ch from hook, 1 hdc in each of next 12 chs—12 sts.

Row 2: Ch 2, TW, 1 hdc in each st to end of row—12 sts. Fasten off, leaving a 24" (61cm) tail. Whip stitch nose stripe on face as shown (Fig. 1). Tie off and weave in ends.

Eyebrows

Make 2.

Row 1: With C, ch 16, TW, starting with 3rd ch from hook, 1 hdc in each of next 14 chs—14 sts.

Row 2: Ch 2, TW, 1 hdc in each of next 8 sts—8 sts.

Row 3: Ch 2, TW, 1 hdc in each of next 6 sts, sc next 2 sts tog—7 sts.

Row 4: Ch 1, TW, 1 sc in next 3 sts, sc next 2 sts tog—4 sts. Fasten off, leaving a 24" (61cm) tail. Position eyebrows as shown and whip stitch in place (Fig. 1). Tie off and weave in ends.

Note: If using a furry novelty yarn, trim as desired. The eyebrows, nose stripe and snout on this raccoon were trimmed.

Inner Ear

Make 2.

Row 1 (base): With B, ch 6, TW, 2 hdc in 3rd ch from hook, 1 hdc in each of next 2 chs, 2 hdc in next ch—6 sts.

Rows 2–5: Ch 2, TW, 1 hdc in each st to end of row—6 sts.

Row 6: Ch 1, TW, hdc next 2 sts tog, 1 hdc in each of next 2 sts, hdc next 2 sts tog—4 sts.

Row 7: Ch 1, TW, hdc next 2 sts tog, hdc next 2 sts tog—2 sts. Fasten off, weave in ends.

Outer Ear

Make 2.

With A and B held tog, leaving a 20" (51cm) tail, work as for inner ear. Align base ends of inner and outer ear and whip stitch tog with C leaving base ends unattached. Whip stitch base end of completed ear to head using excess lengths of A and B (Fig. 1). Tie off and weave in ends.

Tail

Make 1.

Rnd 1: With 2 strands of B held tog, stuffing as work progresses, ch 3, sl st last ch to first ch to make a loop.

Rnd 2: Ch 2, TW, work 8 hdc in center of loop, sl st last hdc to first hdc—8 sts.

Rnd 3: Ch 2, TW, 2 hdc in each st to end of rnd, sl st last hdc to first hdc—16 sts.

Rnd 4: Ch 2, TW, * 1 hdc in next st, 2 hdc in next st; rep from * seven more times to end of rnd, sl st last hdc to first hdc—24 sts.

Rnds 5–6: Ch 2, TW, 1 hdc in each st to end of rnd, sl st last hdc to first hdc—24 sts. At the end of Rnd 6, drop one strand of B and pick up one strand of A.

Rnds 7–10: Ch 2, TW, 1 hdc in each st to end of rnd, sl st last hdc to first hdc—24 sts. At the end of Rnd 10, drop A and pick up 2nd strand of B.

Rnds 11–14: Ch 2, TW, 1 hdc in each st to end of rnd, sl st last hdc to first hdc—24 sts. At the end of Rnd 14, drop 1 strand of B and pick up 1 strand of A.

Rnds 15–18: Ch 2, TW, 1 hdc in each st to end of rnd, sl st last hdc to first hdc—24 sts. At the end of Rnd 18, cut A and pick up 2nd strand of B.

Rnds 19–22: Ch 2, TW, 1 hdc in each st to end of rnd, sl st last hdc to first hdc—24 sts. Fasten off, leaving a 24" (61cm) tail. Stuff. Whip stitch tail to body (Fig. 1). Tie off and weave in ends.

Back Leg

Make 2.

Rnd 1 (foot end): With A and B held tog, leaving an 18" (46cm) tail, ch 16, sl st last ch to first ch.

Rnds 2–3: Ch 2, TW, 1 hdc in each ch to end of rnd, sl st last hdc to first hdc—16 sts.

Rnd 4: Ch 2, TW, * 1 hdc in each of next 7 sts, 2 hdc in next st; rep from * one more time, sl st last hdc to first hdc—18 sts.

Rnds 5–6: Ch 2, TW, 1 hdc in each st to end of rnd, sl st last hdc to first hdc—18 sts.

Rnd 7: Ch 2, TW, * 1 hdc in each of next 5 sts, 2 hdc in next st; rep from * two more times to end of rnd, sl st last hdc to first hdc—21 sts.

Rnd 8: Ch 2, TW, 1 hdc in each st to end of rnd, sl st last hdc to first hdc—21 sts.

Rnd 9: Ch 2, TW, * 1 hdc in each of next 6 sts, 2 hdc in next st; rep from * two more times to end of rnd, sl st last hdc to first hdc—24 sts.

Rnd 10: Ch 2, TW, 1 hdc in each st to end of rnd, sl st last hdc to first hdc—24 sts.

Rnd 11: Ch 1, TW, 1 sc in each of next 4 sts, 1 hdc in each of next 16 sts, 1 sc in each of next 4 sts, sl st last sc to first sc—24 sts. Beg working in rows.

Row 1: Ch 1, TW, 1 sc in each of next 4 sts, 1 hdc in each of next 16 sts—20 sts.

Row 2: Ch 2, TW, 2 hdc in next st, 1 hdc in each of next 14 sts, 2 hdc in next st—18 sts.

Rows 3–5: Ch 2, TW, 1 hdc in each st to end of row—18 sts.

Row 6: Ch 1, TW, hdc next 2 sts tog, 1 hdc in each of next 14 sts, hdc next 2 sts tog—16 sts.

Row 7: Ch 1, TW, hdc next 2 sts tog, 1 hdc in each of next 12 sts, hdc next 2 sts tog—14 sts.

Row 8 (hip end): Ch 1, TW, hdc next 2 sts tog, 1 hdc in each of next 10 sts, hdc next 2 sts tog—12 sts. Fasten off, leaving a 36" (91cm) tail. Whip stitch leg in place (Fig. 1). Stuff. Tie off and weave in ends.

Front Leg

Make 2.

Rnd 1 (foot end): With A and B held tog, leaving an 18" (46cm) tail, ch 12, sl st last ch to first ch.

Rnds 2–4: Ch 2, TW, 1 hdc in each ch/st to end of rnd, sl st last hdc to first hdc—12 sts.

Rnd 5: Ch 2, TW, * 1 hdc in each of next 5 sts, 2 hdc in next st; rep from * one more time to end of rnd, sl st last hdc to first hdc—14 sts.

Rnd 6: Ch 2, TW, 1 hdc in each st to end of rnd—14 sts.

Rnd 7: Ch 2, TW, * 1 hdc in each of next 6 sts, 2 hdc in next st; rep from * one more time to end of rnd, sl st last hdc to first hdc—16 sts.

Rnd 8: Ch 2, TW, * 1 hdc in each of next 7 sts, 2 hdc in next st; rep from * one more time to end of rnd, sl st last hdc to first hdc—18 sts.

Rnd 9: Ch 2, TW, * 1 hdc in each of next 8 sts, 2 hdc in next st; rep from * one more time to end of rnd, sl st last hdc to first hdc—20 sts.

Rnd 10: Ch 2, TW, 1 hdc in each st to end of rnd, sl st last hdc to first hdc—20 sts. Beg working in rows.

Row 1: Ch 1, TW, 1 sc in each of next 4 sts, 1 hdc in each of next 12 sts—16 sts.

Row 2: Ch 2, TW, 2 hdc in next st, 1 hdc in each of next 10 sts, 2 hdc in next st—14 sts.

Row 3: Ch 2, TW, 1 hdc in each st to end of row—14 sts.

Row 4: Ch 1, TW, hdc next 2 sts tog, 1 hdc in each of next 10 sts, hdc next 2 sts tog—12 sts.

Rows 5–9: Ch 2, TW, 1 hdc in each st to end of rnd—12 sts.

Row 10: Ch 1, TW, hdc next 2 sts tog, 1 hdc in each of next 8 sts, hdc next 2 sts tog—10 sts.

Row 11 (hip end): Ch 1, TW, hdc next 2 sts tog, 1 hdc in each of next 6 sts, hdc next 2 sts tog—8 sts. Fasten off, leaving a 36" (91cm) tail. Whip stitch leg in place (Fig. 1). Stuff. Tie off and weave in ends.

Top of Foot

Make 4.

Row 1 (heel end): With A and B held tog, leaving a 36" (91cm) tail, ch 6, TW, starting with 3rd ch from hook, work 1 hdc in each of next 4 sts—4 sts.

Rows 2–3: Ch 2, TW, 1 hdc in each st to end of row—4 sts.

Row 4: Ch 2, TW, 2 hdc in next st, 1 hdc in each of next 2 sts, 2 hdc in next st—6 sts.

Rows 5–6: Ch 2, TW, 1 hdc in each of next 6 sts—6 sts.

Row 7: Ch 2, TW, 2 hdc in next st, 1 hdc in each of next 4 sts, 2 hdc in next st—8 sts.

Row 8: Ch 2, TW, 1 hdc in each st to end of row—8 sts.

Row 9: Ch 1, TW, hdc next 2 sts tog, 1 hdc in each of next 4 sts, hdc next 2 sts tog—6 sts.

Row 10: Ch 1, TW, hdc next 2 sts tog, 1 hdc in each of next 2 sts, hdc next 2 sts tog—4 sts. Fasten off.

Bottom of Foot

Make 4.

With D and leaving a 5" (13cm) tail, work as for top of foot. Align top and bottom pieces and whip stitch around, lightly stuffing as work progresses. Tie off and weave in ends. Using the 18" (46cm) tail at foot end of each leg, whip stitch each leg opening to top of heel end of top-of-foot piece (Fig. 1).

Tiger Lily the Snail

Tiger Lily the Snail

If the first thing that comes to mind when you think of a snail is how slowly they move, then you've never met Tiger Lily! Nothing makes her happier than using her stealth and smarts to play a spirited game of hide-and-seek. Just when her opponent is about to find her, Tiger Lily sneaks off to a new hiding spot, quietly giggling as the endless search for her continues.

YARN

Bulky (5) yarn in 4 colors; 185 yds (169m) of color **A**, 185 yds (169m) of color **B**, 185 yds (169m) of color **C** and 185 yds (169m) of color **D**

Medium (4) yarn in 1 color; 1 yd (1m) of color **E**

*The project shown on page 21 uses Lion Brand Homespun (98% acrylic/2% polyester, 185 yds [169m], 6 oz [170g]) in Grape (**A**), Coral Gables (**B**), Golden (**C**) and Covered Bridge Red (**D**) and Lion Brand Vanna's Choice (acrylic, 170 yds [155m], 3.5 oz [100g]) in White (**E**).*

HOOKS AND NOTIONS

H/8 (5mm) crochet hook • Size 13 darning needle • Polyester fiberfill • Stuffing stick

GAUGE

5 hdc and 4 rows = 2" (5cm) using size H/8 (5mm) hook

FINISHED SIZE

Approx 8" (20cm) tall, 14" (36cm) long

Body

Make 1.

Row 1 (head end): With A, ch 10, TW, starting with 3rd ch from hook, 1 hdc in each ch to end of row—8 sts.

Row 2: Ch 2, TW, 1 hdc in each st to end of row—8 sts.

Row 3: Ch 2, TW, hdc next 2 sts tog, 1 hdc in each of next 4 sts, hdc next 2 sts tog—6 sts.

Row 4: Ch 2, TW, hdc next 2 sts tog, 1 hdc in each of next 2 sts, hdc next 2 sts tog—4 sts.

Row 5: Ch 2, TW, 1 hdc in each st to end of row—4 sts. This is the forehead end of the head. Beg working in rnds, moderately stuffing the tube you're making every 6 rows or so as work progresses, keeping it more flat than round. Keep the seam (where the last st and first st are joined in each rnd) centered on one of the tube's wide, flat sides.

Rnd 1: Ch 2, TW, 1 hdc in each of next 4 sts of Row 5, work 1 hdc in the end of Rows 5–1, work 1 hdc in each of 8 sts of Row 1, work 1 hdc in the end of Rows 1–5, sl st last hdc to first hdc—22 sts.

Rnds 2–6: Ch 2, TW, 1 hdc in each st to end of rnd, sl st last hdc to first hdc—22 sts.

Rnd 7: Ch 2, TW, hdc next 2 sts tog, 1 hdc in each of next 14 sts, * hdc next 2 sts tog; rep from * two more times, sl st last hdc to first hdc—18 sts.

Rnd 8: Ch 2, TW, 1 hdc in each of next 4 sts, * 2 hdc in each of next 3 sts, 1 hdc in each of next 4 sts; rep from * one more time, sl st last hdc to first hdc—24 sts.

Rnds 9–29: Ch 2, TW, 1 hdc in each st to end of rnd, sl st last hdc to first hdc—24 sts.

Rnd 30: Ch 2, TW, * 1 hdc in each of next 10 sts, hdc next 2 sts tog; rep from * one more time, sl st last hdc to first hdc—22 sts.

Rnd 31: Ch 2, TW, * 1 hdc in each of next 9 sts, hdc next 2 sts tog; rep from * one more time, sl st last hdc to first hdc—20 sts.

Rnd 32: Ch 2, TW, * 1 hdc in each of next 8 sts, hdc next 2 sts tog; rep from * one more time, sl st last hdc to first hdc—18 sts.

Rnd 33: Ch 2, TW, * 1 hdc in each of next 7 sts, hdc next 2 sts tog; rep from * one more time, sl st last hdc to first hdc—16 sts.

Rnd 34: Ch 2, TW, * 1 hdc in each of next 6 sts, hdc next 2 sts tog; rep from * one more time, sl st last hdc to first hdc—14 sts.

Rnd 35: Ch 2, TW, * 1 hdc in each of next 5 sts, hdc next 2 sts tog; rep from * one more time, sl st last hdc to first hdc—12 sts.

Rnd 36: Ch 2, TW, * 1 hdc in each of next 4 sts, hdc next 2 sts tog; rep from * one more time, sl st last hdc to first hdc—10 sts.

Rnd 37: Ch 2, TW, * 1 hdc in each of next 3 sts, hdc next 2 sts tog; rep from * one more time, sl st last hdc to first hdc—8 sts.

Rnd 38: Ch 2, TW, * 1 hdc in each of next 2 sts, hdc next 2 sts tog; rep from * one more time, sl st last hdc to first hdc—6 sts. Fasten off, leaving a 6" (15cm) tail. Whip stitch opening closed. Tie off and weave in ends.

Shell

Make 1.

Note: Tie the cut ends from color changes as the work progresses to secure them; no need to weave in those ends. Yarn can be carried up along side of the piece for color changes instead of cutting and joining if preferred; however, with 3 colors the yarns may tangle easily.

Rnd 1 (last B stripe): With B, stuffing as work progresses, ch 55, sl st last ch to first ch to make loop.

Rnds 2-3: Ch 2, TW, 1 hdc in each ch/st to end of rnd, sl st last hdc to first hdc—55 sts.

Rnd 4: Ch 2, TW, * 1 hdc in each of next 3 sts, hdc next 2 sts tog; rep from * ten more times, sl st last hdc to first hdc—44 sts.

Rnd 5: Ch 2, TW, * 1 hdc in each of next 9 sts, hdc next 2 sts tog; rep from * three more times, sl st last hdc to first hdc—40 sts. Cut B, join C.

Rnd 6: Ch 2, TW, 1 hdc in each st to end of rnd, sl st last hdc to first hdc—40 sts. Cut C, join D.

Rnd 7: Ch 2, TW, * 1 hdc in each of next 6 sts, hdc next 2 sts tog; rep from * four more times to end of rnd, sl st last hdc to first hdc—35 sts.

Rnd 8: Ch 2, TW, * 1 hdc in each of next 5 sts, hdc next 2 sts tog; rep from * four more times to end of rnd, sl st last hdc to first hdc—30 sts. Cut D, join C.

Rnd 9: Ch 2, TW, 1 hdc in each st to end of rnd, sl st last hdc to first hdc—30 sts. Cut C, join B.

Rnds 10-11: Ch 2, TW, 1 hdc in each st to end of rnd, sl st last hdc to first hdc—30 sts. At the end of Rnd 11, cut B, join C.

Note: As length increases, check that tube is stuffed so that it lies more flat than round for easier coiling later.

Rnd 12: Ch 2, TW, 1 hdc in each st to end of rnd, sl st last hdc to first hdc—30 sts. Cut C, join D.

Rnds 13-14: Ch 2, TW, 1 hdc in each st to end of rnd, sl st last hdc to first hdc—30 sts. At the end of Rnd 14, cut D, join C.

Rnd 15: Ch 2, TW, * 1 hdc in each of next 4 sts, hdc next 2 sts tog; rep from * four more times, sl st last hdc to first hdc—25 sts. Cut C, join B.

Rnds 16-17: Ch 2, TW, 1 hdc in each st to end of rnd, sl st last hdc to first hdc—25 sts. At the end of Rnd 17, cut B, join C.

Rnd 18: Ch 2, TW, 1 hdc in each st to end of rnd, sl st last hdc to first hdc—25 sts. Cut C, join D.

Rnds 19-20: Ch 2, TW, 1 hdc in each st to end of rnd, sl st last hdc to first hdc—25 sts. At the end of Rnd 20, cut D, join C.

Rnd 21: Ch 2, TW, 1 hdc in each st to end of rnd, sl st last hdc to first hdc—25 sts. Cut C, join B.

Rnds 22-23: Ch 2, TW, 1 hdc in each st to end of rnd, sl st last hdc to first hdc—25 sts. At the end of Rnd 23, cut B, join C.

Rnd 24: Ch 2, TW, 1 hdc in each st to end of rnd, sl st last hdc to first hdc—25 sts. Cut C, join D.

Rnds 25-26: Ch 2, TW, 1 hdc in each st to end of rnd, sl st last hdc to first hdc—25 sts. At the end of Rnd 26, cut D, join C.

Rnd 27: Ch 2, TW, 1 hdc in each st to end of rnd, sl st last hdc to first hdc—25 sts. Cut C, join B.

Rnds 28-29: Ch 2, TW, 1 hdc in each st to end of rnd, sl st last hdc to first hdc—25 sts. At the end of Rnd 29, cut B, join C.

Rnd 30: Ch 2, TW, 1 hdc in each st to end of rnd, sl st last hdc to first hdc—25 sts. Cut C, join D.

Rnds 31-32: Ch 2, TW, 1 hdc in each st to end of rnd, sl st last hdc to first hdc—25 sts. At the end of Rnd 32, cut D, join C.

Rnd 33: Ch 2, TW, 1 hdc in each st to end of rnd, sl st last hdc to first hdc—25 sts. Cut C, join B.

Rnds 34-35: Ch 2, TW, 1 hdc in each st to end of rnd, sl st last hdc to first hdc—25 sts. At the end of Rnd 35, cut B, join C.

Rnd 36: Ch 2, TW, 1 hdc in each st to end of rnd, sl st last hdc to first hdc—25 sts. Cut C, join D.

Rnd 37: Ch 2, TW, * 1 hdc in each of next 4 sts, 2 hdc in next st; rep from * four more times, sl st last hdc to first hdc—30 sts.

Rnd 38: Ch 2, TW, 1 hdc in each st to end of rnd, sl st last hdc to first hdc—30 sts. Cut D, join C.

Rnd 39: Ch 2, TW, * 1 hdc in each of next 5 sts, 2 hdc in next st; rep from * four more times, sl st last hdc to first hdc—35 sts. Cut C, join B.

Rnd 40: Ch 2, TW, 1 hdc in each st to end of rnd, sl st last hdc to first hdc—35 sts.

Rnd 41: Ch 2, TW, * 1 hdc in each of next 6 sts, 2 hdc in next st; rep from * four more times, sl st last hdc to first hdc—40 sts. Cut B, join C.

Rnd 42: Ch 2, TW, 1 hdc in each st to end of rnd, sl st last hdc to first hdc—40 sts. Cut C, join D.

Rnds 43-44: Ch 2, TW, 1 hdc in each st to end of rnd, sl st last hdc to first hdc—40 sts. At the end of Rnd 44, cut D, join C.

Rnd 45: Ch 2, TW, * 1 hdc in each of next 7 sts, 2 hdc in next st; rep from * four more times, sl st last hdc to first hdc—45 sts. Cut C, join B.

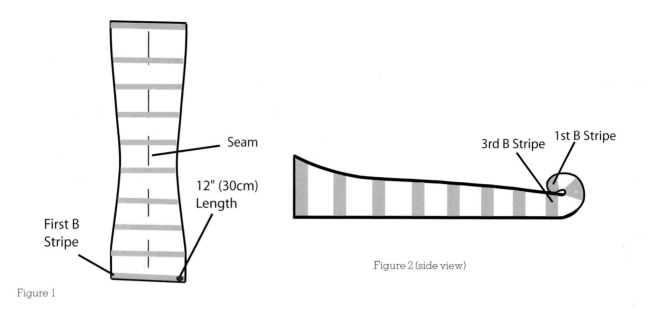

Seam

12" (30cm) Length

First B Stripe

Figure 1

3rd B Stripe   1st B Stripe

Figure 2 (side view)

Rnds 46–47: Ch 2, TW, 1 hdc in each st to end of rnd, sl st last hdc to first hdc—45 sts. At the end of Rnd 47, cut B, join C.

Rnd 48: Ch 2, TW, 1 hdc in each st to end of rnd, sl st last hdc to first hdc—45 sts. Cut C, join D.

Rnds 49–50: Ch 2, TW, 1 hdc in each st to end of rnd, sl st last hdc to first hdc—45 sts. At the end of Rnd 50, cut D, join C.

Rnd 51: Ch 2, TW, 1 hdc in each st to end of rnd, sl st last hdc to first hdc—45 sts. Cut C, join B.

Rnds 52–53: Ch 2, TW, 1 hdc in each st to end of rnd, sl st last hdc to first hdc—45 sts. At the end of Rnd 53, cut B, join C.

Rnd 54: Ch 2, TW, 1 hdc in each st to end of rnd, sl st last hdc to first hdc—45 sts. Cut C, join D.

Rnd 55: Ch 2, TW, * 1 hdc in each of next 7 sts, hdc next 2 sts tog; rep from * four more times to end, sl st last hdc to first hdc—40 sts.

Rnd 56: Ch 2, TW, * 1 hdc in each of next 6 sts, hdc next 2 sts tog; rep from * four more times to end, sl st last hdc to first hdc—35 sts. Cut D, join C.

Rnd 57: Ch 2, TW, 1 hdc in each st to end of rnd, sl st last hdc to first hdc—35 sts. Cut C, join B.

Rnd 58: Ch 2, TW, * 1 hdc in each of next 5 sts, hdc next 2 sts tog; rep from * four more times to end, sl st last hdc to first hdc—30 sts.

Rnd 59 (first B stripe): Ch 2, TW, * 1 hdc in each of next 4 sts, hdc next 2 sts tog; rep from * four more times, sl st last hdc to first hdc—25 sts. Fasten off, leaving a 12" (30cm) tail. Whip stitch opening closed. Tie off and weave in ends.

To curl the shell, lay the flat shell tube seam side up. Tie a 12" (30cm) length of B ½" (1cm) in from the outer edge of the first B stripe (Fig. 1). Roll in toward the seam to meet the 3rd B stripe (Fig. 2) and whip stitch in place. Tie another 12" (30cm) length of B to the outer edge of the 6th B stripe (Fig. 3). Continue rolling until the 2nd B stripe meets the 6th (Fig. 4) and whip stitch in place.

Tie a 12" (30cm) length of B to the outer edge of the last B stripe. Roll until the 4th B stripe meets the last (Fig. 5) and whip stitch in place. Tie off and weave in ends.

Belly

Make 1.

Row 1 (head end): With C, leaving a 48" (122cm) tail, ch 6, TW, work 2 hdc in the 3rd ch from the hook, 1 hdc in each of next 2 chs, 2 hdc in next ch—6 sts.

Row 2: Ch 2, TW, 2 hdc in next st, 1 hdc in each of next 4 sts, 2 hdc in next st—8 sts.

Rows 3–8: Ch 2, TW, 1 hdc in each st to end of row—8 sts.

Row 9: Ch 2, TW, 2 hdc in next st, 1 hdc in each of next 6 sts, 2 hdc in next st—10 sts.

Rows 10–30: Ch 2, TW, 1 hdc in each st to end of row—10 sts.

Row 31: Ch 1, TW, hdc next 2 sts tog, 1 hdc in each of next 6 sts, hdc next 2 sts tog—8 sts.

Row 32: Ch 2, TW, 1 hdc in each st to end of row—8 sts.

Row 33: Ch 1, TW, hdc next 2 sts tog, 1 hdc in each of next 4 sts, hdc next 2 sts tog—6 sts.

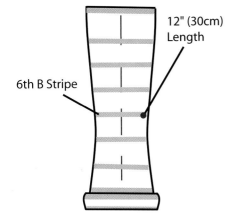

12" (30cm) Length

6th B Stripe

Figure 3 (top view)

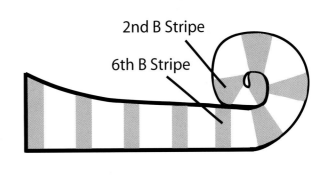

2nd B Stripe

6th B Stripe

Figure 4 (side view)

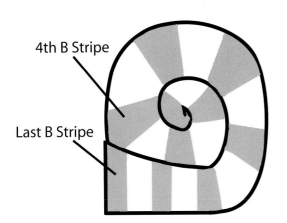

4th B Stripe

Last B Stripe

Figure 5 (side view)

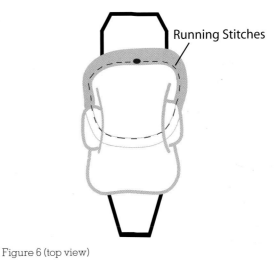

Running Stitches

Figure 6 (top view)

Row 34: Ch 2, TW, 1 hdc in each st to end of row—6 sts.

Row 35: Ch 1, TW, hdc next 2 sts tog, 1 hdc in each of next 2 sts, hdc next 2 sts tog—4 sts.

Row 36: Ch 1, TW, hdc next 2 sts tog, hdc next 2 sts tog—2 sts. Fasten off. Center belly on underside of body and whip stitch in place. Tie off and weave in ends.

To attach the shell to the body, center the wide opening of the shell over the center of the back. Tie a 36" (91cm) length of B to the inside edge of last B stripe. Work a running stitch around the circumference of last B stripe, approx 1" (3cm) in from the edge (Fig. 6). Tie off and weave in ends.

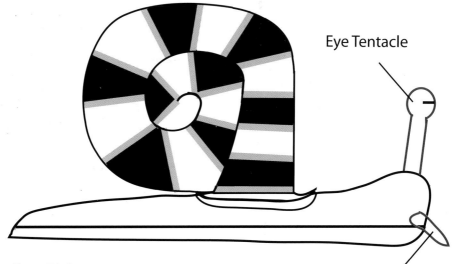

Eye Tentacle

Nose Tentacle

Figure 7 (side view)

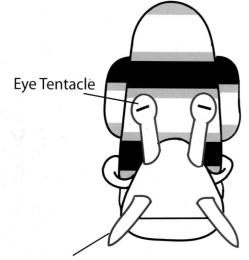

Eye Tentacle

Nose Tentacle

Figure 7 (front view)

Eye Tentacle

Make 2.

Rnd 1: With A, leaving a 10" (25cm) tail, ch 5, sl st last ch to first ch to make a loop.

Rnds 2–6: Ch 2, TW, 1 hdc in each st to end of rnd, sl st last hdc to first hdc—5 sts.

Rnd 7: Ch 2, TW, * 2 hdc in next st, 1 hdc in next st; rep from * one more time, 2 hdc in next st, sl st last hdc to first hdc—8 sts.

Rnd 8: Ch 2, TW, 1 hdc in each st to end of rnd, sl st last hdc to first hdc—8 sts.

Rnd 9: Ch 1, TW, * hdc next 2 sts tog; rep from * three more times, sl st last hdc to first hdc—4 sts. Fasten off. Whip stitch opening closed. Tie off and weave in ends. Stuff firmly. Whip stitch in place on face (Fig. 7). Tie off and weave in ends.

Nose Tentacle

Make 2.

Rnd 1: With A, leaving a 10" (25cm) tail, ch 4, sl st last ch to first ch to make a loop.

Rnds 2–5: Ch 2, TW, 1 hdc in each st to end of rnd, sl st last hdc to first hdc—4 sts. After Rnd 5, fasten off. Whip stitch opening closed. Tie off and weave in ends. Stuff. Whip stitch in place on face (Fig. 7). Tie off and weave in ends.

Eyes

With darning needle and E, embroider eyes on the eye tentacles as shown (Fig. 7).

See page 126 for the yarn colors used to make these versions.

CHAPTER 2

The Covert Operatives: Farm Friends

Visit a few farms and you'll find that they have an idyllic quality about them. Trees sway gently in the breeze, birds soar steadily through the sky and animals graze lazily in the fields—or do they? Is that cow just eating grass, or is she keeping an ear out for unwanted visitors? Is that sheep really just taking a stroll on the back forty, or is she collecting top-secret intel? How about the pig? Is he just super hungry, or is he using that sniffer to seek out more than food? And why is that horse always going on midnight runs? Let's investigate.

Dottie the Cow

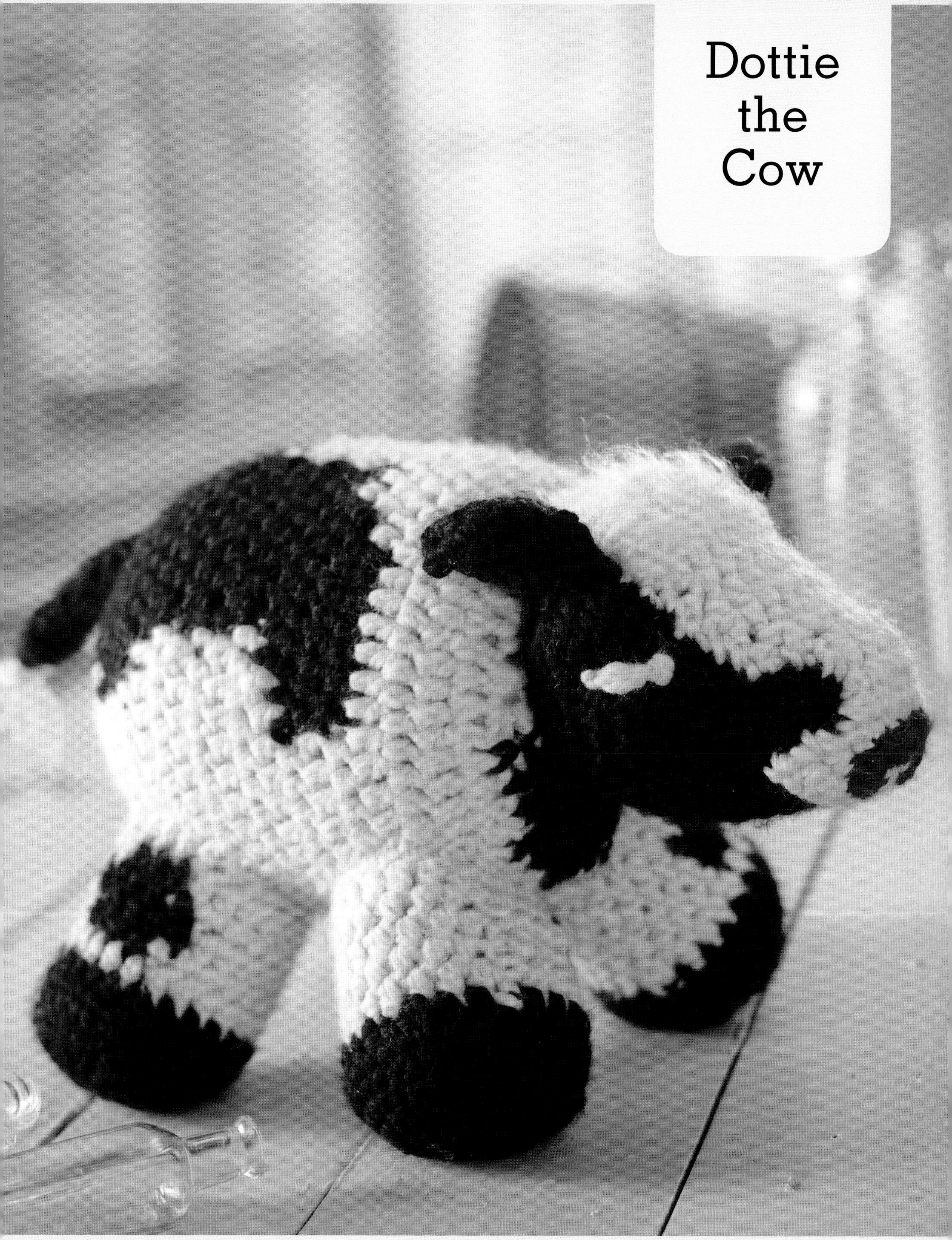

Dottie the Cow

Dottie (code name "Mayday") is the security officer on the farm. You will often spot her standing in the middle of a field, sleeping—or is she? Her hearing is so finely tuned that she can actually detect intruders more quickly with her eyes closed. Trespasser detected! If she senses the threat is high, Dottie bellows out the loudest "MOO" she can muster to alert the rest of the farm animals to the impending danger.

YARN

Super bulky (6) yarn in 2 colors; 216 yds (198m) of color **A** and 216 yds (198m) of color **B**

Medium (4) yarn in 1 color; 10 yds (9m) of color **C**

Bulky (5) yarn in 1 color; 40 yds (37m) of color **D**

*The project shown on page 29 uses Lion Brand Wool-Ease Thick & Quick (80% acrylic/20% wool, 106 yds [97m], 6 oz [170g]) in Black (**A**) and Fisherman (**B**); Lion Brand Vanna's Choice (acrylic, 170 yds [155m], 3.5 oz [100g]) in Magenta (**C**); and Patons Divine (76.5% Acrylic/10.5% Wool/10.5% Mohair/2.5% Polyester, 142 yds [130m], 3.5 oz [100g]) in Icicle White (**D**).*

HOOKS AND NOTIONS

F/5 (3.75mm), H/8 (5mm) and I/9 (5.5mm) crochet hooks • Size 13 darning needle • Polyester fiberfill • Stuffing stick

GAUGE

5 hdc and 4 rows = 2" (5cm) using size I/9 (5.5mm) hook

FINISHED SIZE

Approx 10" (25cm) tall, 13" (33cm) long

Head

Make 1.

Row 1: With I/9 (5.5mm) hook and A, ch 7, TW, starting with 3rd ch from hook, 1 hdc in each of next 5 chs—5 sts.

Rows 2–3: Ch 2, TW, 1 hdc in each st to end of row—5 sts. Beg working in rnds as follows, stuffing as work progresses.

Rnd 1: Ch 2, work 1 hdc each in the end of Rows 3–1, 1 hdc in the first ch of Row 1, 1 hdc in next ch, 2 hdc in next ch, 1 hdc in each of next 2 chs, work 1 hdc each in the end of Rows 1–3, 1 hdc in next st of Row 3, 1 hdc in next st, 2 hdc in next st, 1 hdc in each of next 2 sts, sl st last hdc to first hdc—18 sts.

Rnd 2: Ch 2, TW, 1 hdc in each of next 18 sts, sl st last hdc to first hdc—18 sts.

Rnd 3: Ch 2, 1 hdc in each of next 12 sts, 2 hdc in next st, 1 hdc in next st, 2 hdc in each of next 2 sts, 1 hdc in each of next 2 sts, sl st last hdc to first hdc—21 sts.

Rnd 4: Ch 2, TW, 2 hdc in next st, 1 hdc in each of next 7 sts, 2 hdc in next st, 1 hdc in each of next 12 sts, sl st last hdc to first hdc—23 sts.

Rnd 5: Ch 2, TW, 1 hdc in each st to end of rnd, sl st last hdc to first hdc—23 sts.

Rnd 6: Ch 2, TW, 2 hdc in each of next 2 sts, 1 hdc in each of next 2 sts, 2 hdc in each of next 2 sts, 1 hdc in each of next 2 sts, 2 hdc in each of next 2 sts, 1 hdc in each of next 13 sts, sl st last hdc to first hdc—29 sts.

Rnd 7: Ch 2, TW, 1 hdc in each of next 13 sts, 2 hdc in each of next 2 sts, 1 hdc in each of next 2 sts, 2 hdc in each of next 8 sts, 1 hdc in each of next 2 sts, 2 hdc in each of next 2 sts, sl st last hdc to first hdc—41 sts.

Rnds 8–9: Ch 2, TW, 1 hdc in each st to end of rnd, sl st last hdc to first hdc—41 sts.

Rnd 10: Ch 2, TW, * hdc next 2 sts tog, 1 hdc in next st; rep from * twelve more times, hdc next 2 sts tog, sl st last hdc to first hdc—27 sts.

Rnds 11–12: Ch 2, TW, 1 hdc in each st to end of rnd, sl st last hdc to first hdc—27 sts.

Rnd 13: Ch 2, TW, * hdc next 2 sts tog; rep from * twelve more times, 1 hdc in next st, sl st last hdc to first hdc—14 sts.

Rnd 14: Ch 2, TW, * hdc next 2 sts tog; rep from * six more times to end of rnd, sl st last hdc to first hdc—7 sts. Fasten off, leaving a 10" (25cm) tail. With tail, whip stitch opening closed. Tie off and weave in ends.

Body

Make 1.

Rnd 1: With I/9 (5.5mm) hook and B, stuffing as work progresses, ch 4, sl st last ch to first ch to make a loop.

Rnd 2: Ch 2, work 8 hdc in center of loop, sl st last hdc to first hdc—8 sts.

Rnd 3: Ch 2, TW, 2 hdc in each st to end of rnd, sl st last hdc to first hdc—16 sts.

Rnd 4: Ch 2, TW, 2 hdc in each st to end of rnd, sl st last hdc to first hdc—32 sts.

Rnd 5: Ch 2, TW, * 1 hdc in next st, 2 hdc in next st; rep from * fifteen more times to end of rnd, sl st last hdc to first hdc—48 sts.

Rnd 6: Ch 2, TW, * 1 hdc in each of next 11 sts, 2 hdc in next st; rep from * three more times to end of rnd, sl st last hdc to first hdc—52 sts.

Rnd 7: Ch 2, TW, 1 hdc in each of next 12 sts, drop B, pick up A, 1 hdc in each of next 10 sts, drop A, pick up B, 1 hdc in each of next 30 sts, sl st last hdc to first hdc—52 sts.

Rnd 8: Ch 2, TW, 1 hdc in each of next 30 sts, drop B, pick up A, 1 hdc in each of next 10 sts, drop A, pick up B, 1 hdc in each of next 12 sts, sl st last hdc to first hdc—52 sts.

Rnd 9: Ch 2, TW, 1 hdc in each of next 10 sts, drop B, pick up A, 1 hdc in each of next 13 sts, drop A, pick up B, 1 hdc in each of next 9 sts, drop B, pick up A, 1 hdc in each of next 6 sts, drop A, pick up B, 1 hdc in each of next 14 sts, sl st last hdc to first hdc—52 sts.

Rnd 10: Ch 2, TW, 1 hdc in each of next 12 sts, drop B, pick up A, 1 hdc in each of next 8 sts, drop A, pick up B, 1 hdc in each of next 9 sts, drop B, pick up A, 1 hdc in each of next 14 sts, drop A, pick up B, 1 hdc in each of next 9 sts, sl st last hdc to first hdc—52 sts.

Rnd 11: Ch 2, TW, 1 hdc in each of next 9 sts, drop B, pick up A, 1 hdc in each of next 13 sts, drop A, pick up B, 1 hdc in each of next 10 sts, drop B, pick up A, 1 hdc in each of next 8 sts, drop A, pick up B, 1 hdc in each of next 12 sts, sl st last hdc to first hdc—52 sts.

Rnd 12: Ch 2, TW, 1 hdc in each of next 12 sts, drop B, pick up A, 1 hdc in each of next 7 sts, drop A, pick up B, 1 hdc in each of next 12 sts, drop B, pick up A, 1 hdc in each of next 12 sts, drop A, pick up B, 1 hdc in each of next 9 sts, sl st last hdc to first hdc—52 sts.

Rnd 13: Drop B, pick up A, ch 2, TW, 1 hdc in each of next 4 sts, drop A, pick up B, 1 hdc in each of next 7 sts, drop B, pick up A, 1 hdc in each of next 9 sts, drop A, pick up B, 1 hdc in each of next 13 sts, drop B, pick up A, 1 hdc in each of next 7 sts, drop A, pick up B, 1 hdc in each of next 10 sts, drop B, pick up A, 1 hdc in each of next 2 sts, sl st last hdc to first hdc—52 sts.

Rnd 14: Ch 2, TW, 1 hdc in each of next 2 sts, drop A, pick up B, 1 hdc in each of next 10 sts, drop B, pick up A, 1 hdc in each of next 6 sts, drop A, pick up B, 1 hdc in each of next 13 sts, drop B, pick up A, 1 hdc in each of next 9 sts, drop A, pick up B, 1 hdc in each of next 7 sts, drop B, pick up A, 1 hdc in each of next 5 sts, sl st last hdc to first hdc—52 sts.

Rnd 15: Ch 2, TW, 1 hdc in each of next 5 sts, drop A, pick up B, 1 hdc in each of next 7 sts, drop B, pick up A, 1 hdc in each of next 8 sts, drop A, pick up B, 1 hdc in each of next 15 sts, drop B, pick up A, 1 hdc in each of next 4 sts, drop A, pick up B, 1 hdc in each of next 10 sts, drop B, pick up A, 1 hdc in each of next 3 sts, sl st last hdc to first hdc—52 sts.

Rnd 16: Ch 2, TW, 1 hdc in each of next 5 sts, drop A, pick up B, 1 hdc in each of next 26 sts, drop B, pick up A, 1 hdc in each of next 9 sts, drop A, pick up B, 1 hdc in each of next 7 sts, drop B, pick up A, 1 hdc in each of next 5 sts, sl st last hdc to first hdc—52 sts.

Rnd 17: Ch 2, TW, 1 hdc in each of next 4 sts, drop A, pick up B, 1 hdc in each of next 8 sts, drop B, pick up A, 1 hdc in each of next 8 sts, drop A, pick up B, 1 hdc in each of next 26 sts, drop B, pick up A, 1 hdc in each of next 6 sts, sl st last hdc to first hdc—52 sts.

Rnd 18: Ch 2, TW, 1 hdc in each of next 6 sts, drop A, pick up B, 1 hdc in each of next 24 sts, drop B, pick up A, 1 hdc in each of next 10 sts, drop A, pick up B, 1 hdc in each of next 8 sts, drop B, pick up A, 1 hdc in each of next 4 sts, sl st last hdc to first hdc—52 sts.

Rnd 19: Ch 2, TW, 1 hdc in each of next 4 sts, drop A, pick up B, 1 hdc in each of next 10 sts, drop B, pick up A, 1 hdc in each of next 10 sts, drop A, pick up B, 1 hdc in each of next 20 sts, drop B, pick up A, 1 hdc in each of next 8 sts, sl st last hdc to first hdc—52 sts.

Rnd 20: Ch 2, TW, 1 hdc in each of next 10 sts, drop A, pick up B, 1 hdc in each of next 18 sts, drop B, pick up A, 1 hdc in each of next 9 sts, drop A, pick up B, 1 hdc in each of next 11 sts, drop B, pick up A, 1 hdc in each of next 4 sts, sl st last hdc to first hdc—52 sts.

Rnd 21: Ch 2, TW, 1 hdc in each of next 3 sts, drop A, pick up B, 1 hdc in each of next 13 sts, drop B, pick up A, 1 hdc in each of next 7 sts, drop A, pick up B, 1 hdc in each of next 19 sts, drop B, pick up A, 1 hdc in each of next 10 sts, sl st last hdc to first hdc—52 sts.

Rnd 22: Ch 2, TW, 1 hdc in each of next 10 sts, drop A, pick up B, 1 hdc in each of next 42 sts, sl st last hdc to first hdc—52 sts.

Rnd 23: Ch 2, TW, 1 hdc in each of next 43 sts, drop B, pick up A, 1 hdc in each of next 9 sts, sl st last hdc to first hdc—52 sts.

Rnd 24: Ch 2, TW, 1 hdc in each of next 7 sts, drop A, pick up B, 1 hdc in each of next 9 sts, drop B, pick up A, 1 hdc in each

Figure 1 (front view)

of next 4 sts, drop A, pick up B, 1 hdc in each of next 32 sts, sl st last hdc to first hdc—52 sts.

Rnd 25: Ch 2, TW, * 1 hdc in each of next 2 sts, hdc next 2 sts tog; rep from * six more times, 1 hdc in each of next 2 sts, drop B, pick up A, ** hdc next 2 sts tog, 1 hdc in each of next 2 sts; rep from ** one more time, drop A, pick up B, hdc next 2 sts tog, *** 1 hdc in each of next 2 sts, hdc next 2 sts tog; rep from *** two more times, sl st last hdc to first hdc—39 sts.

Rnd 26: Ch 2, TW, * 1 hdc in next st, hdc next 2 sts tog; rep from * two more times, drop B, pick up A, ** 1 hdc in next st, hdc next 2 sts tog; rep from ** three more times, drop A, pick up B, *** 1 hdc in next st, hdc next 2 sts tog; rep from *** five more times, sl st last hdc to first hdc—26 sts.

Rnd 27: Ch 2, TW, * hdc next 2 sts tog; rep from * five more times, drop B, pick up A, ** hdc next 2 sts tog; rep from ** four more times, cut A, pick up B, tie off A, *** hdc next 2 sts tog; rep from *** one more time, sl st last hdc to first hdc—13 sts.

Rnd 28 (neck): Ch 2, TW, 1 hdc in next st, * hdc next 2 sts tog; rep from * five more times, sl st last hdc to first hdc—7 sts. Fasten off, leaving a 12" (30cm) tail. With tail, whip stitch opening closed. Tie off and weave in ends. Whip stitch head to neck (Fig. 1). Tie off and weave in ends.

Bridge of Nose

Make 1.

Row 1 (forehead end): With I/9 (5.5mm) hook and B, ch 10, TW, starting with 3rd ch from hook, 1 hdc in each of next 8 chs—8 sts.

Rows 2–10: Ch 2, TW, 1 hdc in each st to end of row—8 sts.

Row 11: Ch 2, TW, hdc next 2 sts tog, 1 hdc in each of next 4 sts, hdc next 2 sts tog—6 sts.

Row 12: Ch 2, TW, hdc next 2 sts tog, 1 hdc in each of next 2 sts, hdc next 2 sts tog—4 sts.

Rows 13–16: Ch 2, TW, 1 hdc in each st to end of row—4 sts.

Row 17: Ch 2, TW, 3 hdc in next st, 1 hdc in each of next 2 sts, 3 hdc in next st—8 sts.

Row 18: Ch 2, TW, 2 hdc in next st, 1 hdc in each of next 6 sts, 2 hdc in next st—10 sts.

Row 19: Ch 2, TW, 1 hdc in each st to end of row—10 sts. Fasten off, leaving a 36" (91cm) tail. Whip stitch bridge of nose to face, starting at top of forehead (Fig. 1). Fasten off, weave in ends.

Figure 1 (side view)

Eye

With darning needle and B, embroider eyes as shown (Fig. 1).

Eyelid

Make 2.

Row 1: With I/9 (5.5mm) hook and A, leaving a 10" (25cm) tail, ch 7, TW, starting with 3rd ch from hook, work 1 hdc in each ch to end of row—5 sts.

Row 2: Ch 1, TW, hdc next 2 sts tog, 1 hdc in next st, hdc next 2 sts tog—3 sts. Fasten off. Align straight edge of eyelid along top of eye (Fig. 1) and whip stitch in place around, stuffing lightly as work progresses. Tie off and weave in ends.

Nose

Make 1.

Row 1: With F/5 (3.75mm) hook and C, leaving a 20" (51cm) tail, ch 16, TW, starting with 3rd ch from hook, work 1 hdc in each of next 14 chs. Fasten off. Using long tail, whip stitch in place as shown (Fig. 1). Tie off and weave in ends.

Hair

Make 1.

Row 1: With H/8 (5mm) hook and D, ch 12, TW, starting with 3rd ch from hook, 1 hdc in each of next 10 chs—10 sts.

Rows 2–9: Ch 2, TW, 1 hdc in each of next 10 sts—10 sts. Fasten off, leaving a 36" (91cm) tail. Whip stitch hair on top of head as shown (Fig. 1). Tie off and weave in ends.

Ear

Make 4.

Row 1 (base end): With I/9 (5.5mm) hook and A, leaving a 20" (51cm) tail, ch 6, TW, starting with 3rd ch from hook, 1 hdc in each of next 4 chs—4 sts.

Row 2: Ch 2, TW, 2 hdc in next st, 1 hdc in each of next 2 sts, 2 hdc in next st—6 sts.

Row 3: Ch 2, TW, 1 hdc in each st to end of row—6 sts.

Row 4: Ch 2, TW, hdc next 2 sts tog, 1 hdc in each of next 2 sts, hdc next 2 sts tog—4 sts.

Row 5: Ch 2, TW, 1 hdc in each st to end of row—4 sts.

Row 6 (tip of ear): Ch 2, TW, hdc next 2 sts tog, hdc next 2 sts tog—2 sts. Fasten off. Align two ear pieces and whip stitch tog. Whip stitch base of ear to head as shown (Fig. 1). Tie off and weave in ends.

Leg

Make 4.

Rnd 1: With I/9 (5.5mm) hook and B, leaving a 24" (61cm) tail, ch 22, sl st last ch to first ch to make a loop.

Rnd 2: Ch 2, TW, 1 hdc in each of next 22 sts, sl st last hdc to first hdc—22 sts.

Rnd 3: Ch 2, TW, 1 hdc in each of next 4 sts, drop B, pick up A, 1 hdc in each of next 3 sts, drop A, pick up B, 1 hdc in each of next 15 sts, sl st last hdc to first hdc—22 sts.

Rnd 4: Ch 2, TW, 1 hdc in each of next 14 sts, drop B, pick up A, 1 hdc in each of next 5 sts, drop A, pick up B, 1 hdc in each of next 3 sts, sl st last hdc to first hdc—22 sts.

Rnd 5: Ch 2, TW, 1 hdc in each of next 3 sts, drop B, pick up A, 1 hdc in each of next 5 sts, drop A, pick up B, 1 hdc in each of next 14 sts, sl st last hdc to first hdc—22 sts.

Rnd 6: Ch 2, TW, 1 hdc in each of next 15 sts, drop B, pick up A, 1 hdc in each of next 3 sts, cut A, pick up B, tie off A, 1 hdc in each of next 4 sts, sl st last hdc to first hdc—22 sts.

Rnd 7: Ch 2, TW, 1 hdc in each of next 22 sts, sl st last hdc to first hdc—22 sts.

Rnd 8: Cut B, join A, tie off B, ch 2, TW, * 1 hdc in each of next 3 sts, 2 hdc in next st; rep from * four more times, 1 hdc in each of next 2 sts, sl st last hdc to first hdc—27 sts.

Rnd 9 (hoof end of leg): Ch 2, TW, 1 hdc in each st to end of rnd, sl st last hdc to first hdc—27 sts. Fasten off.

Bottom of Hoof

Make 4.

Rnd 1: With I/9 (5.5mm) hook and A, ch 4, sl st last ch to first ch to make a loop.

Rnd 2: Ch 2, work 9 hdc in center of loop, sl st last hdc to first hdc—9 sts.

Rnd 3: Ch 2, TW, 2 hdc in each st to end of rnd, sl st last hdc to first hdc—18 sts.

Rnd 4: Ch 2, TW, * 1 hdc in next st, 2 hdc in next st; rep from * eight more times to end of rnd, sl st last hdc to first hdc—27 sts. Fasten off, leaving a 24" (61cm) tail. Sew bottom of hoof to hoof end of leg. Tie off and weave in ends. Stuff. Whip stitch legs to body (Fig. 1). Tie off and weave in ends.

Tail

Make 1.

Rnd 1 (base of tail): With I/9 (5.5mm) hook and A, leaving a 12" (30cm) tail, ch 8, sl st last ch to first ch to make a loop.

Rnd 2: Ch 2, TW, 1 hdc in each of next 8 chs, sl st last hdc to first hdc—8 sts.

Rnds 3-4: Ch 2, TW, 1 hdc in each st to end of rnd, sl st last hdc to first hdc—8 sts.

Rnd 5: Ch 2, TW, * 1 hdc in each of next 2 sts, hdc next 2 sts tog; rep from * one more time to end of rnd, sl st last hdc to first hdc—6 sts.

Rnds 6-9: Ch 2, TW, 1 hdc in each of next 6 sts, sl st last hdc to first hdc—6 sts.

Rnd 10: Ch 2, TW, * hdc next 2 sts tog; rep from * two more times to end of rnd, sl st last hdc to first hdc—3 sts. Fasten off, leaving a 10" (25cm) tail. Tie end of tail closed with a double knot, without stuffing tail. Whip stitch base of tail to body as shown (Fig. 1).

Tail Hair

Make 1.

Rnd 1: With H/8 (5mm) hook and D, leaving a 6" (15cm) tail, ch 8, sl st last ch to first ch to make first loop.

Rnd 2: Ch 10, sl st last ch to first ch of first loop to make 2nd loop.

Rnd 3: Ch 14, sl st last ch to first ch of first loop to make 3rd loop.

Rnd 4: Ch 8, sl st last ch to first ch of first loop to make 4th loop. Fasten off, leaving a 6" (15cm) tail. Tie beg and ending tails tog. Thread both through darning needle and attach hair to tip of tail. Tie off and weave in ends.

Trixie the Sheep

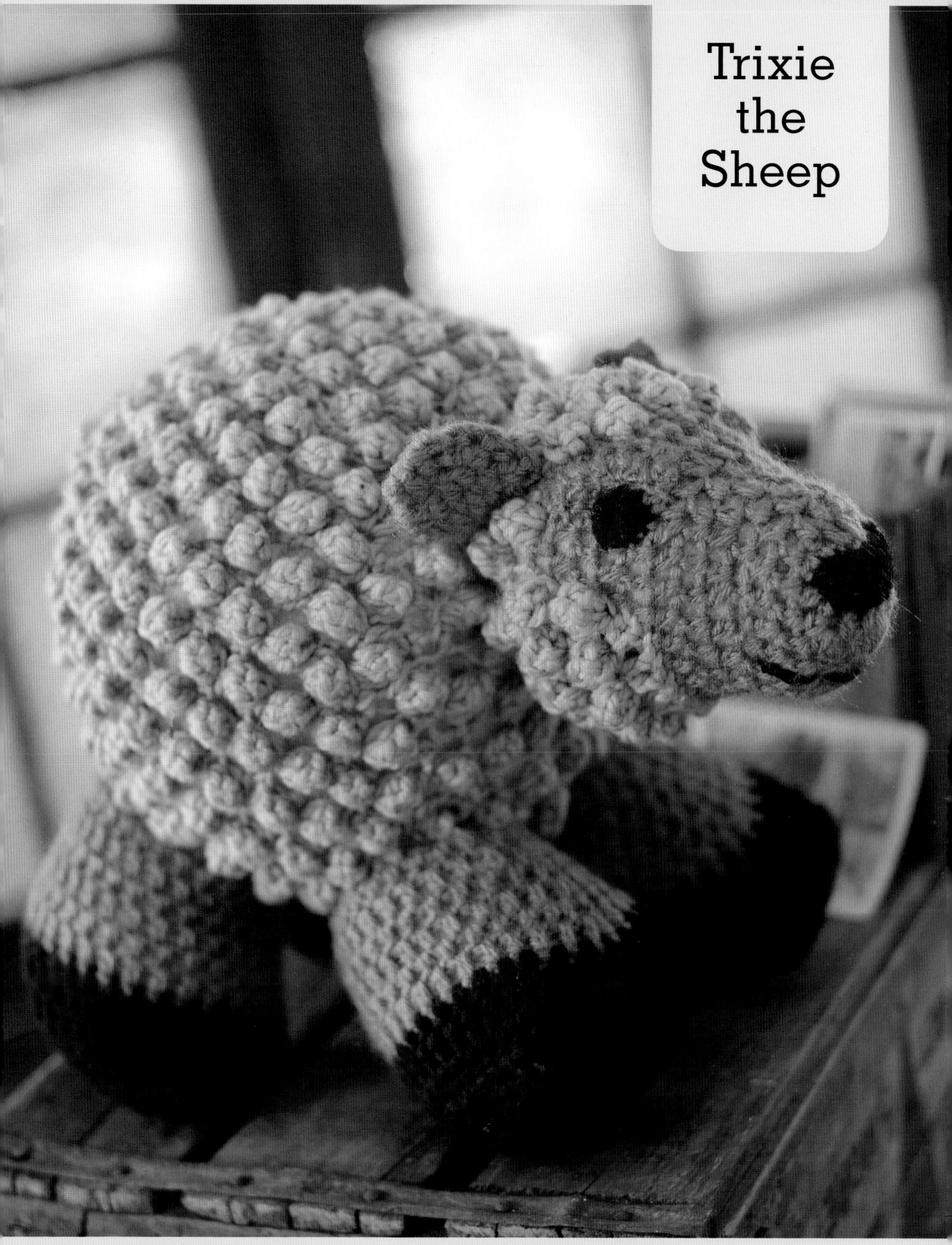

Trixie the Sheep

Trixie (code name "Shadow") is the information officer on the farm. Her unassuming manner allows her to blend easily into any situation. As she grazes in the fields, she eavesdrops on her farming family and their workers, then reports back to the other animals when she hears that they need help. When the family is low on food, for instance, she calls upon the hens for more eggs and the cows for more milk. Caring for her family is always Trixie's first priority.

YARN

Medium (4) yarn in 2 colors; 170 yds (156m) of color **A** and 180 yds (165m) of color **C**

Bulky (5) yarn in 1 color; 324 yds (297m) of color **B**

*The project shown on page 35 uses Lion Brand Vanna's Choice (acrylic, 170 yds [155m], 3.5 oz [100g]) in Honey (**A**) and Black (**C**) and Patons Shetland Chunky Tweeds (72% Acrylic/25% Wool/3% Viscose, 125 yds [114m], 3 oz [85g]) in Biscuit Tweeds (**B**).*

HOOKS AND NOTIONS

G/6 (4mm) and I/9 (5.5mm) crochet hooks • Size 13 darning needle • Polyester fiberfill • Stuffing stick

GAUGE

6 hdc and 6 rows = 2" (5cm) using size I/9 (5.5mm) hook and Color A

FINISHED SIZE

Approx 10" (25cm) tall, 13" (33cm) long

Head

Make 1.

Row 1: With I/9 (5.5mm) hook and A, ch 6, TW, starting with 3rd ch from hook, 1 hdc in each of next 4 chs—4 sts.

Rows 2-4: Ch 2, TW, 1 hdc in each st to end of row—4 sts. Beg working in rnds, stuffing as work progresses.

Rnd 1: Ch 2, TW, 2 hdc in next st, 1 hdc in each of next 2 sts, 2 hdc in next st, 1 hdc in the end of Row 3, 2 hdc in the end of Row 2, 1 hdc in next ch, 1 hdc in each of next 2 chs, 2 hdc in next ch, 2 hdc in the end of Row 2, 1 hdc in the end of Row 3, sl st last hdc to first hdc—18 sts.

Rnds 2-3: Ch 2, TW, 1 hdc in each st to end of rnd, sl st last hdc to first hdc—18 sts.

Rnd 4: Ch 2, TW, * 1 hdc in each of next 4 sts, hdc next 2 sts tog; rep from * two more times to end of rnd, sl st last hdc to first hdc—15 sts.

Rnd 5: Ch 2, TW, 2 hdc in next st, 1 hdc in each of next 2 sts, 2 hdc in each of next 2 sts, 1 hdc in each of next 9 sts, 2 hdc in next st, sl st last hdc to first hdc—19 sts.

Rnd 6: Ch 2, TW, 1 hdc in each of next 13 sts, 2 hdc in next st, 1 hdc in each of next 4 sts, 2 hdc in next st, sl st last hdc to first hdc—21 sts.

Rnd 7: Ch 2, TW, * 2 hdc in next st, 1 hdc in next st; rep from * two more times, 2 hdc in next st, 1 hdc in each of next 6 sts, 2 hdc in each of next 2 sts, 1 hdc in each of next 6 sts, sl st last hdc to first hdc—27 sts.

Rnd 8: Ch 2, TW, 1 hdc in each of next 18 sts, 2 hdc in next st, 1 hdc in each of next 3 sts, 2 hdc in next st, 1 hdc in each of next 3 sts, 2 hdc in next st, sl st last hdc to first hdc—30 sts.

Rnds 9-12: Ch 2, TW, 1 hdc in each st to end of rnd, sl st last hdc to first hdc—30 sts.

Rnd 13: Cut A, join B, tie off A, ch 2, TW, 1 hdc in next st, * 1 popcorn in next st, ch 1, 1 hdc in each of next 2 sts; rep from * eight more times, 1 popcorn in next st, ch 1, 1 hdc in next st, sl st last hdc to first hdc—30 sts.

Rnd 14: Ch 2, TW, * 1 popcorn in next st, ch 1, hdc next 2 sts tog; rep from * nine more times, sl st last hdc to top of first popcorn—20 sts.

Rnd 15: Ch 2, TW, * 1 popcorn in next st, ch 1, 1 hdc in next st, 1 popcorn in next st, ch 1, 1 hdc in next st, hdc next 2 sts tog; rep from * twice more, 1 popcorn in next st, ch 1, 1 hdc in next st, sl st last hdc to top of first popcorn—17 sts.

Rnd 16: Ch 2, TW, * 1 popcorn in next st, ch 1, hdc next 2 sts tog; rep from * four more times, 1 popcorn in next st, ch 1, 1 hdc in next st, sl st last hdc to top of first popcorn—12 sts.

Rnd 17 (back of head): Ch 2, TW, * hdc next 2 sts tog; rep from * five more times to end of rnd, sl st last hdc to first hdc—6 sts. Fasten off, leaving a 12" (30cm) tail. Whip stitch opening closed. Tie off and weave in ends.

Body

Make 1.

Rnd 1 (hind end): With I/9 (5.5mm) hook and B, stuffing as work progresses, ch 4, sl st last ch to first ch to make a loop.

Rnd 2: Ch 2, TW, work 6 hdc in center of loop, sl st last hdc to first hdc—6 sts.

Rnd 3: Ch 2, TW, * 2 hdc in next st, 1 popcorn in next st, ch 1; rep from * two more times, sl st last ch to first hdc—9 sts.

Rnd 4: Ch 2, TW, 1 popcorn in next st, ch 1, * 2 hdc in next st, 1 popcorn in next st, ch 1; rep from * three more times, sl st last ch to top of first popcorn—13 sts.

Rnd 5: Ch 2, TW, 1 hdc in next st, * 1 popcorn in next st, ch 1, 2 hdc in next st; rep from * five more times, sl st last hdc to first hdc—19 sts.

Rnd 6: Ch 2, TW, 1 popcorn in next st, ch 1, * 2 hdc in next st, 1 popcorn in next st, ch 1; rep from * eight more times, sl st last ch to top of first popcorn—28 sts.

Rnd 7: Ch 2, TW, * 2 hdc in next st, 1 popcorn in next st, ch 1; rep from * thirteen more times, sl st last ch to first hdc—42 sts.

Rnd 8: Ch 2, TW, * 1 popcorn in next st, ch 1, 1 hdc in next st, 1 popcorn in next st, ch 1, 1 hdc in next st, 1 popcorn in next st, ch 1, 2 hdc in next st; rep from * five more times, ** 1 popcorn in next st, ch 1, 1 hdc in next st; rep from ** two more times, sl st last hdc to top of first popcorn—48 sts.

Rnd 9: Ch 2, TW, * 1 popcorn in next st, ch 1, 1 hdc in next st, 1 popcorn in next st, ch 1, 1 hdc in next st, 1 popcorn in next st, ch 1, 1 hdc in next st, 1 popcorn in next st, ch 1, 2 hdc in next st; rep from * five more times, sl st last hdc to top of first popcorn—54 sts.

Rnds 10-17: Ch 2, TW, * 1 hdc in next st, 1 popcorn in next st, ch 1; rep from * twenty-six more times, sl st last ch to first hdc—54 sts.

Rnd 18: Ch 2, TW, skip first st, * 1 hdc in next st, 1 popcorn in next st, ch 1, 1 hdc in next st, 1 popcorn in next st, hdc next 2 sts tog, 1 popcorn in next st, ch 1, 1 hdc in next st, 1 popcorn in next st, ch 1, 1 hdc in next st, 1 popcorn decrease over next 2 sts, ch 1, 1 hdc in next st; rep from * three more times, skip next st, sl st last hdc to first hdc—44 sts.

Rnd 19: Ch 2, TW, * 1 hdc in each of next 2 sts, 1 popcorn decrease over next 2 sts, ch 1; rep from * ten more times, sl st last ch to first hdc—33 sts.

Rnd 20: Ch 2, TW, * 1 hdc in next st, 1 popcorn decrease over next 2 sts, ch 1; rep from * ten more times, sl st last ch to first hdc—22 sts.

Rnd 21: Ch 2, TW, * 1 popcorn decrease over next 2 sts, ch 1; rep from * ten more times, sl st last ch to top of first popcorn—11 sts.

Rnd 22 (head end): Ch 2, TW, 1 hdc in next st, * hdc next 2 sts tog; rep from * four more times, sl st last hdc to first hdc—6 sts. Fasten off, leaving a 12" (30cm) tail to whip stitch remaining hole closed. Tie off and weave in ends. With a 36" (91cm) length of B, whip stitch back of head to head end of body (Fig. 1). Tie off and weave in ends.

Forehead Wool

Make 1.

Row 1: With I/9 (5.5mm) hook and B, leaving a 36" (91cm) tail, ch 9, starting with 3rd ch from hook, * 1 popcorn in next ch, ch 1, 1 hdc in next ch; rep from * two more times, 1 popcorn in next ch—7 sts.

Row 2: Ch 2, TW, skip first st, * 1 popcorn in next st, ch 1, 1 hdc in next st; rep from * one more time, 1 popcorn in next st—5 sts. Fasten off. Center Row 1 to line up with existing hairline on top of head. Whip stitch forehead wool in place on top of head (Fig. 1). Tie off and weave in ends.

Chin Wool

Make 1.

Row 1: With I/9 (5.5mm) hook and B, leaving a 36" (91cm) tail, ch 21, starting with 3rd ch from hook, 1 popcorn in next ch, ch 1, * 1 hdc in next ch, 1 popcorn in next ch, ch 1; rep from * eight more times to end of row—19 sts.

Row 2: Ch 2, TW, skip first st, 1 popcorn in next st, ch 1, * 1 hdc in next st, 1 popcorn in next st, ch 1; rep from * seven more times to end of row—17 sts.

Row 3: Ch 1, TW, hdc next 2 sts tog, 1 hdc in each of next 13 sts, hdc next 2 sts tog—15 sts. Fasten off. Line up Row 1 with neckline under head. Whip stitch chin wool in place on chin (Fig. 1). Weave in ends.

Mouth

With darning needle and C, embroider mouth as shown (Fig. 1).

Eye

Make 2.

Rnd 1: With G/6 (4mm) hook and C, ch 3, sl st last ch to first ch to make a loop.

Rnd 2: Ch 1, TW, work 6 sc in center of loop, sl st last sc to first sc—6 sts. Fasten off, leaving an 18" (46cm) tail. Whip stitch eye to head (Fig. 1). Tie off and weave in ends.

Eyelid

Make 2.

Row 1: With I/9 (5.5mm) hook and A, leaving a 20" (51cm) tail, ch 8, TW, starting with 3rd ch from hook, 1 hdc in each of next 6 chs—6 sts. Fasten off. Whip stitch eyelid just above eye (Fig. 1), stuffing lightly as work progresses. Tie off and weave in ends.

Figure 1 (front view)

Figure 1 (side view)

Nose

Make 1.

Row 1: With G/6 (4mm) hook and C, leaving a 20" (51cm) tail, ch 8, TW, starting with 3rd ch from hook, 1 hdc in each of next 6 chs—6 sts. Fasten off. Whip stitch nose to head in a slight U shape (Fig. 1). Tie off and weave in ends.

Ear

Make 4.

Row 1 (base): With I/9 (5.5mm) hook and A, leaving a 24" (61cm) tail on 2 of the pieces, ch 7, TW, starting with 3rd ch from hook, 1 hdc in each ch to end of row—5 sts.

Rows 2–4: Ch 2, TW, 1 hdc in each st to end of row—5 sts.

Row 5: Ch 1, TW, hdc next 2 sts tog, 1 hdc in next st, hdc next 2 sts tog—3 sts.

Row 6: Ch 1, TW, 1 hdc in each st to end of row—3 sts. Fasten off. Align one piece with 24" (61cm) tail and one without and whip stitch around. Whip stitch base end of completed ear to head. Tie off and weave in ends.

Leg

Make 4.

Rnd 1: With I/9 (5.5mm) hook and A, leaving a 36" (91cm) tail, ch 25, sl st last ch to first ch to make a loop.

Rnds 2–3: Ch 2, TW, 1 hdc in each ch/st to end of rnd, sl st last hdc to first hdc—25 sts.

Rnd 4: Ch 2, TW, 1 hdc in each of next 12 sts, 2 hdc in next st, 1 hdc in each of next 12 sts, sl st last hdc to first hdc—26 sts.

Rnd 5: Ch 2, TW, 1 hdc in each of next 12 sts, 2 hdc in next st, 1 hdc in each of next 13 sts, sl st last hdc to first hdc—27 sts.

Rnd 6: Ch 2, TW, 1 hdc in each of next 13 sts, 2 hdc in next st, 1 hdc in each of next 13 sts, sl st last hdc to first hdc—28 sts.

Rnd 7: Ch 2, TW, 1 hdc in each of next 14 sts, 2 hdc in next st, 1 hdc in each of next 13 sts, sl st last hdc to first hdc—29 sts.

Rnd 8: Ch 2, TW, 1 hdc in each of next 14 sts, 2 hdc in next st, 1 hdc in each of next 14 sts, sl st last hdc to first hdc—30 sts.

Rnd 9: Cut A, join C, tie off A, ch 2, TW, 1 hdc in each st to end of rnd, sl st last hdc to first hdc—30 sts.

Rnd 10: Ch 2, TW, 1 hdc in each of next 12 sts, 2 hdc in each of next 6 sts, 1 hdc in each of next 12 sts, sl st last hdc to first hdc—36 sts.

Rnd 11 (hoof end): Ch 2, TW, 1 hdc in each of next 15 sts, 2 hdc in each of next 6 sts, 1 hdc in each of next 15 sts, sl st last hdc to first hdc—42 sts. Fasten off.

Bottom of Hoof

Make 4.

Row 1: With I/9 (5.5mm) hook and C, ch 6, TW, starting with 3rd ch from hook, 2 hdc in next ch, 1 hdc in each of next 2 chs, 2 hdc in next ch—6 sts.

Row 2: Ch 2, TW, 3 hdc in next st, 1 hdc in each of next 4 sts, 3 hdc in next st—10 sts.

Row 3: Ch 2, TW, 3 hdc in next st, 1 hdc in each of next 9 sts—12 sts.

Row 4: Ch 2, TW, 2 hdc in next st, 1 hdc in each of next 9 sts, hdc next 2 sts tog—12 sts.

Figure 2

Row 5: Ch 1, TW, hdc next 2 sts tog, 1 hdc in each of next 10 sts—11 sts.

Row 6: Ch 2, TW, 1 hdc in each of next 10 sts, ch 3—13 sts.

Row 7: TW, starting with 3rd ch from hook, 2 hdc in next ch, 1 hdc in each of next 10 sts—12 sts.

Row 8: Ch 1, TW, hdc next 2 sts tog, 1 hdc in each of next 9 sts, 2 hdc in next st—12 sts.

Row 9: Ch 1, TW, skip next st, hdc next 2 sts tog, 1 hdc in each of next 7 sts, hdc next 2 sts tog—9 sts.

Row 10: Ch 1, TW, hdc next 2 sts tog, 1 hdc in each of next 3 sts, [hdc next 2 sts tog] twice—6 sts. Fasten off, weave in ends. Align bottom of hoof with hoof end of leg, folding the extra portion of color C on the leg opposite the seam to form the "toes" as shown (Fig. 2 above and Figs. 2-4 on page 44). Whip stitch in place. Tie off and weave in ends. Stuff. Whip stitch leg on body (Fig. 1). Tie off and weave in ends.

Tail

Make 1.

Rnd 1 (base): With I/9 (5.5mm) hook and B, leaving a 24" (61cm) tail, ch 16, sl st last ch to first ch.

Rnd 2: Ch 2, TW, * 1 popcorn in next ch, ch 1, 1 hdc in next ch; rep from * four more times, 1 hdc in each of next 6 chs, sl st last hdc to top of first popcorn—16 sts.

Rnd 3: Ch 2, TW, 1 hdc in next st, hdc next 2 sts tog, 1 hdc in next st, hdc next 2 sts tog, 1 hdc in next st, * 1 popcorn decrease over next 2 sts, ch 1, 1 hdc in next st; rep from * one more time, 1 popcorn in next st, ch 1, 1 popcorn decrease over next 2 sts, ch 1, sl st last ch to first hdc—11 sts.

Rnd 4: Ch 2, TW, 1 popcorn decrease over next 2 sts, ch 1, 1 hdc in next st, 1 popcorn in next st, ch 1, 1 hdc in next st, 1 popcorn in next st, ch 1, *hdc next 2 sts tog; rep from * one more time, 1 hdc in next st, sl st last hdc to top of first popcorn—8 sts.

Rnd 5: Ch 2, TW, hdc next 2 sts tog, 1 hdc in next st, hdc next 2 sts tog, 1 popcorn in next st, ch 1, 1 popcorn decrease over next 2 sts, ch 1, sl st last ch to first hdc—5 sts. Fasten off, leaving an 8" (20cm) tail. Whip stitch opening closed. Tie off and weave in ends. With popcorn side facing out, pinch base end of tail tog and whip stitch to hind end of body (Fig. 1). Tie off and weave in ends.

Otis
the
Pig

Otis the Pig

Otis (code name "Seeker") finds anything and everything that the farmer and his family may need. When the farmer is low on funds, Otis goes into the forest and finds him some truffles to sell at the market. If the farmer's daughter loses her toy in a haystack, Otis finds it for her. In fact, he can help you find pretty much anything. Keep him away from peanut butter, though—it throws off his sense of smell.

YARN

Medium (4) yarn in 3 colors; 40 yds (37m) of color **A**, 290 yds (266m) of color **B** and 170 yds (156m) of color **C**

*The project shown on page 40 uses Lion Brand Vanna's Choice (acrylic, 170 yds [155m], 3.5 oz [100g]) in Antique Rose (**A**), Pink (**B**) and Black (**C**).*

HOOKS AND NOTIONS

G/6 (4mm) crochet hook • Size 13 darning needle • Polyester fiberfill • Stuffing stick

GAUGE

7 hdc and 6 rows = 2" (5cm) using size G/6 (4mm) hook

FINISHED SIZE

Approx 8" (20cm) tall, 13" (33cm) long

Head

Make 1.

Row 1: With A, ch 10, TW, starting with 3rd ch from hook, 1 hdc in each of next 8 chs—8 sts.

Row 2: Ch 2, TW, hdc next 2 sts tog, 1 hdc in each of next 4 sts, hdc next 2 sts tog—6 sts.

Row 3: Ch 2, TW, hdc next 2 sts tog, 1 hdc in each of next 2 sts, hdc next 2 sts tog—4 sts.

Row 4: Ch 2, TW, hdc next 2 sts tog, hdc next 2 sts tog—2 sts.

Row 5: Ch 2, TW, hdc next 2 sts tog—1 st. Beg working in rnds, stuffing as work progresses.

Rnd 1: Ch 2, TW, work 2 hdc in same st, work 1 hdc each in the end of Rows 5–1, work 2 hdc in next st of Row 1, 1 hdc in each of next 6 sts, 2 hdc in next st, work 1 hdc each in the end of Rows 1–5, sl st last hdc to first hdc—22 sts.

Rnds 2–6: Cut A, join B, tie off A, ch 2, TW, 1 hdc in each st to end of rnd, sl st last hdc to first hdc—22 sts.

Rnd 7: Ch 2, TW, 1 hdc in each of next 2 sts, 3 hdc in each of next 2 sts, 1 hdc in each of next 3 sts, 3 hdc in next st, 1 hdc in each of next 6 sts, 3 hdc in next st, 1 hdc in each of next 3 sts, 3 hdc in each of next 2 sts, 1 hdc in each of next 2 sts, sl st last hdc to first hdc—34 sts.

Rnd 8: Ch 2, TW, 1 hdc in each of next 4 sts, 3 hdc in next st, 1 hdc in each of next 6 sts, 3 hdc in next st, 1 hdc in each of next 10 sts, 3 hdc in next st, 1 hdc in each of next 6 sts, 3 hdc in next st, 1 hdc in each of next 4 sts, sl st last hdc to first hdc—42 sts.

Rnd 9: Ch 2, TW, 1 hdc in each st to end of rnd, sl st last hdc to first hdc—42 sts.

Rnd 10: Ch 2, TW, 2 hdc in next st, 1 hdc in each of next 5 sts, 2 hdc in next st, 1 hdc in each of next 29 sts, 2 hdc in next st, 1 hdc in each of next 5 sts, sl st last hdc to first hdc—45 sts.

Rnds 11–16: Ch 2, TW, 1 hdc in each st to end of rnd, sl st last hdc to first hdc—45 sts.

Rnd 17: Ch 2, TW, * 1 hdc in each of next 3 sts, hdc next 2 sts tog; rep from * eight more times to end of rnd, sl st last hdc to first hdc—36 sts.

Rnd 18: Ch 2, TW, * 1 hdc in each of next 4 sts, hdc next 2 sts tog; rep from * five more times to end of rnd, sl st last hdc to first hdc—30 sts.

Rnd 19: Ch 2, TW, * 1 hdc in each of next 3 sts, hdc next 2 sts tog; rep from * five more times to end of rnd, sl st last hdc to first hdc—24 sts.

Rnd 20: Ch 2, TW, * 1 hdc in each of next 2 sts, hdc next 2 sts tog; rep from * five more times to end of rnd, sl st last hdc to first hdc—18 sts.

Rnd 21: Ch 2, TW, * 1 hdc in next st, hdc next 2 sts tog; rep from * five more times to end of rnd, sl st last hdc to first hdc—12 sts.

Rnd 22: Ch 2, TW, * hdc next 2 sts tog; rep from * five more times to end of rnd, sl st last hdc to first hdc—6 sts. Fasten off, leaving a 12" (30cm) tail. Whip stitch opening closed. Tie off and weave in ends.

Figure 1 (front view)

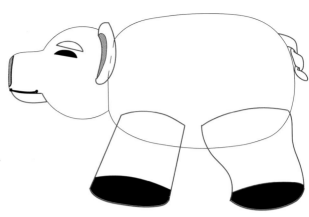

Figure 1 (side view)

Body

Make 1.

Rnd 1: With B, stuffing as work progresses, ch 4, sl st last ch to first ch to make loop.

Rnd 2: Ch 2, work 10 hdc in center of loop, sl st last hdc to first hdc—10 sts.

Rnd 3: Ch 2, TW, * 1 hdc in next st, 2 hdc in next st; rep from * four more times to end of rnd, sl st last hdc to first hdc—15 sts.

Rnd 4: Ch 2, TW, * 1 hdc in each of next 2 sts, 2 hdc in next st; rep from * four more times, sl st last hdc to first hdc—20 sts.

Rnd 5: Ch 2, TW, * 1 hdc in next st, 2 hdc in next st; rep from * nine more times, sl st last hdc to first hdc—30 sts.

Rnd 6: Ch 2, TW, * 1 hdc in each of next 2 sts, 2 hdc in next st; rep from * nine more times, sl st last hdc to first hdc—40 sts.

Rnd 7: Ch 2, TW, * 1 hdc in each of next 3 sts, 2 hdc in next st; rep from * nine more times, sl st last hdc to first hdc—50 sts.

Rnd 8: Ch 2, TW, * 1 hdc in each of next 9 sts, 2 hdc in next st; rep from * four more times, sl st last hdc to first hdc—55 sts.

Rnds 9–29: Ch 2, TW, 1 hdc in each st to end of rnd, sl st last hdc to first hdc—55 sts.

Rnd 30: Ch 2, TW, * 1 hdc in each of next 3 sts, hdc next 2 sts tog; rep from * ten more times to end of rnd, sl st last hdc to first hdc—44 sts.

Rnd 31: Ch 2, TW, * 1 hdc in each of next 9 sts, hdc next 2 sts tog; rep from * three more times to end of rnd, sl st last hdc to first hdc—40 sts.

Rnd 32: Ch 2, TW, * 1 hdc in each of next 2 sts, hdc next 2 sts tog; rep from * nine more times to end of rnd, sl st last hdc to first hdc—30 sts.

Rnd 33: Ch 2, TW, * 1 hdc in each of next 3 sts, hdc next 2 sts tog; rep from * five more times to end of rnd, sl st last hdc to first hdc—24 sts.

Rnd 34: Ch 2, TW, * 1 hdc in each of next 4 sts, hdc next 2 sts tog; rep from * three more times to end of rnd, sl st last hdc to first—20 sts.

Rnd 35: Ch 2, TW, * 1 hdc in each of next 2 sts, hdc next 2 sts tog; rep from * four more times to end of rnd, sl st last hdc to first hdc—15 sts.

Rnd 36: Ch 2, TW, * 1 hdc in next st, hdc next 2 sts tog; rep from * four more times to end of rnd, sl st last hdc to first hdc—10 sts.

Rnd 37: Ch 2, TW, * hdc next 2 sts tog; rep from * four more times to end of rnd, sl st last hdc to first hdc—5 sts. Fasten off, leaving a 12" (30cm) tail. Whip stitch opening closed. Tie off and weave in ends. Whip stitch head to body (Fig. 1). Tie off and weave in ends.

Eyes and Nose

With darning needle and C, embroider eyes and nostrils as shown (Fig. 1).

Eyelid

Make 2.

Row 1: With B, leaving a 15" (38cm) tail, ch 10, TW, starting with 3rd ch from hook, 1 hdc in each of next 8 chs—8 sts.

Row 2: Ch 1, TW, hdc next 2 sts tog, 1 hdc in each of next 4 sts, hdc next 2 sts tog—6 sts.

Row 3: Ch 1, TW, hdc next 2 sts tog, 1 hdc in each of next 2 sts, hdc next 2 sts tog—4 sts. Fasten off. Align Row 1 above eye and whip stitch around, stuffing as work progresses (Fig. 1). Tie off and weave in ends.

Bottom Lip

Make 1.

Row 1: With B, ch 9, TW, starting with 3rd ch from hook, 1 hdc in each of next 7 chs—7 sts.

Rows 2–3: Ch 2, TW, 1 hdc in each st to end of row—7 sts.

Row 4: Ch 2, TW, hdc next 2 sts tog, 1 hdc in each of next 3 sts, hdc next 2 sts tog—5 sts.

Row 5: Ch 2, TW, hdc next 2 sts tog, 1 hdc in next st, hdc next 2 sts tog—3 sts. Fasten off, leaving a 20" (51cm) tail. Whip stitch lip beneath snout, keeping Row 1 toward the back (Fig. 1), stuffing as work progresses. Tie off and weave in ends. With darning needle and C, embroider mouth along seam (Fig. 1).

Inner Ear

Make 2.

Row 1 (base): With A, ch 7, TW, starting with 3rd ch from hook, 1 hdc in each of next 5 chs—5 sts.

Row 2: Ch 2, TW, 3 hdc in next st, 1 hdc in each of next 3 sts, 2 hdc in next st—8 sts.

Row 3: Ch 2, TW, 1 hdc in each of next 7 sts, 3 hdc in next st—10 sts.

Row 4: Ch 2, TW, 1 hdc in each st to end of row—10 sts.

Row 5: Ch 2, TW, 1 hdc in each of next 8 sts, hdc next 2 sts tog—9 sts.

Row 6: Ch 2, TW, hdc next 2 sts tog, 1 hdc in each of next 7 sts—8 sts.

Row 7: Ch 2, TW, hdc next 2 sts tog, 1 hdc in each of next 3 sts, hdc next 2 sts tog—5 sts.

Row 8: Ch 2, TW, hdc next 2 sts tog, 1 hdc in next st, hdc next 2 sts tog—3 sts.

Row 9: Ch 2, TW, 1 hdc in next st, hdc next 2 sts tog—2 sts. Fasten off. Join B to base corner and work next rnd as follows.

Rnd 1: Ch 2, work 2 hdc in the end of Row 1 of inner ear piece, work 1 hdc in the end of Rows 2-9, work 1 hdc in each st of Row 9, work 1 hdc in the end of Rows 9-2, work 2 hdc in the end of Row 1—22 sts. Fasten off, weave in ends.

Outer Ear

Make 2.

Row 1 (base): With B, leaving a 36" (91cm) tail, ch 9, TW, starting with 3rd ch from hook, 1 hdc in each of next 7 chs—7 sts.

Row 2: Ch 2, TW, 2 hdc in each of next 2 sts, 1 hdc in each of next 4 sts, 2 hdc in next st—10 sts.

Row 3: Ch 2, TW, 1 hdc in each of next 9 sts, 3 hdc in next st—12 sts.

Row 4: Ch 2, TW, 1 hdc in each st to end of row—12 sts.

Row 5: Ch 2, TW, 1 hdc in each of next 10 sts, hdc next 2 sts tog—11 sts.

Row 6: Ch 2, TW, hdc next 2 sts tog, 1 hdc in each of next 9 sts—10 sts.

Row 7: Ch 2, TW, hdc next 2 sts tog, 1 hdc in each of next 6 sts, hdc next 2 sts tog—8 sts.

Row 8: Ch 2, TW, hdc next 2 sts tog, 1 hdc in each of next 4 sts, hdc next 2 sts tog—6 sts.

Row 9: Ch 2, TW, hdc next 2 sts tog, 1 hdc in each of next 2 sts, hdc next 2 sts tog—4 sts.

Row 10: Ch 2, TW, hdc next 2 sts tog, hdc next 2 sts tog—2 sts. Fasten off. Align inner and outer ear pieces so you clearly have one right and one left ear and whip stitch each tog. Whip stitch completed ear to head (Fig. 1). Tie off and weave in ends.

Front Leg

Make 2.

Rnd 1: With B, leaving a 36" (91cm) tail, ch 28, sl st last ch to first ch to make a loop.

Rnd 2: Ch 2, TW, 1 hdc in each ch to end of rnd, sl st last hdc to first hdc—28 sts.

Rnds 3–11: Ch 2, TW, 1 hdc in each st to end of rnd, sl st last hdc to first hdc—28 sts.

Rnd 12: Cut B, join C, tie off B, ch 2, TW, 1 hdc in each of next 7 sts, * 2 hdc in next st, 1 hdc in next st; rep from * six more times, 1 hdc in each of next 7 sts, sl st last hdc to first hdc—35 sts.

Rnd 13: Ch 2, TW, 1 hdc in each of next 14 sts, * 2 hdc in next st, 1 hdc in next st; rep from * two more times, 1 hdc in each of next 15 sts, sl st last hdc to first hdc—38 sts.

Rnd 14 (hoof end): Ch 2, TW, 1 hdc in each of next 15 sts, * 2 hdc in next st, 1 hdc in next st; rep from * three more times, 1 hdc in each of next 15 sts, sl st last hdc to first hdc—42 sts. Fasten off.

Back Legs

Make 2.

Rnd 1: With B, leaving a 36" (91cm) tail, ch 38, sl st last ch to first ch.

Rnd 2: Ch 2, TW, 1 hdc in each ch to end of rnd, sl st last hdc to first hdc—38 sts.

Rnd 3: Ch 2, TW, * 1 hdc in each of next 7 sts, hdc next 2 sts tog; rep from * three more times, 1 hdc in each of next 2 sts—34 sts.

Rnd 4: Ch 2, TW, * 1 hdc in each of next 9 sts, hdc next 2 sts tog; rep from * two more times, 1 hdc in next st, sl st last hdc to first hdc—31 sts.

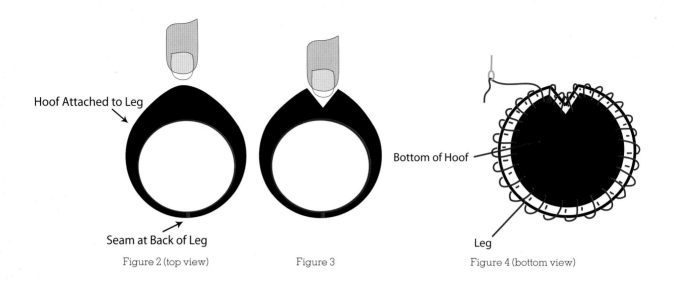

Hoof Attached to Leg

Seam at Back of Leg

Figure 2 (top view)

Figure 3

Bottom of Hoof

Leg

Figure 4 (bottom view)

Rnd 5: Ch 2, TW, 1 hdc in each of next 14 sts, hdc next 2 sts tog, 1 hdc in each of next 15 sts, sl st last hdc to first hdc—30 sts.

Rnd 6: Ch 2, TW, 1 hdc in each of next 14 sts, hdc next 2 sts tog, 1 hdc in each of next 14 sts, sl st last hdc to first hdc—29 sts.

Rnd 7: Ch 2, TW, 2 hdc in next st, 1 hdc in each of next 27 sts, 2 hdc in next st, sl st last hdc to first hdc—31 sts.

Rnd 8: Ch 2, TW, 1 hdc in each of next 10 sts, * hdc next 2 sts tog, 1 hdc in next st; rep from * two more times, 1 hdc in each of next 12 sts, sl st last hdc to first hdc—28 sts.

Rnds 9–11: Ch 2, TW, 1 hdc in each st to end of rnd, sl st last hdc to first hdc—28 sts.

Rnd 12: Cut B, join C, tie off B, ch 2, TW, 1 hdc in each of next 7 sts, * 2 hdc in next st, 1 hdc in next st; rep from * six more times, 1 hdc in each of next 7 sts, sl st last hdc to first hdc—35 sts.

Rnd 13: Ch 2, TW, 1 hdc in each of next 14 sts, * 2 hdc in next st, 1 hdc in next st; rep from * two more times, 1 hdc in each of next 15 sts, sl st last hdc to first hdc—38 sts.

Rnd 14 (hoof end): Ch 2, TW, 1 hdc in each of next 15 sts, * 2 hdc in next st, 1 hdc in next st; rep from * three more times, 1 hdc in each of next 15 sts, sl st last hdc to first hdc—42 sts. Fasten off.

Bottom of Hoof

Make 4.

Row 1: With C, ch 7, TW, starting with 3rd ch from hook, 2 hdc in next ch, 1 hdc in each of next 3 chs, 2 hdc in next ch—7 sts.

Row 2: Ch 2, TW, 2 hdc in next st, 1 hdc in each of next 5 sts, 2 hdc in next st—9 sts.

Row 3: Ch 2, TW, 2 hdc in next st, 1 hdc in each of next 7 sts, 2 hdc in next st—11 sts.

Row 4: Ch 2, TW, 1 hdc in each of next 9 sts, hdc next 2 sts tog—10 sts.

Row 5: Ch 2, TW, hdc next 2 sts tog, 1 hdc in each of next 8 sts—9 sts.

Row 6: Ch 2, TW, 1 hdc in each of next 8 sts, 2 hdc in next st—10 sts.

Row 7: Ch 2, TW, 2 hdc in next st, 1 hdc in each of next 9 sts—11 sts.

Row 8: Ch 2, TW, hdc next 2 sts tog, 1 hdc in each of next 7 sts, hdc next 2 sts tog—9 sts.

Row 9: Ch 2, TW, hdc next 2 sts tog, 1 hdc in each of next 5 sts, hdc next 2 sts tog—7 sts.

Row 10: Ch 2, TW, hdc next 2 sts tog, 1 hdc in each of next 3 sts, hdc next 2 sts tog—5 sts. Fasten off. Holding leg with seam at back center of leg, align bottom of hoof with hoof end of leg, folding as shown to create "toes" (Figs. 2 and 3) and whip stitch around (Fig. 4). Stuff. Whip stitch leg to body (Fig. 1). Tie off and weave in ends.

Tail

Make 1.

Row 1: With B, ch 22, starting with 2nd ch from hook, 1 sc in each of next 21 chs. Fasten off, leaving an 8" (20cm) tail. Whip stitch in place on body (Fig. 1). Tie off and weave in ends.

Nelly
the
Horse

Nelly the Horse

Nelly (code name "Retriever") helps recruit outside help when the farmer and his family are unable to work. The farm can't simply shut down when the family falls ill. Corn still needs to be shucked and eggs must be collected. It is Nelly's job to go out at night to nearby farms and round up extra animals that are willing to help out. She then leads them back to the farm and takes them to the areas where they are needed most.

YARN

Super bulky (6) yarn in 2 colors; 320 yds (293m) of color **A** and 100 yds (92m) of color **B**

*The project shown on page 45 uses Lion Brand Wool-Ease Thick & Quick (80% acrylic/20% wool, 106 yds [97m], 6 oz [170g]) in Hazelnut (**A**) and Fisherman (**B**).*

HOOKS AND NOTIONS

I/9 (5.5mm) crochet hook • Size 13 darning needle • Polyester fiberfill • Stuffing stick

GAUGE

5 hdc and 4 rows = 2" (5cm) using size I/9 (5.5mm) hook

FINISHED SIZE

Approx 12" (30cm) tall, 17" (43cm) long

Head

Make 1.

Row 1: With A, ch 6, TW, starting with 3rd ch from hook, 1 hdc in each of next 4 chs—4 sts.

Row 2: Ch 2, TW, 1 hdc in each st to end of row—4 sts. Beg working in rnds, stuffing as work progresses.

Rnd 1: Ch 2, TW, 1 hdc in next 4 sts, work 1 hdc each in the end of Rows 2–1, work 1 hdc in next 4 chs, work 1 hdc each in the end of Rows 1–2, sl st last hdc to first hdc—12 sts.

Rnd 2: Ch 2, TW, 2 hdc in next st, 1 hdc in each of next 8 sts, 2 hdc in next st, 1 hdc in each of next 2 sts, sl st last hdc to first hdc—14 sts.

Rnd 3: Ch 2, TW, 1 hdc in next st, 2 hdc in each of next 2 sts, 1 hdc in each of next 11 sts, sl st last hdc to first hdc—16 sts.

Rnd 4: Ch 2, TW, 1 hdc in each st to end of rnd, sl st last hdc to first hdc—16 sts.

Rnd 5: Ch 2, TW, 1 hdc in each of next 2 sts, 2 hdc in next st, 1 hdc in each of next 13 sts, sl st last hdc to first hdc—17 sts.

Rnd 6: Ch 2, TW, 2 hdc in each of next 2 sts, 1 hdc in each of next 2 sts, 2 hdc in each of next 3 sts, 1 hdc in each of next 2 sts, 2 hdc in each of next 2 sts, 1 hdc in each of next 6 sts, sl st last hdc to first hdc—24 sts.

Rnd 7: Ch 2, TW, * 2 hdc in next st, 1 hdc in each of next 2 sts; rep from * two more times, 2 hdc in next st, 1 hdc in each of next 11 sts, 2 hdc in next st, 1 hdc in each of next 2 sts, sl st last hdc to first hdc—29 sts.

Rnds 8–9: Ch 2, TW, 1 hdc in each st to end of rnd, sl st last hdc to first hdc—29 sts.

Rnd 10: Ch 2, TW, * 1 hdc in each of next 3 sts, hdc next 2 sts tog; rep from * four more times, 1 hdc in each of next 4 sts, sl st last hdc to first hdc—24 sts.

Rnd 11: Ch 2, TW, * 1 hdc in each of next 2 sts, hdc next 2 sts tog; rep from * five more times to end of rnd, sl st last hdc to first hdc—18 sts.

Rnd 12: Ch 2, TW, * 1 hdc in next st, hdc next 2 sts tog; rep from * five more times to end of rnd, sl st last hdc to first hdc—12 sts.

Rnd 13: Ch 2, TW, * hdc next 2 sts tog; rep from * five more times to end of rnd, sl st last hdc to first hdc—6 sts. Fasten off, leaving a 10" (25cm) tail. Whip stitch opening closed. Tie off and weave in ends.

Body

Make 1.

Rnd 1 (hind end): With A, stuffing as work progresses, ch 4, sl st last ch to first ch to make loop.

Rnd 2: Ch 2, TW, work 8 hdc in center of loop, sl st last hdc to first hdc—8 sts.

Rnd 3: Ch 2, TW, * 1 hdc in next st, 2 hdc in next st; rep from * three more times to end of rnd, sl st last hdc to first hdc—12 sts.

Rnd 4: Ch 2, TW, * 2 hdc in next st, 1 hdc in next st; rep from * five more times to end of rnd, sl st last hdc to first hdc—18 sts.

Rnd 5: Ch 2, TW, * 1 hdc in next st, 2 hdc in next st; rep from * eight more times to end of rnd, sl st last hdc to first hdc—27 sts.

Rnd 6: Ch 2, TW, * 1 hdc in each of next 2 sts, 2 hdc in next st; rep from * eight more times to end of rnd, sl st last hdc to first hdc—36 sts.

Rnd 7: Ch 2, TW, * 1 hdc in each of next 8 sts, 2 hdc in next st; rep from * three more times to end of rnd, sl st last hdc to first hdc—40 sts.

Rnds 8–14: Ch 2, TW, 1 hdc in each st to end of rnd, sl st last hdc to first hdc—40 sts.

Rnd 15: Ch 2, TW, * 1 hdc in each of next 8 sts, hdc next 2 sts tog; rep from * three more times, sl st last hdc to first hdc—36 sts.

Rnds 16–20: Ch 2, TW, 1 hdc in each st to end of rnd, sl st last hdc to first hdc—36 sts.

Rnd 21: Ch 2, TW, 1 hdc in each of next 16 sts, 2 hdc in each of next 4 sts, 1 hdc in each of next 16 sts, sl st last hdc to first hdc—40 sts.

Rnds 22–25: Ch 2, TW, 1 hdc in each st to end of rnd, sl st last hdc to first hdc—40 sts.

Rnd 26: Ch 2, TW, * 1 hdc in each of next 3 sts, hdc next 2 sts tog; rep from * seven more times to end of rnd, sl st last hdc to first hdc—32 sts.

Rnd 27: Ch 2, TW, * 1 hdc in each of next 2 sts, hdc next 2 sts tog; rep from * seven more times to end of rnd—24 sts.

Rnd 28: Ch 2, TW, * 1 hdc in next st, hdc next 2 sts tog; rep from * seven more times to end of rnd, sl st last hdc to first hdc—16 sts.

Rnd 29: Ch 2, TW, * hdc next 2 sts tog; rep from * seven more times to end of rnd, sl st last hdc to first hdc—8 sts.

Rnd 30 (neck end): Ch 2, TW, * hdc next 2 sts tog; rep from * three more times to end of rnd, sl st last hdc to first hdc—4 sts. Fasten off, leaving an 8" (20cm) tail. Whip stitch opening closed. Tie off and weave in ends.

Neck

Make 1.

Row 1 (head end): With A, leaving a 36" (91cm) tail, ch 6, starting with 3rd ch from hook, 2 hdc in next st, 1 hdc in each of next 2 sts, 2 hdc in next st—6 sts. Beg working in rnds.

Rnd 1: Ch 2, TW, 2 hdc in next st, 1 hdc in each of next 4 sts, 2 hdc in next st, ch 16, sl st last ch to first hdc to make loop.

Rnds 2–5: Ch 2, TW, 1 hdc in each ch/st to end of row, sl st last hdc to first hdc—24 sts.

Rnd 6: Ch 2, TW * 1 hdc in each of next 5 sts, 2 hdc in next st; rep from * three more times to end of rnd, sl st last hdc to first hdc—28 sts.

Rnd 7: Ch 2, TW, * 1 hdc in each of next 6 sts, 2 hdc in next st; rep from * three more times to end of rnd, sl st last hdc to first hdc—32 sts.

Rnd 8 (body end): Ch 2, TW, * hdc next 2 sts tog, 1 hdc in each of next 13 sts; rep from * one more time, hdc next 2 sts tog, sl st last hdc to first hdc—29 sts. Fasten off, leaving a 36" (91cm) tail. Insert back of head into head opening of neck and rotate until horse appears to be looking straight ahead, and whip stitch in place (Fig. 1). (Note: The seam of the head should run diagonally from center of face up to outside corner of horse's left eyelid.) Tie off and weave in ends. Stuff neck. Align neck and body, turning body so the seam is centered under belly, and whip stitch in place (Fig. 1). Tie off and weave in ends.

Nose Diamond

Make 1.

Row 1 (forehead end): With B, leaving a 36" (91cm) tail, ch 4, TW, starting with 3rd ch from hook, 1 hdc in each of next 2 chs—2 sts.

Row 2: Ch 2, TW, 2 hdc in each of next 2 sts—4 sts.

Row 3: Ch 2, TW, 1 hdc in each st to end of row—4 sts.

Row 4: Ch 1, TW, hdc next 2 sts tog, hdc next 2 sts tog—2 sts.

Rows 5–7: Ch 2, TW, 1 hdc in each of next 2 sts—2 sts.

Row 8: Ch 1, TW, hdc next 2 sts tog—1 st. Fasten off. Position on snout as shown (Fig. 1) and whip stitch in place. Tie off and weave in ends.

Eyes and Mouth

With darning needle and B, embroider eyes and mouth as shown (Fig. 1).

Eyelid

Make 2.

Row 1: With A, leaving an 18" (46cm) tail, ch 7, TW, starting with 2nd ch from hook, 1 sc in each of next 6 chs—6 sts.

Row 2: Ch 1, TW, sc next 2 sts tog, 1 sc in each of next 2 sts, sc next 2 sts tog—4 sts. Fasten off. Align Row 1 parallel to eye and whip stitch around, stuffing as work progresses (Fig. 1). Tie off and weave in ends.

Nostril

Make 2.

Row 1: With A, leaving an 18" (46cm) tail, ch 5, TW, starting with 2nd ch from hook, 1 sc in each of next 4 chs—4 sts.

Figure 1 (front view)

Fasten off, weave in ends. Pinch nostril tog in the shape of an upside-down U. Position on face as shown and whip stitch in place (Fig. 1), taking care not to stitch down the front edge of the nostrils. Tie off and weave in ends.

Ear

Make 4. Leave a 36" (91cm) tail on 2 pieces and a 5" (13cm) tail on the other 2.

Row 1 (base): With A, ch 8, TW, starting with 3rd ch from hook, 1 hdc in each of next 6 chs—6 sts.

Row 2: Ch 2, TW, 1 hdc in each st to end of row—6 sts.

Row 3: Ch 2, TW, hdc next 2 sts tog, 1 hdc in each of next 2 sts, hdc next 2 sts tog—4 sts.

Row 4: Ch 2, TW, hdc next 2 sts tog, hdc next 2 sts tog—2 sts.

Row 5: Ch 2, TW, hdc next 2 sts tog—1 st. Fasten off. Align one piece with a 36" (91cm) tail with one without, and whip stitch tog. Whip stitch ear to head, pinching bottom corners of the ear as shown to shape (Fig. 1). Tie off and weave in ends.

Front Leg

Make 2.

Row 1 (hip end): With A, leaving a 36" (91cm) tail, ch 6, TW, starting with 3rd ch from hook, 2 hdc in next st, 1 hdc in each of next 2 sts, 2 hdc in next st—6 sts.

Row 2: Ch 2, TW, 2 hdc in next st, 1 hdc in each of next 4 sts, 2 hdc in next st—8 sts.

Row 3: Ch 2, TW, 2 hdc in next st, 1 hdc in each of next 6 sts, 2 hdc in next st—10 sts. Beg working in rnds.

Rnd 1: Ch 2, TW, 2 hdc in next st, 1 hdc in each of next 8 sts, 2 hdc in next st, ch 14, sl st last ch to first hdc to make a loop—26 sts.

Rnds 2–3: Ch 2, TW, 1 hdc in each ch/st to end of rnd, sl st last hdc to first hdc—26 sts.

Rnd 4: Ch 2, TW, 1 hdc in next st, * hdc next 2 sts tog, 1 hdc in each of next 4 sts; rep from * three more times, 1 hdc in next st, sl st last hdc to first hdc—22 sts.

Rnds 5–6: Ch 2, TW, 1 hdc in each st to end of rnd, sl st last hdc to first hdc—22 sts.

Rnd 7: Ch 2, TW, 1 hdc in next st, * hdc next 2 sts tog, 1 hdc in each of next 3 sts; rep from * three more times, 1 hdc in next st, sl st last hdc to first hdc—18 sts.

Rnd 8: Ch 2, TW, * 1 hdc in each of next 4 sts, hdc next 2 sts tog; rep from * two more times, sl st last hdc to first hdc—15 sts.

Rnd 9: Ch 2, TW, 1 hdc in each st to end of rnd, cut A, join B, tie off A, sl st last hdc to first hdc—15 sts.

Rnd 10: Ch 2, TW, 1 hdc in each st to end of rnd, sl st last hdc to first hdc—15 sts.

Rnd 11: Ch 2, TW, * 1 hdc in each of next 4 sts, 2 hdc in next st; rep from * two more times to end of rnd, sl st last hdc to first hdc—18 sts.

Figure 1 (side view)

Rnd 12: Ch 2, TW, * 2 hdc in next st, 1 hdc in each of next 8 sts; rep from * one more time, sl st last hdc to first hdc—20 sts.

Rnd 13: Ch 2, TW, * 2 hdc in next st, 1 hdc in each of next 9 sts; rep from * one more time, sl st last hdc to first hdc—22 sts.

Rnds 14–15 (hoof end of leg): Ch 2, TW, 1 hdc in each st to end of rnd, sl st last hdc to first hdc—22 sts. Fasten off.

Back Leg

Make 2.

Row 1 (hip end): With A, leaving a 36" (91cm) tail, ch 10, TW, starting with 3rd ch from hook, 2 hdc in next st, 1 hdc in each of next 6 sts, 2 hdc in next st—10 sts.

Row 2: Ch 2, TW, 2 hdc in next st, 1 hdc in each of next 8 sts, 2 hdc in next st—12 sts.

Row 3: Ch 2, TW, 2 hdc in next st, 1 hdc in each of next 10 sts, 2 hdc in next st—14 sts.

Rows 4–6: Ch 2, TW, 1 hdc in each st to end of row—14 sts. Beg working in rnds.

Rnd 1: Ch 2, TW, 1 hdc in each st to end of row, ch 14, sl st last ch to first hdc—28 sts.

Rnd 2: Ch 2, TW, 1 hdc in each ch/st to end of rnd, sl st last hdc to first hdc—28 sts.

Rnd 3: Ch 2, TW, hdc next 2 sts tog, 1 hdc in each of next 12 sts, hdc next 2 sts tog, 1 hdc in each of next 12 sts, sl st last hdc to first hdc—26 sts.

Rnd 4: Ch 2, TW, hdc next 2 sts tog, 1 hdc in each of next 11 sts, hdc next 2 sts tog, 1 hdc in each of next 11 sts, sl st last hdc to first hdc—24 sts.

Rnd 5: Ch 2, TW, hdc next 2 sts tog, 1 hdc in each of next 10 sts, hdc next 2 sts tog, 1 hdc in each of next 10 sts, sl st last hdc to first hdc—22 sts.

Rnd 6: Ch 2, TW, hdc next 2 sts tog, 1 hdc in each of next 9 sts, hdc next 2 sts tog, 1 hdc in each of next 9 sts, sl st last hdc to first hdc—20 sts.

Rnd 7: Ch 2, TW, hdc next 2 sts tog, 1 hdc in each of next 8 sts, hdc next 2 sts tog, 1 hdc in each of next 8 sts, sl st last hdc to first hdc—18 sts.

Rnd 8: Ch 2, TW, hdc next 2 sts tog, 1 hdc in each of next 7 sts, hdc next 2 sts tog, 1 hdc in each of next 7 sts, sl st last hdc to first hdc—16 sts.

Rnd 9: Ch 2, TW, 1 hdc in each of next 7 sts, hdc next 2 sts tog, 1 hdc in each of next 7 sts, cut A, join B, tie off A, sl st last hdc to first hdc—15 sts.

Rnd 10: Ch 2, TW, 1 hdc in each st to end of rnd, sl st last hdc to first hdc—15 sts.

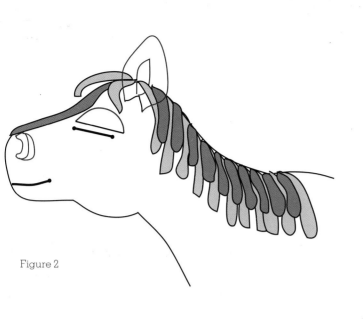

Figure 2

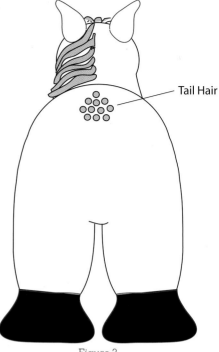

Tail Hair

Figure 3

Rnd 11: Ch 2, TW, * 1 hdc in each of next 4 sts, 2 hdc in next st; rep from * two more times to end of rnd, sl st last hdc to first hdc—18 sts.

Rnd 12: Ch 2, TW, * 2 hdc in next st, 1 hdc in each of next 8 sts; rep from * one more time, sl st last hdc to first hdc—20 sts.

Rnd 13: Ch 2, TW, * 2 hdc in next st, 1 hdc in each of next 9 sts; rep from * one more time, sl st last hdc to first hdc—22 sts.

Rnds 14–15 (hoof end of leg): Ch 2, TW, 1 hdc in each st to end of rnd, sl st last hdc to first hdc—22 sts. Fasten off.

Bottom of Hoof

Make 4.

Rnd 1: With A, ch 4, sl st last ch to first ch to make a loop.

Rnd 2: Ch 2, work 10 hdc in center of loop, sl st last hdc to first hdc—10 sts.

Rnd 3: Ch 2, TW, * 2 hdc in next st; rep from * nine times to end of rnd, sl st last hdc to first hdc—20 sts.

Rnd 4: Ch 2, TW, * 2 hdc in next st, 1 hdc in each of next 9 sts; rep from * one more time, sl st last hdc to first hdc—22 sts. Fasten off, leaving a 20" (51cm) tail. Whip stitch bottom of hoof to hoof end of leg. Tie off and weave in ends. Stuff. Whip stitch hip end of leg to body (Fig. 1). Tie off and weave in ends.

First Layer of Mane

Make 11.

Row 1: With B, leaving a 10" (25cm) tail, ch 12. Fasten off. Whip stitch short end of pieces in a line down center of neck and upper back, spacing ⅛" (3mm) apart (Fig. 2). Tie off and weave in ends.

Second Layer of Mane

Make 10.

Row 1: With B, leaving a 10" (25cm) tail, ch 10. Fasten off. Whip stitch between first layer pieces (Fig. 2). Tie off and weave in ends.

Forehead Hair

Make 3.

Row 1: With B, leaving a 10" (25cm) tail, ch 8. Fasten off. Whip stitch across forehead, like bangs (Fig. 1). Tie off and weave in ends.

Tail Hair

Make 11.

Row 1: With B, leaving a 10" (25cm) tail, ch 22. Fasten off. Whip stitch in a circular pattern on hind end (Fig. 3). Tie off and weave in ends.

See page 126 for the yarn colors used to make these versions.

CHAPTER 3

The Entertainers: Ocean Dwellers

If you've ever seen a nature documentary, you know that sea creatures are some of the most interesting and entertaining animals on the planet. Some, like the dolphin, are brilliant yet playful, while others, like the octopus, seem to dance gracefully through the water, like a ballerina. There are also a few, like the penguin, who seem to be all business, in appearance and action—but deep down, I think he's just always ready for a party!

Waddlesworth the Penguin

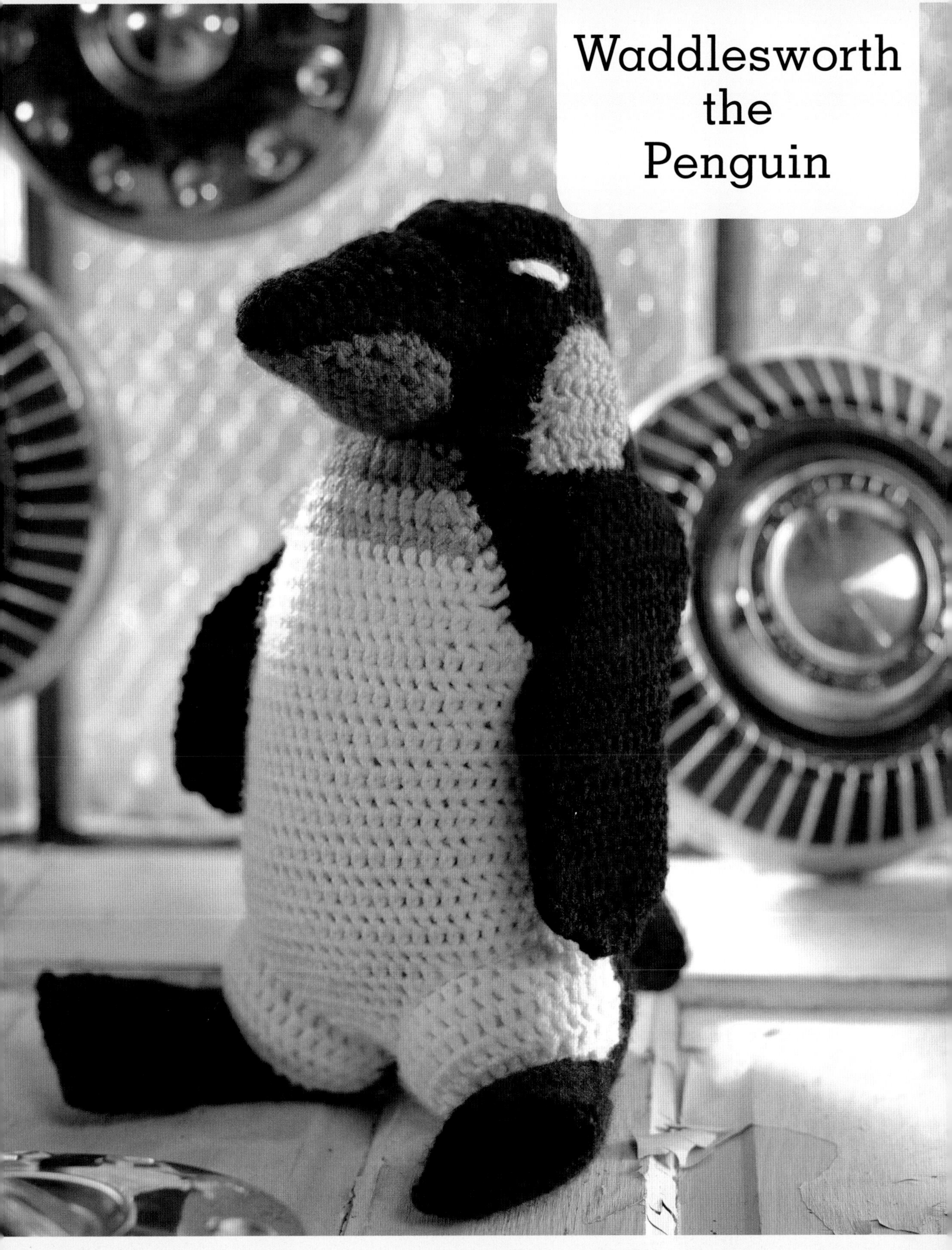

Waddlesworth the Penguin

Planning a special event, but the details are just too overwhelming? Then Waddlesworth is the bird for you! He is an event coordinator extraordinaire, planning all of the most important events of the underwater world: charity concerts, talent shows, birthday parties. You name it, and Waddlesworth can make it unforgettable. But, book him as soon as possible—his calendar fills up quickly!

YARN

Medium (4) yarn in 4 colors; 670 yds (613m) of color **A**, 50 yds (46m) of color **B**, 50 yds (46m) of color **C** and 130 yds (119m) of color **D**

*The project shown on page 53 uses Lion Brand Vanna's Choice (acrylic, 170 yds [155m], 3.5 oz [100g]) in Black (**A**), Rust (**B**), Mustard (**C**) and White (**D**).*

HOOKS AND NOTIONS

G/6 (4mm) crochet hook • Size 13 darning needle • Polyester fiberfill • Stuffing stick

GAUGE

7 hdc and 6 rows = 2" (5cm) using size G/6 (4mm) hook

FINISHED SIZE

Approx 13.5" (34cm) tall

Head/Body

Make 1.

Rnd 1: With A and stuffing as work progresses, ch 3, sl st last ch to first ch to make loop.

Rnd 2: Ch 2, TW, work 8 hdc in center of loop, sl st last hdc to first hdc—8 sts.

Rnd 3: Ch 2, TW, 2 hdc in each st to end of rnd, sl st last hdc to first hdc—16 sts.

Rnd 4: Ch 2, TW, 2 hdc in each st to end of rnd, sl st last hdc to first hdc—32 sts.

Rnd 5: Ch 2, TW, * 1 hdc in each of next 3 sts, 2 hdc in next st; rep from * seven more times, sl st last hdc to first hdc—40 sts.

Rnds 6-16: Ch 2, TW, 1 hdc in each st to end of rnd, sl st last hdc to first hdc—40 sts.

Rnd 17: Ch 2, TW, * 1 hdc in each of next 3 sts, 2 hdc in next st; rep from * nine more times to end of rnd, sl st to first hdc—50 sts.

Rnd 18: Ch 2, TW, * 1 hdc in each of next 9 sts, 2 hdc in next st; rep from * four more times to end of rnd, sl st last hdc to first hdc—55 sts.

Rnds 19-25: Ch 2, TW, 1 hdc in each st to end of rnd, sl st last hdc to first hdc—55 sts.

Rnd 26: Ch 2, TW, * 1 hdc in each of next 10 sts, 2 hdc in next st; rep from * four more times to end of rnd, sl st last hdc to first hdc—60 sts.

Rnd 27: Ch 2, TW, * 1 hdc in each of next 9 sts, 2 hdc in next st; rep from * five more times to end of rnd, sl st last hdc to first hdc—66 sts.

Rnds 28-48: Ch 2, TW, 1 hdc in each st to end of rnd, sl st last hdc to first hdc—66 sts.

Rnd 49: Ch 2, TW, * 1 hdc in each of next 9 sts, hdc next 2 sts tog; rep from * five more times to end of rnd, sl st last hdc to first hdc—60 sts.

Rnd 50: Ch 2, TW, * 1 hdc in each of next 4 sts, hdc next 2 sts tog; rep from * nine more times to end of rnd, sl st last hdc to first hdc—50 sts.

Rnd 51: Ch 2, TW, * 1 hdc in each of next 3 sts, hdc next 2 sts tog; rep from * nine more times to end of rnd, sl st last hdc to first hdc—40 sts.

Rnd 52: Ch 2, TW, * 1 hdc in each of next 2 sts, hdc next 2 sts tog; rep from * nine more times to end of rnd, sl st last hdc to first hdc—30 sts.

Rnd 53: Ch 2, TW, * 1 hdc in each of next 4 sts, hdc next 2 sts tog; rep from * four more times to end of rnd, sl st last hdc to first hdc—25 sts.

Rnd 54: Ch 2, TW, 1 hdc in each of next 3 sts, hdc next 2 sts tog; rep from * four more times to end of rnd, sl st last hdc to first hdc—20 sts.

Rnd 55: Ch 2, TW, * 1 hdc in each of next 2 sts, hdc next 2 sts tog; rep from * four more times to end of rnd, sl st last hdc to first hdc—15 sts.

Rnd 56: Ch 2, TW, * 1 hdc in next st, hdc next 2 sts tog; rep from * four more times to end of rnd, sl st last hdc to first hdc—10 sts. Fasten off, leaving an 8" (20cm) tail. Whip stitch opening closed. Tie off and weave in ends.

Beak

Make 1.

Rnd 1: With A, leaving a 24" (61cm) tail, ch 30, sl st last ch to first ch.

Rnd 2: Ch 2, TW, 1 hdc in each ch to end of rnd, sl st last hdc to first hdc—30 sts.

Rnd 3: Ch 2, TW, 1 hdc in each of next 28 sts, hdc next 2 sts tog, sl st last hdc to first hdc—29 sts.

Rnd 4: Ch 2, TW, 1 hdc in each of next 27 sts, hdc next 2 sts tog, sl st last hdc to first hdc—28 sts.

Rnd 5: Ch 2, TW, * 1 hdc in each of next 5 sts, hdc next 2 sts tog; rep from * three more times to end of rnd, sl st last hdc to first hdc—24 sts.

Rnd 6: Ch 2, TW, * 1 hdc in each of next 2 sts, hdc next 2 sts tog; rep from * five more times, sl st last hdc to first hdc—18 sts.

Rnd 7: Ch 2, TW, 1 hdc in each st to end of rnd, sl st last hdc to first hdc—18 sts.

Rnd 8: Ch 2, TW, * hdc next 2 sts tog, 1 hdc in each of next 7 sts; rep from * one more time to end of rnd, sl st last hdc to first hdc—16 sts.

Rnd 9: Ch 2, TW, * hdc next 2 sts tog, 1 hdc in each of next 6 sts; rep from * one more time to end of rnd, sl st last hdc to first hdc—14 sts.

Rnd 10: Ch 2, TW, 1 hdc in each st to end of rnd, sl st last hdc to first hdc—14 sts.

Rnd 11: Ch 2, TW, * hdc next 2 sts tog, 1 hdc in each of next 5 sts; rep from * one more time to end of rnd, sl st last hdc to first hdc—12 sts.

Rnd 12: Ch 2, TW, 1 hdc in each st to end of rnd, sl st last hdc to first hdc—12 sts.

Rnd 13: Ch 2, TW, * 1 hdc in next st, hdc next 2 sts tog; rep from * three more times to end of rnd, sl st last hdc to first hdc—8 sts.

Rnd 14: Ch 2, TW, * 1 hdc in each of next 2 sts, hdc next 2 sts tog; rep from * one more time to end of rnd, sl st last hdc to first hdc—6 sts. Fasten off, leaving an 8" (20cm) tail. Whip stitch opening closed. Stuff. Whip stitch beak to head, keeping seam centered at bottom (Fig. 1). Tie off and weave in ends.

Beak Accent

Make 1.

Row 1: With B, ch 8, TW, 2 hdc in 3rd ch from hook, 1 hdc in each of next 4 chs, 2 hdc in next ch—8 sts.

Row 2: Ch 2, TW, 2 hdc in next st, 1 hdc in each of next 6 sts, 2 hdc in next st—10 sts.

Row 3: Ch 2, TW, 2 hdc in next st, 1 hdc in each of next 8 sts, 2 hdc in next st—12 sts.

Rows 4–5: Ch 2, TW, 1 hdc in each st to end of row—12 sts.

Row 6: Ch 2, TW, hdc next 2 sts tog, 1 hdc in each of next 8 sts, hdc next 2 sts tog—10 sts.

Row 7: Ch 2, TW, hdc next 2 sts tog, 1 hdc in each of next 6 sts, hdc next 2 sts tog—8 sts.

Row 8: Ch 2, TW, hdc next 2 sts tog, 1 hdc in each of next 4 sts, hdc next 2 sts tog—6 sts.

Row 9: Ch 2, TW, hdc next 2 sts tog, 1 hdc in each of next 2 sts, hdc next 2 sts tog—4 sts.

Row 10: Ch 2, TW, hdc next 2 sts tog, hdc next 2 sts tog—2 sts.

Row 11 (tip of beak): Ch 2, TW, hdc next 2 sts tog—1 st. Fasten off, leaving a 24" (61cm) tail. Whip stitch in place on underside of beak (Fig. 1). Tie off and weave in ends.

Eyes

With darning needle and D, embroider eyes as shown (Fig. 1).

Eyelid

Make 2.

Row 1: With A, leaving a 12" (30cm) tail, ch 8, TW, starting with 3rd ch from hook, 1 hdc in each ch to end of row—6 sts.

Row 2: Ch 1, TW, hdc next 2 sts tog, 1 hdc in each of next 2 sts, hdc next 2 sts tog—4 sts. Fasten off. Align Row 1 of eyelid parallel to eye and whip stitch in place, stuffing as work progresses (Fig. 1). Tie off and weave in ends.

Cheek Accent

Make 2.

Row 1: With C, leaving a 20" (51cm) tail, ch 5, TW, 2 hdc in 3rd ch from hook, 1 hdc in next ch, 2 hdc in next ch—5 sts.

Row 2: Ch 2, TW, 3 hdc in next st, 1 hdc in each of next 4 sts—7 sts.

Row 3: Ch 2, TW, 1 hdc in each st to end of row—7 sts.

Row 4: Ch 2, TW, hdc next 2 sts tog, 1 hdc in each of next 5 sts—6 sts.

Row 5: Ch 2, TW, 3 hdc in next st, 1 hdc in each of next 3 sts, hdc next 2 sts tog—7 sts.

Row 6: Ch 2, TW, * hdc next 2 sts tog; rep from * two more times, 2 hdc in next st—5 sts. Fasten off. Whip stitch in place (Fig. 1). Tie off and weave in ends.

Belly

Make 1.

Row 1 (neck end): With B, ch 10, TW, 2 hdc in 3rd ch from hook, 1 hdc in each of next 6 chs, 2 hdc in next ch—10 sts.

Row 2: Ch 2, TW, 2 hdc in next st, 1 hdc in each of next 8 sts, 2 hdc in next st—12 sts.

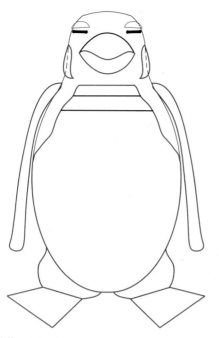

Figure 1 (front view)

Figure 1 (side view)

Row 3: Cut B, join C, ch 2, TW, 2 hdc in next st, 1 hdc in each of next 10 sts, 2 hdc in next st—14 sts.

Row 4: Ch 2, TW, 2 hdc in next st, 1 hdc in each of next 12 sts, 2 hdc in next st—16 sts.

Row 5: Ch 2, TW, 2 hdc in next st, 1 hdc in each of next 14 sts, 2 hdc in next st—18 sts.

Row 6: Cut C, join D, ch 2, TW, 2 hdc in next st, 1 hdc in each of next 16 sts, 2 hdc in next st—20 sts.

Rows 7–8: Ch 2, TW, 1 hdc in each st to end of row—20 sts.

Row 9: Ch 2, TW, 2 hdc in next st, 1 hdc in each of next 18 sts, 2 hdc in next st—22 sts.

Row 10: Ch 2, TW, 2 hdc in next st, 1 hdc in each of next 20 sts, 2 hdc in next st—24 sts.

Row 11: Ch 2, TW, 2 hdc in next st, 1 hdc in each of next 22 sts, 2 hdc in next st—26 sts.

Rows 12–15: Ch 2, TW, 1 hdc in each st to end of row—26 sts.

Row 16: Ch 2, TW, 2 hdc in next st, 1 hdc in each of next 24 sts, 2 hdc in next st—28 sts.

Row 17: Ch 2, TW, 2 hdc in next st, 1 hdc in each of next 26 sts, 2 hdc in next st—30 sts.

Row 18: Ch 2, TW, 2 hdc in next st, 1 hdc in each of next 28 sts, 2 hdc in next st—32 sts.

Row 19: Ch 2, TW, 2 hdc in next st, 1 hdc in each of next 30 sts, 2 hdc in next st—34 sts.

Rows 20–27: Ch 2, TW, 1 hdc in each st to end of row—34 sts.

Row 28: Ch 1, TW, hdc next 2 sts tog, 1 hdc in each of next 30 sts, hdc next 2 sts tog—32 sts.

Row 29: Ch 1, TW, hdc next 2 sts tog, 1 hdc in each of next 28 sts, hdc next 2 sts tog—30 sts.

Row 30: Ch 1, TW, hdc next 2 sts tog, 1 hdc in each of next 26 sts, hdc next 2 sts tog—28 sts.

Row 31: Ch 1, TW, hdc next 2 sts tog, 1 hdc in each of next 24 sts, hdc next 2 sts tog—26 sts.

Row 32: Ch 1, TW, hdc next 2 sts tog, 1 hdc in each of next 22 sts, hdc next 2 sts tog—24 sts.

Row 33: Ch 1, TW, hdc next 2 sts tog, 1 hdc in each of next 20 sts, hdc next 2 sts tog—22 sts.

Row 34: Ch 1, TW, hdc next 2 sts tog, 1 hdc in each of next 18 sts, hdc next 2 sts tog—20 sts.

Row 35: Ch 1, TW, hdc next 2 sts tog, 1 hdc in each of next 16 sts, hdc next 2 sts tog—18 sts. Fasten off, weave in end. Center neck end of belly under beak and whip stitch around using a 48" (122cm) length of A, stuffing lightly if desired (Fig. 1). Tie off and weave in ends.

Flipper

Make 4.

Row 1 (top edge): With A, leaving a 36" (91cm) tail on 2 of the pieces, ch 10, starting with 3rd ch from hook, 2 hdc in next ch, 1 hdc in each of next 7 chs—9 sts.

Row 2: Ch 2, TW, 1 hdc in each of next 8 sts, 2 hdc in next st—10 sts.

Row 3: Ch 2, TW, 1 hdc in each of next 9 sts, 2 hdc in next st—11 sts.

Rows 4–5: Ch 2, TW, 1 hdc in each st to end of row—11 sts.

Row 6: Ch 2, TW, 2 hdc in next st, 1 hdc in each of next 10 sts—12 sts.

Note: The next two groupings of instruction represent alternating rows.

Rows 7, 9, 11: Ch 2, TW, hdc next 2 sts tog, 1 hdc in each of next 9 sts, 2 hdc in next st—12 sts.

Rows 8, 10, 12: Ch 2, TW, 2 hdc in next st, 1 hdc in each of next 9 sts, hdc next 2 sts tog—12 sts.

Rows 13–14: Ch 2, TW, 1 hdc in each st to end of row—12 sts.

Row 15: Ch 2, TW, hdc next 2 sts tog, 1 hdc in each of next 10 sts—11 sts.

Rows 16–23: Ch 2, TW, 1 hdc in each st to end of row—11 sts.

Row 24: Ch 1, TW, [hdc next 2 sts tog] twice, 1 hdc in each of next 5 sts, hdc next 2 sts tog—8 sts.

Row 25: Ch 1, TW, hdc next 2 sts tog, 1 hdc in each of next 2 sts, [hdc next 2 sts tog] twice—5 sts.

Row 26: Ch 1, TW, [hdc next 2 sts tog] twice, 1 hdc in next st—3 sts.

Row 27: Ch 1, TW, hdc next 2 sts tog, 1 hdc in next st—2 sts. Fasten off. Align one piece with a long tail with one without and whip stitch around. Whip stitch top edge of completed flipper in place on body (Fig. 1). Tie off and weave in ends.

Leg

Make 2 in A and 2 in D.

Row 1 (hip end): Leaving a 24" (61cm) tail, ch 22, TW, starting with 3rd ch from hook, 1 hdc in each ch to end of row—20 sts.

Rows 2–4: Ch 2, TW, 1 hdc in each st to end of row—20 sts.

Row 5: Ch 2, TW, * 1 hdc in each of next 4 sts, hdc next 2 sts tog; rep from * one more time, 1 hdc in each of next 8 sts—18 sts.

Row 6: Ch 2, TW, * 1 hdc in each of next 4 sts, hdc next 2 sts tog; rep from * two more times to end of row—15 sts.

Row 7: Ch 2, TW, * 1 hdc in next st, hdc next 2 sts tog; rep from * four more times to end of row—10 sts.

Row 8 (foot end): Ch 2, TW, * hdc next 2 sts tog; rep from * four more times to end of row—5 sts. Fasten off, leaving a 12" (31cm) tail on each A piece. Lay 1 D piece over 1 A piece and whip stitch tog the row ends of one side of leg, using the 12" (31cm) tail (Fig. 2). Tie another 12" (31cm) length of A onto opposite end of Row 8 of A piece. Use that length to whip stitch tog row ends of other side of leg. Tie off and weave in ends. Turn completed leg right side out. Use lengths of A and D to whip stitch each side of hip end of leg to body, matching colors (Fig. 3). At end of each color panel, tie off and weave in ends. Stuff. Leave foot end of leg open for now.

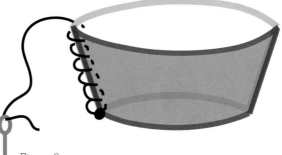

Figure 2

Foot

Make 4.

Row 1 (heel end): With A, leaving a 36" (91cm) tail, ch 8, TW, starting with 3rd ch from hook, 1 hdc in each ch to end of row—6 sts.

Row 2: Ch 2, TW, 2 hdc in next st, 1 hdc in each of next 4 sts, 2 hdc in next st—8 sts.

Row 3: Ch 2, TW, 2 hdc in next st, 1 hdc in each of next 6 sts, 2 hdc in next st—10 sts.

Rows 4–12: Ch 2, TW, 1 hdc in each st to end of row—10 sts.

Row 13: Ch 2, TW, 2 hdc in next st, 1 hdc in each of next 8 sts, 2 hdc in next st—12 sts.

Rows 14–21: Ch 2, TW, 1 hdc in each st to end of row—12 sts. Fasten off. Align two foot pieces and whip stitch around, stuffing lightly as work progresses. Whip stitch top layer of heel end of foot to end of leg. Tie off and weave in ends.

Tail

Make 2.

Row 1 (base): With A, leaving a 36" (91cm) tail, ch 22, TW, starting with 3rd ch from hook, 1 hdc in each ch to end of row—20 sts.

Row 2: Ch 2, TW, hdc next 2 sts tog, 1 hdc in each of next 16 sts, hdc next 2 sts tog—18 sts.

Row 3: Ch 2, TW, hdc next 2 sts tog, 1 hdc in each of next 14 sts, hdc next 2 sts tog—16 sts.

Row 4: Ch 2, TW, 1 hdc in each st to end of row—16 sts.

Row 5: Ch 2, TW, hdc next 2 sts tog, 1 hdc in each of next 12 sts, hdc next 2 sts tog—14 sts.

Row 6: Ch 2, TW, 1 hdc in each st to end of row—14 sts.

Row 7: Ch 2, TW, hdc next 2 sts tog, 1 hdc in each of next 10 sts, hdc next 2 sts tog—12 sts.

Row 8: Ch 2, TW, 1 hdc in each st to end of row—12 sts.

Row 9: Ch 2, TW, hdc next 2 sts tog, 1 hdc in each of next 8 sts, hdc next 2 sts tog—10 sts.

Row 10: Ch 2, TW, 1 hdc in each st to end of row—10 sts.

Row 11: Ch 2, TW, hdc next 2 sts tog, 1 hdc in each of next 6 sts, hdc next 2 sts tog—8 sts.

Row 12: Ch 2, TW, 1 hdc in each st to end of row—8 sts.

Row 13: Ch 2, TW, hdc next 2 sts tog, 1 hdc in each of next 4 sts, hdc next 2 sts tog—6 sts.

Row 14: Ch 2, TW, 1 hdc in each st to end of row—6 sts.

Row 15: Ch 2, TW, hdc next 2 sts tog, 1 hdc in each of next 2 sts, hdc next 2 sts tog—4 sts.

Row 16: Ch 2, TW, 1 hdc in each st to end of row—4 sts. Fasten off. Align pieces and whip stitch around, stuffing as work progresses and leaving base open (Fig. 4). Turn completed tail right side out. Whip stitch opening of tail to body (Fig. 1). Tie off and weave in ends.

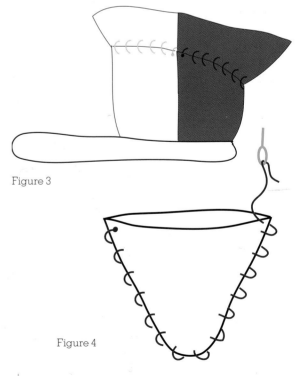

Figure 3

Figure 4

Inky
the
Octopus

Inky the Octopus

There has never been a more graceful ballerina on eight legs than Inky. She has been amazing audiences with her dancing genius since she hatched. Recruited at a young age to be the star dancer of the Russian Coral Reef Ballet, she has been bringing fans to tears with her rendition of *Swan Lake* ever since. If given the opportunity, she will surely twirl her way into your heart, too!

YARN

Super bulky (6) yarn in 1 color; 275 yds (252m) of color **A**

Bulky (5) yarn in 1 color; 185 yds (169m) of color **B**

Medium (4) yarn in 2 colors; 128 yds (117m) of color **C** and 1 yd (1m) of color **D**

*The project shown on page 59 uses Lion Brand Quick & Cozy (nylon, 55 yds [50m], 3.5 oz [100g]) in Raspberry (**A**); Lion Brand Homespun (98% acrylic/2% polyester, 185 yds [169m], 6 oz [170g]) in Sunshine State (**B**); and Lion Brand Vanna's Choice (acrylic, 170 yds [155m], 3.5 oz [100g]) in White (**C**) and Black (**D**).*

HOOKS AND NOTIONS

G/6 (4mm), H/8 (5mm) and I/9 (5.5mm) crochet hooks • Size 13 darning needle • Polyester fiberfill • Stuffing stick

GAUGE

4 hdc and 3 rows = 2" (5cm) using size H/8 (5mm) hook and Color A

FINISHED SIZE

Approx 18" (46cm) tall

Head

Make 1.

Rnd 1: With H/8 (5mm) hook and A, stuffing as work progresses, ch 4, sl st last ch to first ch to make a loop.

Rnd 2: Ch 2, TW, work 8 hdc in center of loop, sl st last hdc to first hdc—8 sts.

Rnd 3: Ch 2, TW, 2 hdc in each st to end of rnd, sl st last hdc to first hdc—16 sts.

Rnd 4: Ch 2, TW, * 1 hdc in next st, 2 hdc in next st; rep from * seven more times to end of rnd, sl st last hdc to first hdc—24 sts.

Rnd 5: Ch 2, TW, * 1 hdc in each of next 2 sts, 2 hdc in next st; rep from * seven more times to end of rnd, sl st last hdc to first hdc—32 sts.

Rnd 6: Ch 2, TW, * 1 hdc in each of next 3 sts, 2 hdc in next st; rep from * seven more times to end of rnd, sl st last hdc to first hdc—40 sts.

Rnd 7: Ch 2, TW, 1 hdc in each st to end of rnd, sl st last hdc to first hdc—40 sts.

Rnd 8: Ch 2, TW, * 1 hdc in each of next 4 sts, 2 hdc in next st; rep from * seven more times to end of rnd, sl st last hdc to first hdc—48 sts.

Rnds 9-12: Ch 2, TW, 1 hdc in each st to end of rnd, sl st last hdc to first hdc—48 sts.

Rnd 13: Ch 2, TW, * 1 hdc in each of next 4 sts, hdc next 2 sts tog; rep from * seven more times to end of rnd, sl st last hdc to first hdc—40 sts.

Rnds 14-16: Ch 2, TW, 1 hdc in each st to end of rnd, sl st last hdc to first hdc—40 sts.

Rnd 17: Ch 2, TW, * 1 hdc in each of next 7 sts, 2 hdc in next st; rep from * four more times to end of rnd, sl st last hdc to first hdc—45 sts. Fasten off. Weave in ends.

Bottom of Head

Make 1.

Rnd 1: With H/8 (5mm) hook and A, ch 4, sl st last ch to first ch to make loop.

Rnd 2: Ch 2, TW, work 10 hdc in center of loop, sl st last hdc to first hdc—10 sts.

Rnd 3: Ch 2, TW, 2 hdc in each st to end of rnd, sl st last hdc to first hdc—20 sts.

Rnd 4: Ch 2, TW, * 1 hdc in next st, 2 hdc in next st; rep from * nine more times to end of rnd, sl st last hdc to first hdc—30 sts.

Rnd 5: Ch 2, TW, * 1 hdc in each of next 2 sts, 2 hdc in next st; rep from * nine more times to end of rnd, sl st last hdc to first hdc—40 sts.

Rnd 6: Ch 2, TW, * 1 hdc in each of next 7 sts, 2 hdc in next st; rep from * four more times to end of rnd, sl st last hdc to first hdc—45 sts. Fasten off, leaving a 36" (91cm) tail. Whip stitch to opening at bottom of head. Tie off and weave in ends.

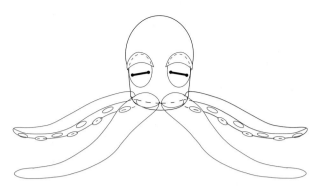

Figure 1 (front view)

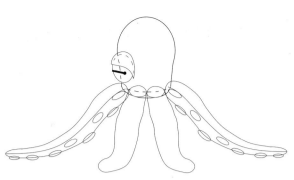

Figure 1 (side view)

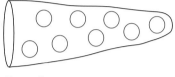

Figure 2

Upper Tentacle

Make 8.

Row 1 (base): With H/8 (5mm) hook and A, ch 10, TW, starting with 3rd ch from hook, 1 hdc in each of next 8 chs—8 sts.

Rows 2–12: Ch 2, TW, 1 hdc in each st to end of row—8 sts.

Row 13: Ch 2, TW, 1 hdc in each of next 3 sts, hdc next 2 sts tog, 1 hdc in each of next 3 sts—7 sts.

Row 14: Ch 2, TW, 1 hdc in each st to end of row—7 sts.

Row 15: Ch 2, TW, 1 hdc in each of next 3 sts, hdc next 2 sts tog, 1 hdc in each of next 2 sts—6 sts.

Row 16: Ch 2, TW, 1 hdc in each st to end of row—6 sts.

Row 17: Ch 2, TW, 1 hdc in each of next 2 sts, hdc next 2 sts tog, 1 hdc in each of next 2 sts—5 sts.

Rows 18–20: Ch 2, TW, 1 hdc in each st to end of row—5 sts.

Row 21: Ch 2, TW, 1 hdc in next st, hdc next 2 sts tog, 1 hdc in each of next 2 sts—4 sts.

Row 22: Ch 2, TW, 1 hdc in each st to end of row—4 sts.

Row 23: Ch 2, TW, 1 hdc in next st, hdc next 2 sts tog, 1 hdc in next st—3 sts.

Row 24: Ch 2, TW, 1 hdc in next st, hdc next 2 sts tog—2 sts.

Row 25: Ch 2, TW, 1 hdc in each st to end of row—2 sts.

Row 26: Ch 1, TW, hdc next 2 sts tog—1 st. Fasten off.

Lower Tentacle

Make 8.

With I/9 (5.5mm) hook and B, leaving a 48" (122cm) tail, work as for Upper Tentacle. Align upper and lower tentacle (lower will stretch to fit). Whip stitch around, leaving base open. Stuff. Tie off and weave in ends.

Suction Cups

Make 64.

Rnd 1: With G/6 (4mm) hook and C, ch 3, sl st last ch to first ch to make a loop.

Rnd 2: Ch 2, TW, work 8 hdc in center of loop, sl st last hdc to first hdc—8 sts. Fasten off, leaving a 12" (30cm) tail. Whip stitch 8 suction cups to B side of each completed tentacle (Fig. 2). Whip stitch tentacles in place, evenly spaced and lined up along seam at bottom of head (Fig. 1). Tie off and weave in ends.

Eyeball

Make 2.

Rnd 1: With I/9 (5.5mm) hook and B, ch 3, TW, sl st last ch to first ch to make a loop.

Rnd 2: TW, work 8 hdc in center of loop, sl st last hdc to first hdc—8 sts.

Rnd 3: TW, 2 hdc in each st to end of rnd, sl st last hdc to first hdc—16 sts.

Rnds 4–5: Ch 2, TW, 1 hdc in each st to end of rnd, sl st last hdc to first hdc—16 sts. Fasten off, leaving a 24" (61cm) tail. Stuff. Whip stitch eyeball to head. Tie off and weave in ends.

Eyelid

Make 2.

Row 1: With I/9 (5.5mm) hook and A, leaving a 24" (61cm) tail, ch 12, TW, starting with 3rd ch from hook, 1 hdc in each ch to end of row—10 sts.

Row 2: Ch 1, TW, hdc next 2 sts tog, 1 hdc in each of next 6 sts, hdc next 2 sts tog—8 sts. Fasten off. Whip stitch eyelid over top quarter of eyeball (Fig. 1). Do not stuff. With darning needle and D, embroider pupil onto eyeball as shown. Tie off and weave in ends.

Skipper
the
Dolphin

Skipper the Dolphin

Skipper is the most famous comedian in the sea. He played small coral reef clubs at first, to work out the kinks in his material. As word of his comic genius began to spread, club owners from all over the Atlantic began to book him. You may recognize Skipper from his most popular joke: "A dolphin, an octopus and a shark swim into a bar..."

YARN

Super bulky (6) yarn in 2 colors; 300 yds (275m) of color **A** and 81 yds (74m) of color **B**

Medium (4) yarn in 1 color; 3 yds (3m) of color **C**

*The project shown on page 62 uses Lion Brand Hometown USA (acrylic, 81 yds [74m], 5 oz [140g]) in Charlotte Blue (**A**) and New York White (**B**); and Lion Brand Vanna's Choice (acrylic, 170 yds [155m], 3.5 oz [100g]) in Charcoal (**C**).*

HOOKS AND NOTIONS

G/6 (4mm) and I/9 (5.5mm) crochet hooks • Size 13 darning needle • Polyester fiberfill • Stuffing stick

GAUGE

5 hdc and 4 rows = 2" (5cm) using size I/9 (5.5mm) hook

FINISHED SIZE

Approx 22" (56cm) long

Body

Make 1.

Rnd 1: With I/9 (5.5mm) hook and A, stuffing as work progresses, ch 3, sl st last ch to first ch to make loop.

Rnd 2: Ch 2, TW, work 5 hdc in center of loop, sl st last hdc to first hdc—5 sts.

Rnd 3: Ch 2, TW, 2 hdc in each st to end of rnd, sl st last hdc to first hdc—10 sts.

Rnd 4: Ch 2, TW, 2 hdc in each st to end of rnd, sl st last hdc to first hdc—20 sts.

Rnd 5: Ch 2, TW, * 1 hdc in next st, 2 hdc in next st; rep from * nine more times to end of rnd, sl st last hdc to first hdc—30 sts.

Rnds 6-7: Ch 2, TW, 1 hdc in each st to end of rnd, sl st last hdc to first hdc—30 sts.

Rnd 8: Ch 2, TW, * 1 hdc in each of next 4 sts, 2 hdc in next st; rep from * five more times to end of rnd, sl st last hdc to first hdc—36 sts.

Rnd 9: Ch 2, TW, * 1 hdc in each of next 5 sts, 2 hdc in next st; rep from * five more times to end of rnd, sl st last hdc to first hdc—42 sts.

Rnd 10: Ch 2, TW, * 1 hdc in each of next 6 sts, 2 hdc in next st; rep from * five more times to end of rnd, sl st last hdc to first hdc—48 sts.

Rnds 11-18: Ch 2, TW, 1 hdc in each st to end of rnd, sl st last hdc to first hdc—48 sts.

Rnd 19: Ch 2, TW, * 1 hdc in each of next 10 sts, hdc next 2 sts tog; rep from * three more times to end of rnd, sl st last hdc to first hdc—44 sts.

Rnd 20: Ch 2, TW, 1 hdc in each st to end of rnd, sl st last hdc to first hdc—44 sts.

Rnd 21: Ch 2, TW, * 1 hdc in each of next 9 sts, hdc next 2 sts tog; rep from * three more times to end of rnd, sl st last hdc to first hdc—40 sts.

Rnd 22: Ch 2, TW, 1 hdc in each st to end of rnd, sl st last hdc to first hdc—40 sts.

Rnd 23: Ch 2, TW, * 1 hdc in each of next 8 sts, hdc next 2 sts tog; rep from * three more times to end of rnd, sl st last hdc to first hdc—36 sts.

Rnd 24: Ch 2, TW, * 1 hdc in each of next 16 sts, hdc next 2 sts tog; rep from * one more time to end of rnd, sl st last hdc to first hdc—34 sts.

Rnd 25: Ch 2, TW, * 1 hdc in each of next 15 sts, hdc next 2 sts tog; rep from * one more time to end of rnd, sl st last hdc to first hdc—32 sts.

Rnd 26: Ch 2, TW, * 1 hdc in each of next 14 sts, hdc next 2 sts tog; rep from * one more time to end of rnd, sl st last hdc to first hdc—30 sts.

Rnd 27: Ch 2, TW, * 1 hdc in each of next 13 sts, hdc next 2 sts tog; rep from * one more time to end of rnd, sl st last hdc to first hdc—28 sts.

Rnd 28: Ch 2, TW, * 1 hdc in each of next 12 sts, hdc next 2 sts tog; rep from * one more time to end of rnd, sl st last hdc to first hdc—26 sts.

Rnd 29: Ch 2, TW, * 1 hdc in each of next 11 sts, hdc next 2 sts tog; rep from * one more time to end of rnd, sl st last hdc to first hdc—24 sts.

Rnd 30: Ch 2, TW, 1 hdc in each st to end of rnd, sl st last hdc to first hdc—24 sts.

Rnd 31: Ch 2, TW, * 1 hdc in each of next 10 sts, hdc next 2 sts tog; rep from * one more time to end of rnd, sl st last hdc to first hdc—22 sts.

Rnd 32: Ch 2, TW, 1 hdc in each st to end of rnd, sl st last hdc to first hdc—22 sts.

Rnd 33: Ch 2, TW, * 1 hdc in each of next 9 sts, hdc next 2 sts tog; rep from * one more time to end of rnd, sl st last hdc to first hdc—20 sts.

Rnd 34: Ch 2, TW, 1 hdc in each st to end of rnd, sl st last hdc to first hdc—20 sts.

Rnd 35: Ch 2, TW, * 1 hdc in each of next 8 sts, hdc next 2 sts tog; rep from * one more time to end of rnd, sl st last hdc to first hdc—18 sts.

Rnd 36: Ch 2, TW, 1 hdc in each st to end of rnd, sl st last hdc to first hdc—18 sts.

Rnd 37: Ch 2, TW, * 1 hdc in each of next 7 sts, hdc next 2 sts tog; rep from * one more time to end of rnd, sl st last hdc to first hdc—16 sts.

Rnd 38: Ch 2, TW, * 1 hdc in each of next 6 sts, hdc next 2 sts tog; rep from * one more time to end of rnd, sl st last hdc to first hdc—14 sts.

Rnd 39: Ch 2, TW, * 1 hdc in each of next 5 sts, hdc next 2 sts tog; rep from * one more time to end of rnd, sl st last hdc to first hdc—12 sts.

Rnd 40: Ch 1, TW, * hdc next 2 sts tog; rep from * five more times to end of rnd, sl st last hdc to first hdc—6 sts. Fasten off, leaving a 10" (25cm) tail. Whip stitch opening closed. Tie off and weave in ends.

Belly

Make 1.

Row 1 (head end): With I/9 (5.5mm) hook and B, leaving a 48" (122cm) tail, ch 12, TW, starting with 3rd ch from hook, 2 hdc in next ch, 1 hdc in each of next 8 chs, 2 hdc in next ch—12 sts.

Row 2: Ch 2, TW, 1 hdc in each st to end of row—12 sts.

Row 3: Ch 2, TW, 2 hdc in next st, 1 hdc in each of next 10 sts, 2 hdc in next st—14 sts.

Rows 4–5: Ch 2, TW, 1 hdc in each st to end of row—14 sts.

Row 6: Ch 2, TW, 2 hdc in next st, 1 hdc in each of next 12 sts, 2 hdc in next st—16 sts.

Rows 7–12: Ch 2, TW, 1 hdc in each st to end of row—16 sts.

Row 13: Ch 2, TW, hdc next 2 sts tog, 1 hdc in each of next 12 sts, hdc next 2 sts tog—14 sts.

Rows 14–15: Ch 2, TW, 1 hdc in each st to end of row—14 sts.

Row 16: Ch 2, TW, hdc next 2 sts tog, 1 hdc in each of next 10 sts, hdc next 2 sts tog—12 sts.

Rows 17–18: Ch 2, TW, 1 hdc in each st to end of row—12 sts.

Row 19: Ch 2, TW, hdc next 2 sts tog, 1 hdc in each of next 8 sts, hdc next 2 sts tog—10 sts.

Row 20: Ch 2, TW, 1 hdc in each st to end of row—10 sts.

Row 21: Ch 2, TW, hdc next 2 sts tog, 1 hdc in each of next 6 sts, hdc next 2 sts tog—8 sts.

Rows 22–23: Ch 2, TW, 1 hdc in each st to end of row—8 sts.

Row 24: Ch 2, TW, hdc next 2 sts tog, 1 hdc in each of next 4 sts, hdc next 2 sts tog—6 sts.

Row 25: Ch 2, TW, 1 hdc in each st to end of row—6 sts.

Row 26: Ch 2, TW, hdc next 2 sts tog, 1 hdc in each of next 2 sts, hdc next 2 sts tog—4 sts.

Row 27: Ch 2, TW, 1 hdc in each st to end of row—4 sts.

Row 28 (tail end): Ch 2, TW, hdc next 2 sts tog, hdc next 2 sts tog—2 sts. Fasten off. Whip stitch belly to underside of body, so that it covers seam of body (Fig. 1). Tie off and weave in ends.

Top of Nose

Make 1.

Row 1: With I/9 (5.5mm) hook and A, ch 4, TW, starting with 3rd ch from hook, 2 hdc in each of next 2 chs—4 sts.

Rows 2–3: Ch 2, TW, 1 hdc in each st to end of row—4 sts.

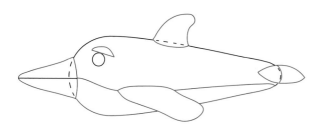

Figure 1 (side view)

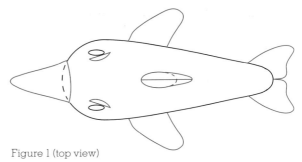

Figure 1 (top view)

Row 4: Ch 2, TW, 2 hdc in next st, 1 hdc in each of next 2 sts, 2 hdc in next st—6 sts.

Rows 5–6: Ch 2, TW, 1 hdc in each st to end of row—6 sts.

Row 7: Ch 2, TW, 2 hdc in next st, 1 hdc in each of next 4 sts, 2 hdc in next st—8 sts.

Row 8: Ch 2, TW, 2 hdc in next st, 1 hdc in each of next 6 sts, 2 hdc in next st—10 sts.

Row 9: Ch 2, TW, 1 hdc in each st to end of row—10 sts.

Row 10 (base): Ch 2, TW, 2 hdc in next st, 1 hdc in each of next 8 sts, 2 hdc in next st—12 sts. Fasten off, leaving a 36" (91cm) tail.

Bottom of Nose

Make 1.

With I/9 (5.5mm) hook and B, work as for top of nose. Fasten off, leaving a 12" (30cm) tail. Align top and bottom of nose and whip stitch tog, leaving base ends open. Stuff. Whip stitch nose to body, matching colors and lining up base of bottom with first row of belly (Fig. 1). Tie off and weave in ends.

Eye

Make 2.

Rnd 1: With G/6 (4mm) hook and C, ch 3, sl st last ch to first ch to make a loop.

Rnd 2: Ch 1, TW, work 6 sc in center of loop, sl st last sc to first sc—6 sts. Fasten off, leaving an 18" (46cm) tail. Whip stitch eye to head (Fig. 1). Tie off and weave in ends.

Eyelid

Make 2.

Row 1 (base): With I/9 (5.5mm) hook and A, leaving a 15" (38cm) tail, ch 7, TW, starting with 3rd ch from hook, hdc next 2 chs tog, 1 hdc in next ch, hdc next 2 chs tog—3 sts. Fasten off. Align eyelid above eye as shown (Fig. 1). Whip stitch around, stuffing lightly as work progresses. Tie off and weave in ends.

Flipper

Make 4.

Row 1 (base): With I/9 (5.5mm) hook and A, leaving a 48" (122cm) tail on 2 of the pieces, ch 10, TW, starting with 3rd ch from hook, 1 hdc in each ch to end of row—8 sts.

Row 2: Ch 2, TW, 1 hdc in each st to end of row—8 sts.

Row 3: Ch 2, TW, 2 hdc in next st, 1 hdc in each of next 5 sts, hdc next 2 sts tog—8 sts.

Row 4: Ch 2, TW, hdc next 2 sts tog, 1 hdc in each of next 6 sts—7 sts.

Row 5: Ch 2, TW, 2 hdc in next st, 1 hdc in each of next 4 sts, hdc next 2 sts tog—7 sts.

Row 6: Ch 2, TW, hdc next 2 sts tog, 1 hdc in each of next 4 sts, 2 hdc in next st—7 sts.

Row 7: Ch 2, TW, 1 hdc in each of next 5 sts, hdc next 2 sts tog—6 sts.

Row 8: Ch 2, TW, hdc next 2 sts tog, 1 hdc in each of next 3 sts, 2 hdc in next st—6 sts.

Row 9: Ch 2, TW, 1 hdc in each of next 4 sts, hdc next 2 sts tog—5 sts.

Row 10: Ch 2, TW, hdc next 2 sts tog, 1 hdc in each of next 3 sts—4 sts.

Row 11: Ch 1, TW, hdc next 2 sts tog, hdc next 2 sts tog—2 sts. Fasten off. Align one piece with long tail with one piece without and whip stitch around, leaving base ends open. Stuff lightly. Sew open base end of flipper to side of body (Fig. 1).

Top Fin

Make 2.

Row 1 (base): With I/9 (5.5mm) hook and A, leaving a 36" (91cm) tail on 1 of the pieces, ch 10, TW, starting with 3rd ch from hook, 1 hdc in each ch to end of row—8 sts.

Row 2: Ch 2, TW, hdc next 2 sts tog, 1 hdc in each of next 4 sts, hdc next 2 sts tog—6 sts.

Row 3: Ch 2, TW, 1 hdc in each st to end of row—6 sts.

Row 4: Ch 1, TW, hdc next 2 sts tog, 1 hdc in each of next 3 sts, 2 hdc in next st—6 sts.

Row 5: Ch 2, TW, 2 hdc in next st, 1 hdc in each of next 3 sts, hdc next 2 sts tog—6 sts.

Row 6: Ch 1, TW, hdc next 2 sts tog, hdc next 2 sts tog, 1 hdc in next st, 2 hdc in next st—5 sts.

Row 7: Ch 2, TW, 2 hdc in next st, hdc next 2 sts tog, hdc next 2 sts tog—4 sts. Fasten off. Align pieces and whip stitch around, stuffing lightly and leaving base ends open. Pull base ends apart slightly and whip stitch to top of body (Fig. 1). Tie off and weave in ends.

Tail Fin

Make 4.

Row 1 (base): With I/9 (5.5mm) hook and A, leaving a 36" (91cm) tail on 2 of the pieces, ch 8, work 2 hdc in the 3rd ch from hook, 1 hdc in each of next 5 chs—7 sts.

Row 2: Ch 2, TW, 1 hdc in each of next 6 sts, 2 hdc in next st—8 sts.

Row 3: Ch 2, TW, 1 hdc in each st to end of row—8 sts.

Row 4: Ch 2, TW, 1 hdc in each of next 6 sts, hdc next 2 sts tog—7 sts.

Row 5: Ch 1, TW, hdc next 2 sts tog, 1 hdc in each of next 5 sts—6 sts.

Row 6: Ch 2, TW, 1 hdc in each of next 4 sts, hdc next 2 sts tog—5 sts.

Row 7: Ch 2, TW, 1 hdc in each st to end of row—5 sts.

Row 8: Ch 2, TW, 1 hdc in each of next 3 sts, hdc next 2 sts tog—4 sts.

Row 9: Ch 1, TW, hdc next 2 sts tog, hdc next 2 sts tog—2 sts.

Row 10: Ch 1, TW, hdc next 2 sts tog—1 st. Fasten off. Align one piece with long tail with one piece without and whip stitch around, stuffing lightly and leaving base ends open. Sew fins to end of tail (Fig. 1). Tie off and weave in ends.

See page 126 for the yarn colors used to make these versions.

CHAPTER 4

The Protectors:
Safari Animals

The lion is the king and protector of the jungle, but he can't do it alone. There is a lot to be done in the jungle and out on the open plains. There are babies of all kinds to watch over. Daily threats of intruders are always looming. Even Mother Nature needs to be considered when overseeing the safety of a kingdom. Unfortunately, this king is only one cat with four paws. He can't do it all! So, at the advice of his queen, he has enlisted the help of a trustworthy trio—a hippo, elephant and giraffe—to keep his kingdom secure.

Byron
the Lion

Byron the Lion

Byron is truly the ruler of his kingdom. He makes sure that all of his loyal subjects are safe and well fed. He likes to relax and hang out with the family, but he spends most of his time roaming the open plains to ensure that his territory is clear of intruders. Once you bring him into your family, he'll do the same for you!

YARN

Super bulky (6) yarn in 4 colors; 300 yds (275m) of color **A**, 10 yds (10m) of color **B**, 90 yds (83m) of color **C** and 75 yds (69m) of color **D**

Medium (4) yarn in 1 color; 2 yds (2m) of color **E**

*The project shown on page 69 uses Lion Brand Hometown USA (acrylic, 81 yds [74m], 5 oz [140g]) in Los Angeles Tan (**A**), New York White (**B**), Billings Chocolate (**C**) and Cleveland Brown (**D**); and Lion Brand Vanna's Choice (acrylic, 170 yds [155m], 3.5 oz [100g]) in Black (**E**).*

HOOKS AND NOTIONS

I/9 (5.5mm) crochet hook • Size 13 darning needle • Polyester fiberfill • Stuffing stick

GAUGE

5 hdc and 4 rows = 2" (5cm) using size I/9 (5.5mm) hook

FINISHED SIZE

Approx 16" (41cm) tall

Head

Make 1.

Row 1: With A, ch 7, TW, starting with 3rd ch from hook, 1 hdc in each ch to end of row—5 sts.

Rows 2–4: Ch 2, TW, 1 hdc in each st to end of row—5 sts. Beg working in rnds, stuffing as work progresses.

Rnd 1: Ch 2, TW, starting on side A (Fig. 1), 2 hdc in first st, 1 hdc in each of next 3 sts, 2 hdc in next st, work 1 hdc in the end of Rows 2 and 3 of side B, work 2 hdc in first st of side C, 1 hdc in each of next 3 sts, 2 hdc in next st, work 1 hdc in the end of Rows 2 and 3 of side D, sl st last hdc to first hdc—18 sts.

Rnds 2–5: Ch 2, TW, 1 hdc in each st to end of rnd, sl st last hdc to first hdc—18 sts.

Rnd 6: Ch 2, TW, 1 hdc in next st, 2 hdc in each of next 4 sts, 1 hdc in next 3 sts, 2 hdc in each of next 4 sts, 1 hdc in each of next 6 sts, sl st last hdc to first hdc—26 sts.

Rnd 7: Ch 2, TW, 1 hdc in each of next 7 sts, 2 hdc in each of next 2 sts, 1 hdc in next st, 2 hdc in each of next 3 sts, 1 hdc in each of next 2 sts, 2 hdc in next st, 1 hdc in each of next 2 sts, 2 hdc in each of next 3 sts, 1 hdc in next st, 2 hdc in each of next 2 sts, 1 hdc in each of next 2 sts, sl st last hdc to first hdc—37 sts.

Rnds 8–10: Ch 2, TW, 1 hdc in each st to end of rnd, sl st last hdc to first hdc—37 sts.

Rnd 11: Ch 2, TW, * 1 hdc in each of next 2 sts, hdc next 2 sts tog; rep from * eight more times, 1 hdc in last st, sl st last hdc to first hdc—28 sts.

Rnd 12: Ch 2, TW, * 1 hdc in each of next 2 sts, hdc next 2 sts tog; rep from * six more times, sl st last hdc to first hdc—21 sts.

Rnd 13: Ch 2, TW, * 1 hdc in next st, hdc next 2 sts tog; rep from * six more times to end of rnd, sl st last hdc to first hdc—14 sts.

Rnd 14: Ch 2, TW, * hdc next 2 sts tog; rep from * six more times to end of rnd, sl st last hdc to first hdc—7 sts.

Rnd 15: Ch 1, TW, * sc next 2 sts tog; rep from * two more times, 1 sc in last st, sl st last sc to first sc—4 sts. Fasten off, leaving an 8" (20cm) tail. Whip stitch opening closed. Tie off and weave in ends. (Note: Don't worry if you have any visible gaps in the back of the head. They will be covered by hair later.)

Eyes and Nose

With darning needle and E, embroider eyes and nose as shown (Fig. 2).

Chin

Make 1.

Row 1: With B and leaving a 24" (61cm) tail, ch 12, TW, starting with 3rd ch from hook, 1 hdc in each of next 10 chs—10 sts.

Rows 2–3: Ch 2, TW, 1 hdc in each st to end of row—10 sts.

Row 4: Ch 1, TW, 1 sl st in first st, 1 hdc in each of next 8 sts, 1 sl st in next st—10 sts.

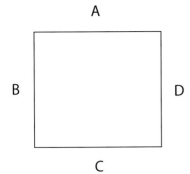

Figure 1

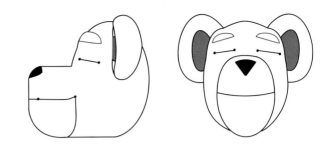

Figure 2

Row 5: Ch 1, TW, 1 sl st in each of next 2 sts, 1 sc in next st, 1 hdc in each of next 4 sts, 1 sc in next st, 1 sl st in each of next 2 sts—10 sts.

Row 6: Ch 1, TW, sc next 2 sts tog, 1 hdc in next 6 sts, sc next 2 sts tog—8 sts. Fasten off. Whip stitch chin to bottom of snout, centering rounded edge of the chin horizontally across the front of the snout and stuffing as work progresses. (Note: To create the illusion of chin hair rather than just a flush chin, use more stuffing rather than less.) Weave in ends.

Mouth

With darning needle and E, embroider mouth as shown, following curve of chin (Fig. 2).

Eyelid

Make 2.

Row 1: With A and leaving a 20" (51cm) tail, ch 7, starting with 3rd ch from hook, 1 hdc in each of next 5 chs—5 sts.

Row 2: Ch 1, TW, hdc next 2 sts tog, 1 sl st in next st—2 sts. Fasten off. Align Row 1 of eyelid above eye and whip stitch around, stuffing as work progresses (Fig. 2). Tie off and weave in ends.

Inner Ear

Make 2.

Row 1 (base): With B, ch 7, starting with 3rd ch from hook, 1 hdc in each of next 5 chs—5 sts.

Row 2: Ch 1, TW, 1 sc in first st, 1 hdc in each of next 3 sts, 1 sc in last st—5 sts.

Row 3: Ch 1, TW, sc next 2 sts tog, 1 hdc in next st, sc next 2 sts tog—3 sts. Fasten off, weave in ends.

Inner Ear Edging

Row 1: With A, join yarn in first st in first row of inner ear, ch 2, work 1 hdc in the end of Rows 1-3, 1 hdc in each st of Row 3, work 1 hdc in the end of Rows 3-1—9 sts.

Row 2: Ch 1, TW, 1 sc in each st around arc, back to starting point—9 sts. Fasten off, leaving a 36" (91cm) tail for sewing.

Outer Ear

Make 2.

Row 1 (base): With A, ch 12, starting with 3rd ch from hook, 1 hdc in each of next 10 chs—10 sts.

Row 2: Ch 1, TW, 1 sc in first st, 1 hdc in each of next 8 sts, 1 sc in last st—10 sts.

Row 3: Ch 1, TW, hdc next 2 sts tog, 1 hdc in each of next 6 sts, hdc last 2 sts tog—8 sts.

Row 4: Ch 1, TW, hdc next 2 sts tog, 1 hdc in each of next 4 sts, hdc last 2 sts tog—6 sts.

Row 5: Ch 1, TW, hdc next 2 sts tog, 1 hdc in each of next 2 sts, hdc last 2 sts tog—4 sts. Fasten off, weave in ends. Align inner and outer ear, whip stitch around. Whip stitch base end of completed ear in place on head (Fig. 2).

Small Hair

Make 4.

Row 1: With C, ch 6, starting with 3rd ch from hook, 1 hdc in each of next 4 chs—4 sts.

Rows 2-4: Ch 2, TW, 1 hdc in each of next 4 sts—4 sts. Fasten off, weave in ends.

Outer Edge of Small Hair

Rnd 1: With D, join yarn in ending corner of hair piece, ch 2, work 2 hdc in end of Row 1, work 1 hdc each in the end of Rows 2 and 3, work 2 hdc in the end of Row 4, work 2 hdc in next st, 1 hdc in each of next 2 sts, 2 hdc in next st, work 2 hdc in the end of Row 4, work 1 hdc each in the end of Rows 3 and 2, work 2 hdc in the end of Row 1, work 2 hdc in next st, 1 hdc in each of next 2 sts, 2 hdc in next st, sl st last hdc to first hdc—24 sts. Fasten off, leaving a 20" (51cm) tail for sewing. Whip stitch nearest short edge of hair on head (Fig. 3), placing two on top of head at ear line and the other two along neckline, under chin. Weave in ends.

Figure 3

Figure 4

Figure 5

Medium Hair

Make 10.

Row 1: With C, ch 6, starting with 3rd ch from hook, 1 hdc in each of next 4 chs—4 sts.

Rows 2–5: Ch 2, TW, 1 hdc in each of next 4 sts—4 sts. Fasten off. Weave in ends.

Outer Edge of Medium Hair

Rnd 1: With D, join yarn in ending corner of hair piece, ch 2, work 2 hdc in the end of Row 1, work 1 hdc in the end of Rows 2–4, work 2 hdc in the end of Row 5, work 2 hdc in next st, 1 hdc in each of next 2 sts, 2 hdc in next st, work 2 hdc in the end of Row 5, work 1 hdc in the end of Rows 4–2, work 2 hdc in the end of Row 1, work 2 hdc in next st, 1 hdc in each of next 2 sts, 2 hdc in next st, sl st last hdc to first hdc—26 sts. Fasten off, leaving a 20" (51cm) tail for sewing. Whip stitch nearest short edge of hair on head, centering one piece behind hair on top of head and the other two evenly spaced on either side of the hair under the chin (Fig. 4). (Note: Attach the pieces as close to each other as possible, to avoid bald spots.) Set rem medium hair aside. Weave in ends.

Large Hair

Make 2.

Row 1: With C, ch 8, starting with 3rd ch from hook, 1 hdc in each of next 6 chs.

Rows 2–8: Ch 2, TW, 1 hdc in each st to end of row—6 sts. Fasten off, weave in ends.

Outer Edge of Large Hair

Rnd 1: With D, join yarn in ending corner of hair piece, ch 2, work 2 hdc in end of Row 1, work 1 hdc in the end of Rows 2–7, work 2 hdc in the end of Row 8, work 2 hdc in next st, work 1 hdc in each of next 4 sts, 2 hdc in next st, work 2 hdc in the end of Row 8, work 1 hdc in the end of Rows 7–2, work 2 hdc in the end of Row 1, work 2 hdc in the next st, 1 hdc

in each of next 4 sts, 2 hdc in next st, sl st last hdc to first hdc—36 sts. Fasten off, leaving a 20" (51cm) tail for sewing. Whip stitch nearest short edge of hair on head, placing one piece behind each ear (Fig. 5). With rem medium hair, fill in gaps, whip stitching in place (Figs. 6a–6c). Tie off and weave in ends.

Body

Make 1.

Rnd 1: With A, stuffing as work progresses, ch 4, sl st last ch to first ch to make a loop.

Rnd 2: Ch 2, TW, 10 hdc in center of loop, sl st last hdc to first hdc—10 sts.

Rnd 3: Ch 2, TW, * 1 hdc in next st, 2 hdc in next st; rep from * four more times to end of rnd, sl st last hdc to first hdc—15 sts.

Rnd 4: Ch 2, TW, * 1 hdc in each of next 2 sts, 2 hdc in next st; rep from * four more times to end of rnd, sl st last hdc to first hdc—20 sts.

Rnd 5: Ch 2, TW, * 1 hdc in next st, 2 hdc in next st; rep from * nine more times to end of rnd, sl st last hdc to first hdc—30 sts.

Rnd 6: Ch 2, TW, * 1 hdc in each of next 4 sts, 2 hdc in next st; rep from * five more times to end of rnd, sl st last hdc to first hdc—36 sts.

Rnds 7–13: Ch 2, TW, 1 hdc in each st to end of rnd, sl st last hdc to first hdc—36 sts.

Rnd 14: Ch 2, TW, * 1 hdc in next st, hdc next 2 sts tog; rep from * eleven more times to end of rnd, sl st last hdc to first hdc—24 sts.

Rnds 15–17: Ch 2, TW, 1 hdc in each st to end of rnd, sl st last hdc to first hdc—24 sts.

Rnd 18: Ch 2, TW, * 1 hdc in each of next 2 sts, hdc next 2 sts tog; rep from * five more times to end of rnd, sl st last hdc to first hdc—18 sts.

Rnd 19: Ch 2, TW, * hdc next 2 sts tog; rep from * eight more times to end of rnd, sl st last hdc to first hdc—9 sts.

Rnd 20 (head end): Ch 1, TW, * sc next 2 sts tog; rep from * three more times, 1 sc in last st, sl st last sc to first sc—5 sts. Fasten off, leaving an 8" (20cm) tail. Whip stitch opening closed. Tie off and weave in ends. Whip stitch head to body (Fig. 7). Tie off and weave in ends.

Legs

Make 4.

Rnd 1: With A, leaving a 36" (91cm) tail, ch 18, sl st last ch to first ch.

Rnd 2: Ch 2, TW, 1 hdc in each ch to end of rnd, sl st last hdc to first hdc—18 sts.

Rnd 3: Ch 2, TW, * 1 hdc in each of next 8 sts, 2 hdc in next st; rep from * one more time, sl st last hdc to first hdc—20 sts.

Rnds 4–5: Ch 2, TW, 1 hdc in each st to end of rnd, sl st last hdc to first hdc—20 sts.

Rnd 6: Ch 2, TW, * 1 hdc in each of next 9 sts, 2 hdc in next st; rep from * one more time to end of rnd, sl st last hdc to first hdc—22 sts.

Rnds 7–11: Ch 2, TW, 1 hdc in each st to end of rnd, sl st last hdc to first hdc—22 sts. Fasten off, leaving a 30" (76cm) tail.

Paws

Make 4.

Rnd 1: With C, ch 4, sl st last ch to first ch to make a loop.

Rnd 2: Ch 2, TW, work 10 hdc in center of loop, sl st last hdc to first hdc—10 sts.

Rnd 3: Ch 2, TW, * 2 hdc in each of next 4 sts, 3 hdc in next st; rep from * one more time to end of rnd, sl st last hdc to first hdc—22 sts. Fasten off, weave in ends. Turn leg inside out. Whip stitch paw piece to opening at wide end of leg. Tie off and weave in ends. Turn leg right side out. Stuff. Whip stitch leg to body (Fig. 7). Tie off and weave in ends.

Tail

Make 1.

Rnd 1: With A, leaving a 24" (61cm) tail, ch 8, sl st last ch to first ch.

Rnd 2: Ch 2, 1 hdc in each ch to end of rnd, sl st last hdc to first hdc—8 sts.

Rnd 3: Ch 2, 1 hdc in each st to end of rnd, sl st last hdc to first hdc—8 sts.

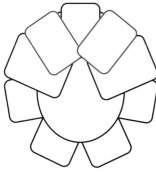

Figure 6a

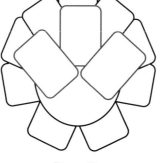

Figure 6b

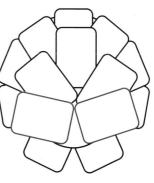

Figure 6c

Figure 7 (front view)　　　　Figure 7 (side view)　　　　Figure 8

Rnd 4: Ch 2, * 1 hdc in each of next 2 sts, hdc next 2 sts tog; rep from * one more time to end of rnd, sl st last hdc to first hdc—6 sts.

Rnd 5: Ch 2, 1 hdc in each st to end of rnd, sl st last hdc to first hdc—6 sts.

Rnd 6: Ch 2, * 1 hdc in next st, hdc next 2 sts tog; rep from * one more time to end of rnd, sl st last hdc to first hdc—4 sts.

Rnd 7: Ch 2, 1 hdc in each st to end of rnd, sl st last hdc to first hdc—4 sts. Fasten off, leaving a 20" (51cm) tail.

Tail Hair

Make 4.

Row 1: With C, leaving a 12" (30cm) tail, ch 6, TW, 2 hdc in 3rd ch from hook—2 sts.

Row 2: Ch 2, TW, 2 hdc in each of next 2 sts—4 sts.

Row 3: Ch 2, TW, 1 hdc in each of next 4 sts—4 sts. Fasten off, weave in ends.

Outer Edge of Tail Hair

Join D to 3rd ch of beg ch-6 on tail hair piece (Fig. 8).

Rnd 1: Ch 1, work 2 sc in the end of Row 1, work 1 sc in the end of each of the next 2 rows, work 2 sc in the first st, 1 sc in each of the next 2 sts, 2 sc in the next st, work 1 sc in the end of each of the next 2 rows, work 2 sc in the end of Row 1, sl st last sc to first sc—14 sts. Fasten off. Thread excess lengths up through center of narrow end of tail (Fig. 9). With A, whip stitch tail hair to end of tail (Fig. 10). Arrange and secure tail hair pieces around end of tail as shown (Fig. 11). Whip stitch tail in place on body (Fig. 7). Tie off and weave in ends.

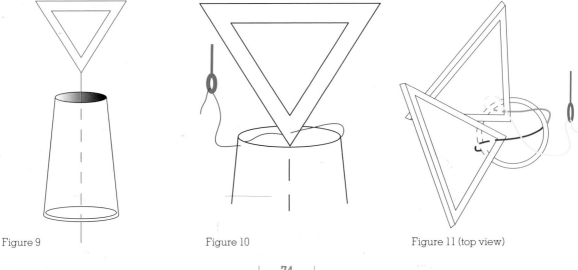

Figure 9　　　　Figure 10　　　　Figure 11 (top view)

Seymour
the
Giraffe

Seymour the Giraffe

Seymour is the first line of defense for the king of the jungle. He operates as the early warning system for any potential threats to the kingdom. Since Seymour is able to see much farther than any of the other animals, he can tell if there are any far-off invaders staging a coup, or if bad weather is approaching. No matter what the danger may be, he is able to warn all, so that everyone can seek safety until the danger passes.

YARN

Bulky (5) yarn in 3 colors; 370 yds (339m) of color **A**, 185 yds (169m) of color **B** and 185 yds (169m) of color **C**

Medium (4) yarn in 1 color; 3 yds (3m) of color **D**

*The project shown on page 75 uses Lion Brand Homespun (98% acrylic/2% polyester, 185 yds [169m], 6 oz [170g]) in Sunshine State (**A**), Ranch (**B**) and Black (**C**); and Lion Brand Vanna's Choice (acrylic, 170 yds [155m], 3.5 oz [100g]) in Black (**D**).*

HOOKS AND NOTIONS

H/8 (5mm) crochet hook • Size 13 darning needle • Polyester fiberfill • Stuffing stick

GAUGE

5 hdc and 4 rows = 2" (5cm) using size H/8 (5mm) hook

FINISHED SIZE

Approx 16" (41cm) tall

Head

Make 1.

Row 1: With A, ch 8, TW, starting with 3rd ch from hook, 1 hdc in each of next 6 chs—6 sts.

Rows 2-3: Ch 2, TW, 1 hdc in each st to end of row—6 sts. Beg working in rnds, stuffing as work progresses.

Rnd 1: Ch 2, TW, 2 hdc in next st, 1 hdc in each of next 4 sts, 2 hdc in next st, 1 hdc in the end of Row 2, 2 hdc in first st of Row 1, 1 hdc in each of next 4 sts, 2 hdc in next st, 1 hdc in the end of Row 2, sl st last hdc to first hdc—18 sts.

Rnds 2-5: Ch 2, TW, 1 hdc in each st to end of rnd, sl st last hdc to first hdc—18 sts.

Rnd 6: Ch 2, TW, 1 hdc in each of next 10 sts, 2 hdc in next st, 1 hdc in each of next 6 sts, 2 hdc in next st, sl st last hdc to first hdc—20 sts.

Rnd 7: Ch 2, TW, 1 hdc in each of next 2 sts, 2 hdc in next st, 1 hdc in next st, 2 hdc in each of next 2 sts, 1 hdc in next st, 2 hdc in next st, 1 hdc in each of next 3 sts, 2 hdc in next st, 1 hdc in each of next 8 sts, sl st last hdc to first hdc—25 sts.

Rnds 8-9: Ch 2, TW, 1 hdc in each st to end of rnd, sl st last hdc to first hdc—25 sts.

Rnd 10: Ch 2, TW, 1 hdc in each of next 10 sts, 2 hdc in next st, 1 hdc in each of next 2 sts, 2 hdc in next st, 1 hdc in each of next 2 sts, 2 hdc in each of next 2 sts, 1 hdc in each of next 2 sts, 2 hdc in next st, 1 hdc in each of next 3 sts, 2 hdc in next st, sl st last hdc to first hdc—31 sts.

Rnd 11: Ch 2, TW, 1 hdc in next st, * 2 hdc in next st, 1 hdc in each of next 2 sts, rep from * nine more times to end of rnd, sl st last hdc to first hdc—41 sts.

Rnd 12: Ch 2, TW, 1 hdc in each of next 25 sts, 2 hdc in next st, 1 hdc in each of next 15 sts, sl st last hdc to first hdc—42 sts.

Rnds 13-15: Ch 2, TW, 1 hdc in each st to end of rnd, sl st last hdc to first hdc—42 sts.

Rnd 16: Ch 2, TW, * 1 hdc in each of next 4 sts, hdc next 2 sts tog; rep from * six more times to end of rnd, sl st last hdc to first hdc—35 sts.

Rnd 17: Ch 2, TW, * 1 hdc in each of next 3 sts, hdc next 2 sts tog; rep from * six more times to end of rnd, sl st last hdc to first hdc—28 sts.

Rnd 18: Ch 2, TW, * 1 hdc in each of next 2 sts, hdc next 2 sts tog; rep from * six more times to end of rnd, sl st last hdc to first hdc—21 sts.

Rnd 19: Ch 2, TW, * 1 hdc in next st, hdc next 2 sts tog; rep from * six more times to end of rnd, sl st last hdc to first hdc—14 sts.

Rnd 20: Ch 2, TW, * 1 hdc in each of next 5 sts, hdc next 2 sts tog; rep from * one more time to end of rnd, sl st last hdc to first hdc—12 sts.

Rnd 21: Ch 2, TW, * hdc next 2 sts tog; rep from * five more times to end of rnd, sl st last hdc to first hdc—6 sts. Fasten off, leaving an 8" (20cm) tail. Whip stitch opening closed. Tie off and weave in ends.

Body

Make 1.

Rnd 1 (hind end): With A, stuffing as work progresses, ch 4, sl st last ch to first ch to make a loop.

Rnd 2: Ch 2, TW, work 10 hdc in center of loop, sl st last hdc to first hdc—10 sts.

Rnd 3: Ch 2, TW, 2 hdc in each of next 7 sts, drop A, pick up B, 2 hdc in each of next 3 sts, sl st last hdc to first hdc—20 sts.

Rnd 4: Ch 2, TW, * 1 hdc in next st, 2 hdc in next st; rep from * two more times, drop B, pick up A, ** 1 hdc in next st, 2 hdc in next st; rep from ** six more times to end of rnd, sl st last hdc to first hdc—30 sts.

Rnd 5: Ch 2, TW, * 1 hdc in next st, 2 hdc in next st; rep from * two more times, drop A, pick up B, ** 1 hdc in next st, 2 hdc in next st; rep from ** two more times, drop B, pick up A, *** 1 hdc in next st, 2 hdc in next st; rep from *** three more times, drop A, pick up B, **** 1 hdc in next st, 2 hdc in next st; rep from **** four more times to end of rnd, sl st last hdc to first hdc—45 sts.

Rnd 6: Ch 2, TW, 1 hdc in each of next 8 sts, 2 hdc in next st, 1 hdc in each of next 5 sts, drop B, pick up A, 1 hdc in each of next 3 sts, 2 hdc in next st, 1 hdc in each of next 8 sts, 2 hdc in next st, drop A, pick up B, 1 hdc in each of next 8 sts, 2 hdc in next st, drop B, pick up A, 1 hdc in each of next 8 sts, 2 hdc in next st, sl st last hdc to first hdc—50 sts.

Rnd 7: Ch 2, TW, 1 hdc in each of next 10 sts, drop A, pick up B, 1 hdc in each of next 10 sts, drop B, pick up A, 1 hdc in each of next 30 sts, sl st last hdc to first hdc—50 sts.

Rnd 8: Ch 2, TW, 1 hdc in each of next 31 sts, drop A, pick up B, 1 hdc in each of next 8 sts, drop B, pick up A, 1 hdc in each of next 11 sts, sl st last hdc to first hdc—50 sts.

Rnd 9: Ch 2, TW, 1 hdc in each of next 25 sts, drop A, pick up B, 1 hdc in each of next 5 sts, drop B, pick up A, 1 hdc in each of next 20 sts, sl st last hdc to first hdc—50 sts.

Rnd 10: Ch 2, TW, 1 hdc in each of next 20 sts, drop A, pick up B, 1 hdc in each of next 5 sts, drop B, pick up A, 1 hdc in each of next 18 sts, drop A, pick up B, 1 hdc in each of next 4 sts, drop B, pick up A, 1 hdc in each of next 3 sts, sl st last hdc to first hdc—50 sts.

Rnd 11: Ch 2, TW, 1 hdc in each of next 3 sts, drop A, pick up B, 1 hdc in each of next 4 sts, drop B, pick up A, 1 hdc in each of next 18 sts, drop A, pick up B, 1 hdc in each of next 5 sts, drop B, pick up A, 1 hdc in each of next 8 sts, drop A, pick up B, 1 hdc in each of next 5 sts, drop B, pick up A, 1 hdc in each of next 7 sts, sl st last hdc to first hdc—50 sts.

Rnd 12: Ch 2, TW, 1 hdc in each of next 7 sts, drop A, pick up B, 1 hdc in each of next 5 sts, drop B, pick up A, 1 hdc in each of next 8 sts, drop A, pick up B, 1 hdc in each of next 5 sts, drop B, pick up A, 1 hdc in each of next 18 sts, drop A, pick up B, 1 hdc in each of next 4 sts, drop B, pick up A, 1 hdc in each of next 3 sts, sl st last hdc to first hdc—50 sts.

Rnd 13: Ch 2, TW, 1 hdc in each of next 3 sts, drop A, pick up B, 1 hdc in each of next 4 sts, drop B, pick up A, 1 hdc in each of next 31 sts, drop A, pick up B, 1 hdc in each of next 5 sts, drop B, pick up A, 1 hdc in each of next 7 sts, sl st last hdc to first hdc—50 sts.

Rnd 14: Ch 2, TW, 1 hdc in each of next 7 sts, drop A, pick up B, 1 hdc in each of next 5 sts, drop B, pick up A, 1 hdc in each of next 17 sts, drop A, pick up B, 1 hdc in each of next 5 sts, drop B, pick up A, 1 hdc in each of next 9 sts, drop A, pick up B, 1 hdc in each of next 4 sts, drop B, pick up A, 1 hdc in each of next 3 sts, sl st last hdc to first hdc—50 sts.

Rnd 15: Ch 2, TW, 1 hdc in each of next 16 sts, drop A, pick up B, 1 hdc in each of next 5 sts, drop B, pick up A, 1 hdc in each of next 17 sts, drop A, pick up B, 1 hdc in each of next 5 sts, drop B, pick up A, 1 hdc in each of next 7 sts, sl st last hdc to first hdc—50 sts.

Rnd 16: Ch 2, TW, 1 hdc in each of next 29 sts, drop A, pick up B, 1 hdc in each of next 5 sts, drop B, pick up A, 1 hdc in each of next 16 sts, sl st last hdc to first hdc—50 sts.

Rnd 17: Ch 2, TW, 1 hdc in each of next 16 sts, drop A, pick up B, 1 hdc in each of next 5 sts, drop B, pick up A, 1 hdc in each of next 7 sts, drop A, pick up B, 1 hdc in each of next 5 sts, drop B, pick up A, 1 hdc in each of next 12 sts, drop A, pick up B, 1 hdc in each of next 5 sts, sl st last hdc to first hdc—50 sts.

Rnd 18: Ch 2, TW, 1 hdc in each of next 5 sts, drop B, pick up A, 1 hdc in each of next 12 sts, drop A, pick up B, 1 hdc in each of next 5 sts, drop B, pick up A, 1 hdc in each of next 7 sts, drop A, pick up B, 1 hdc in each of next 5 sts, drop B, pick up A, 1 hdc in each of next 16 sts, sl st last hdc to first hdc—50 sts.

Rnd 19: Ch 2, TW, 1 hdc in each of next 28 sts, drop A, pick up B, 1 hdc in each of next 5 sts, drop B, pick up A, 1 hdc in each of next 12 sts, drop A, pick up B, 1 hdc in each of next 5 sts, sl st last hdc to first hdc—50 sts.

Rnd 20: Ch 2, TW, 1 hdc in each of next 5 sts, drop B, pick up A, 1 hdc in each of next 12 sts, drop A, pick up B, 1 hdc in each of next 5 sts, drop B, pick up A, 1 hdc in each of next 16 sts, drop A, pick up B, 1 hdc in each of next 5 sts, drop B, pick up A, 1 hdc in each of next 7 sts, sl st last hdc to first hdc—50 sts.

Rnd 21: Ch 2, TW, 1 hdc in each of next 7 sts, drop A, pick up B, 1 hdc in each of next 5 sts, drop B, pick up A, 1 hdc in each of next 33 sts, drop A, pick up B, 1 hdc in each of next 5 sts, sl st last hdc to first hdc—50 sts.

Rnd 22: Ch 2, TW, 1 hdc in each of next 5 sts, drop B, pick up A, 1 hdc in each of next 5 sts, drop A, pick up B, 1 hdc in each of next 4 sts, drop B, pick up A, 1 hdc in each of next 24 sts, drop A, pick up B, 1 hdc in each of next 5 sts, drop B, pick up A, 1 hdc in each of next 7 sts, sl st last hdc to first hdc—50 sts.

Rnd 23: Ch 2, TW, 1 hdc in each of next 7 sts, drop A, pick up B, 1 hdc in each of next 5 sts, drop B, pick up A, 1 hdc in each of next 24 sts, drop A, pick up B, 1 hdc in each of next 4 sts, drop B, pick up A, 1 hdc in each of next 10 sts, sl st last hdc to first hdc—50 sts.

Rnd 24: Ch 2, TW, 1 hdc in each of next 10 sts, drop A, pick up B, 1 hdc in each of next 4 sts, drop B, pick up A, 1 hdc in each of next 12 sts, drop A, pick up B, 1 hdc in each of next 5 sts, drop B, pick up A, 1 hdc in each of next 7 sts, drop A, pick up B, 1 hdc in each of next 5 sts, drop B, pick up A, 1 hdc in each of next 7 sts, sl st last hdc to first hdc—50 sts.

Rnd 25: Ch 2, TW, 1 hdc in each of next 19 sts, drop A, pick up B, 1 hdc in each of next 5 sts, drop B, pick up A, 1 hdc in each of next 12 sts, drop A, pick up B, 1 hdc in each of next 4 sts, drop B, pick up A, 1 hdc in each of next 10 sts, sl st last hdc to first hdc—50 sts.

Rnd 26: Ch 2, TW, 1 hdc in each of next 10 sts, drop A, pick up B, 1 hdc in each of next 4 sts, drop B, pick up A, 1 hdc in each of next 12 sts, drop A, pick up B, 1 hdc in each of next 5 sts, drop B, pick up A, 1 hdc in each of next 19 sts, sl st last hdc to first hdc—50 sts.

Rnd 27: Ch 2, TW, 1 hdc in next st, drop A, pick up B, 1 hdc in each of next 4 sts, drop B, pick up A, 1 hdc in each of next 14 sts, drop A, pick up B, 1 hdc in each of next 5 sts, drop B, pick up A, 1 hdc in each of next 4 sts, drop A, pick up B, 1 hdc in each of next 4 sts, drop B, pick up A, 1 hdc in each of next 18 sts, sl st last hdc to first hdc—50 sts.

Rnd 28: Ch 2, TW, 1 hdc in each of next 18 sts, drop A, pick up B, 1 hdc in each of next 4 sts, drop B, pick up A, 1 hdc in each of next 4 sts, drop A, pick up B, 1 hdc in each of next 5 sts, drop B, pick up A, 1 hdc in each of next 14 sts, drop A, pick up B, 1 hdc in each of next 4 sts, drop B, pick up A, 1 hdc in next st, sl st last hdc to first hdc—50 sts.

Rnd 29: Ch 2, TW, 1 hdc in next st, drop A, pick up B, 1 hdc in each of next 2 sts, hdc next 2 sts tog, drop B, pick up A, * 1 hdc in each of next 3 sts, hdc next 2 sts tog; rep from * three more times, 1 hdc in each of next 3 sts, drop A, pick up B, hdc next 2 sts tog, 1 hdc in each of next 2 sts, drop B, pick up A, 1 hdc in next st, hdc next 2 sts tog, ** 1 hdc in each of next 3 sts, hdc next 2 sts tog; rep from ** two more times to end of rnd, sl st last hdc to first hdc—40 sts.

Rnd 30: Ch 2, TW, * 1 hdc in each of next 2 sts, hdc next 2 sts tog; rep from * two more times, 1 hdc in each of next 2 sts, drop A, pick up B, hdc next 2 sts tog, 1 hdc in next st, drop B, pick up A, 1 hdc in next st, hdc next 2 sts tog, ** 1 hdc in each of next 2 sts, hdc next 2 sts tog; rep from ** three more times, drop A, pick up B, 1 hdc in each of next 2 sts, drop B, pick up A, fasten off B, hdc next 2 sts tog, sl st last hdc to first hdc—30 sts.

Rnd 31: Ch 2, TW, * 1 hdc in each of next 3 sts, hdc next 2 sts tog; rep from * five more times to end of rnd, sl st last hdc to first hdc—24 sts.

Rnd 32: Ch 2, TW, * 1 hdc in each of next 2 sts, hdc next 2 sts tog; rep from * five more times to end of rnd, sl st last hdc to first hdc—18 sts.

Rnd 33: Ch 2, TW, * 1 hdc in next st, hdc next 2 sts tog; rep from * five more times to end of rnd, sl st last hdc to first hdc—12 sts.

Rnd 34 (neck end): Ch 2, TW, * 1 hdc in next st, hdc next 2 sts tog; rep from * three more times, sl st last hdc to first hdc—8 sts. Fasten off, leaving a 10" (25cm) tail. Whip stitch opening closed. Tie off and weave in ends.

Neck

Make 1.

Rnd 1 (head end): With A, leaving a 24" (61cm) tail, ch 28, sl st last ch to first ch to make a loop.

Rnd 2: Ch 2, TW, 1 hdc in each ch to end of rnd, sl st last hdc to first hdc—28 sts.

Rnd 3: Ch 2, TW, 1 hdc in each of next 6 sts, drop A, pick up B, 1 hdc in each of next 4 sts, drop B, pick up A, 1 hdc in each of next 18 sts, sl st last hdc to first hdc—28 sts.

Rnd 4: Ch 2, TW, 1 hdc in each of next 8 sts, drop A, pick up B, 1 hdc in each of next 4 sts, drop B, pick up A, 1 hdc in each of next 6 sts, drop A, pick up B, 1 hdc in each of next 4 sts, drop B, pick up A, 1 hdc in each of next 6 sts, sl st last hdc to first hdc—28 sts.

Rnd 5: Ch 2, TW, 1 hdc in each of next 6 sts, drop A, pick up B, 1 hdc in each of next 4 sts, drop B, pick up A, 1 hdc in each of next 6 sts, drop A, pick up B, 1 hdc in each of next 4 sts, drop B, pick up A, 1 hdc in each of next 8 sts, sl st last hdc to first hdc—28 sts.

Rnd 6: Ch 2, TW, 1 hdc in next st, drop A, pick up B, 1 hdc in each of next 4 sts, drop B, pick up A, 1 hdc in each of next 3 sts, drop A, pick up B, 1 hdc in each of next 4 sts, drop B, pick up A, 1 hdc in each of next 6 sts, drop A, pick up B, 1 hdc in each of next 4 sts, drop B, pick up A, 1 hdc in each of next 6 sts, sl st last hdc to first hdc—28 sts.

Rnd 7: Ch 2, TW, 1 hdc in each of next 16 sts, drop A, pick up B, 1 hdc in each of next 4 sts, drop B, pick up A, 1 hdc in each of next 3 sts, drop A, pick up B, 1 hdc in each of next 4 sts, drop B, pick up A, 1 hdc in next st, sl st last hdc to first hdc—28 sts.

Rnd 8: Ch 2, TW, 1 hdc in next st, drop A, pick up B, 1 hdc in each of next 4 sts, drop B, pick up A, 1 hdc in each of next 3 sts, drop A, pick up B, 1 hdc in each of next 4 sts, drop B, pick up A, 1 hdc in each of next 16 sts, sl st last hdc to first hdc—28 sts.

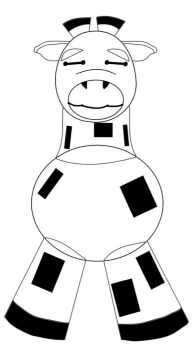

Figure 1 (front view)

Figure 1 (side view)

Rnd 9: Ch 2, TW, 1 hdc in next st, drop A, pick up B, 1 hdc in each of next 4 sts, drop B, pick up A, 1 hdc in each of next 18 sts, drop A, pick up B, 1 hdc in each of next 4 sts, drop B, pick up A, 1 hdc in next st, sl st last hdc to first hdc—28 sts.

Rnd 10: Ch 2, TW, 1 hdc in next st, drop A, pick up B, 1 hdc in each of next 4 sts, drop B, pick up A, 1 hdc in each of next 9 sts, drop A, pick up B, 1 hdc in each of next 4 sts, drop B, pick up A, 1 hdc in each of next 5 sts, drop A, pick up B, 1 hdc in each of next 4 sts, drop B, pick up A, 1 hdc in next st, sl st last hdc to first hdc—28 sts.

Rnd 11: Ch 2, TW, 1 hdc in next st, drop A, pick up B, 1 hdc in each of next 4 sts, drop B, pick up A, 1 hdc in next st, 2 hdc in next st, 1 hdc in each of next 3 sts, drop A, pick up B, 1 hdc in each of next 3 sts, 2 hdc in next st, drop B, pick up A, * 1 hdc in each of next 6 sts, 2 hdc in next st; rep from * one more time, sl st last hdc to first hdc—32 sts.

Rnd 12 (body end): Ch 2, TW, * 1 hdc in each of next 7 sts, 2 hdc in next st; rep from * one more time, drop A, pick up B, 1 hdc in each of next 5 sts, drop B, pick up A, 1 hdc in each of next 2 sts, 2 hdc in next st, 1 hdc in each of next 3 sts, drop A, pick up B, 1 hdc in each of next 4 sts, drop B, pick up A, 2 hdc in next st, sl st last hdc to first hdc—36 sts. Fasten off, leaving a 24" (61cm) tail. Align spots on body with spots on neck and whip stitch neck in place, matching colors (Fig. 2). Stuff neck. Whip stitch head to head end of neck (Fig. 1).

Eyes, Nostrils and Mouth

With darning needle and D, embroider eyes, nostrils and mouth as shown (Fig. 1).

Eyelid

Make 2.

Row 1 (base): With A, leaving a 12" (30cm) tail, ch 8, TW, starting with 3rd ch from hook, hdc next 2 sts tog, 1 hdc in each of next 2 sts, hdc next 2 sts tog—4 sts.

Row 2: Ch 1, TW, hdc next 2 sts tog, hdc next 2 sts tog—2 sts. Fasten off. Align base of eyelid above eye and whip stitch around, stuffing lightly (Fig. 1). Tie off and weave in ends.

Horn

Make 2.

Rnd 1: With A, leaving a 12" (30cm) tail, ch 8, sl st last ch to first ch to make a loop.

Rnd 2: Ch 2, TW, 1 hdc in each ch to end of rnd, sl st last hdc to first hdc—8 sts.

Rnd 3: Ch 2, TW, 1 hdc in each st to end of rnd, sl st last hdc to first hdc—8 sts.

Rnd 4: Cut A, join C, ch 2, TW, * 2 hdc in next st, 1 hdc in next st; rep from * three more times to end of rnd, sl st last hdc to first hdc—12 sts.

Rnd 5: Ch 2, TW, * 1 hdc in each of next 3 sts, 2 hdc in next st; rep from * two more times to end of rnd, sl st last hdc to first hdc—15 sts. Fasten off.

Top of Horn

Make 2.

Rnd 1: With C, ch 3, sl st last ch to first ch to make a loop.

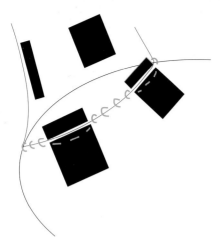

Figure 2

Rnd 2: Ch 2, TW, work 10 hdc in center of loop, sl st last hdc to first hdc—10 sts.

Rnd 3: Ch 1, TW, * 1 sc in next st, 2 sc in next st; rep from * four more times to end of rnd, sl st last sc to first sc—15 sts. Fasten off, leaving a 12" (30cm) tail. Whip stitch top of horn to C end of horn. Tie off and weave in ends. Stuff. Whip stitch horn to top of head as shown (Fig. 1).

Inner Ear

Make 2.

Row 1 (base): With B, leaving a 20" (51cm) tail, ch 6, TW, 2 hdc in 3rd ch from hook, 1 hdc in each of next 2 chs, 2 hdc in next ch—6 sts.

Rows 2–4: Ch 2, TW, 1 hdc in each st to end of row—6 sts.

Row 5: Ch 1, TW, hdc next 2 sts tog, 1 hdc in each of next 2 sts, hdc next 2 sts tog—4 sts.

Row 6: Ch 1, TW, hdc next 2 sts tog, hdc next 2 sts tog—2 sts.

Row 7: Ch 2, TW, 1 hdc in each st to end of row—2 sts. Fasten off.

Outer Ear

Make 2.

With A, work as for inner ear, omitting long tail at beg. Align inner and outer ear and whip stitch tog. Whip stitch base of completed ear to head as shown (Fig. 1). Tie off and weave in ends.

Leg

Make 4.

Rnd 1: With A, leaving a 36" (91cm) tail, ch 25, sl st last ch to first ch to form a loop.

Rnd 2: Ch 2, TW, 1 hdc in each ch to end of rnd, sl st last hdc to first hdc—25 sts.

Rnd 3: Ch 2, TW, 1 hdc in each of next 3 sts, drop A, pick up B, 1 hdc in each of next 4 sts, drop B, pick up A, 1 hdc in each of next 18 sts, sl st last hdc to first hdc—25 sts.

Rnd 4: Ch 2, TW, 1 hdc in each of next 7 sts, drop A, pick up B, 1 hdc in each of next 4 sts, drop B, pick up A, 1 hdc in each of next 7 sts, drop A, pick up B, 1 hdc in each of next 4 sts, drop B, pick up A, 1 hdc in each of next 3 sts, sl st last hdc to first hdc—25 sts.

Rnd 5: Ch 2, TW, 1 hdc in each of next 3 sts, drop A, pick up B, 1 hdc in each of next 4 sts, drop B, pick up A, 1 hdc in each of next 7 sts, drop A, pick up B, 1 hdc in each of next 4 sts, drop B, pick up A, 1 hdc in each of next 3 sts, drop A, pick up B, 1 hdc in each of next 4 sts, sl st last hdc to first hdc—25 sts.

Rnd 6: Ch 2, TW, 1 hdc in each of next 4 sts, drop B, pick up A, 1 hdc in each of next 3 sts, drop A, pick up B, 1 hdc in each of next 4 sts, drop B, pick up A, 1 hdc in each of next 7 sts, drop A, pick up B, 1 hdc in each of next 4 sts, drop B, pick up A, 1 hdc in each of next 3 sts, sl st last hdc to first hdc—25 sts.

Rnd 7: Ch 2, TW, 1 hdc in each of next 3 sts, drop A, pick up B, 1 hdc in each of next 4 sts, drop B, pick up A, 1 hdc in each of next 7 sts, drop A, pick up B, 1 hdc in each of next 4 sts, drop B, pick up A, 1 hdc in each of next 3 sts, drop A, pick up B, 1 hdc in each of next 4 sts, sl st last hdc to first hdc—25 sts.

Rnd 8: Ch 2, TW, 1 hdc in each of next 4 sts, drop B, pick up A, 1 hdc in each of next 3 sts, drop A, pick up B, 1 hdc in each of next 4 sts, drop B, pick up A, 1 hdc in each of next 14 sts, sl st last hdc to first hdc—25 sts.

Rnd 9: Ch 2, TW, 1 hdc in each of next 21 sts, drop A, pick up B, 1 hdc in each of next 4 sts, sl st last hdc to first hdc—25 sts.

Rnd 10: Ch 2, TW, 1 hdc in each of next 4 sts, cut B, pick up A, 1 hdc in each of next 21 sts, sl st last hdc to first hdc—25 sts.

Rnds 11–12: Ch 2, TW, 1 hdc in each st to end of rnd, sl st last hdc to first hdc—25 sts.

Rnd 13: Cut A, join C, ch 2, TW, 1 hdc in each st to end of rnd, sl st last hdc to first hdc—25 sts.

Rnd 14: Ch 2, TW, * 1 hdc in each of next 4 sts, 2 hdc in next st; rep from * four more times to end of rnd, sl st last hdc to first hdc—30 sts.

Rnd 15: Ch 2, TW, * 1 hdc in each of next 5 sts, 2 hdc in next st; rep from * four more times to end of rnd, sl st last hdc to first hdc—35 sts.

Rnd 16: Ch 2, TW, 1 hdc in each st to end of rnd, sl st last hdc to first hdc—35 sts. Fasten off, leaving a 36" (91cm) tail.

Bottom of Hoof

Make 4.

Rnd 1: With C, ch 4, sl st last ch to first ch to make a loop.

Rnd 2: Ch 2, TW, work 10 hdc in the center of the loop, sl st last hdc to first hdc—10 sts.

Rnd 3: Ch 2, TW, 2 hdc in each st to end of rnd, sl st last hdc to first hdc—20 sts.

Rnd 4: Ch 2, TW, * 1 hdc in next st, 2 hdc in next st; rep from * nine more times to end of rnd, sl st last hdc to first hdc—30 sts.

Rnd 5: Ch 2, TW, * 1 hdc in each of next 5 sts, 2 hdc in next st; rep from * four more times, sl st last hdc to first hdc—35 sts. Fasten off. Whip stitch bottom of hoof to C end of leg. Stuff. Whip stitch leg to body (Fig. 1). Tie off and weave in ends.

Tail

Make 1.

Rnd 1 (base): With A, leaving a 12" (30cm) tail, ch 10, sl st last ch to first ch.

Rnd 2: Ch 2, TW, 1 hdc in each ch to end of rnd, sl st last hdc to first hdc—10 sts.

Rnd 3: Ch 2, TW, 1 hdc in each st to end of rnd, sl st last hdc to first hdc—10 sts.

Rnd 4: Ch 2, TW, hdc next 2 sts tog, 1 hdc in each of next 8 sts, sl st last hdc to first hdc—9 sts.

Rnd 5: Ch 2, TW, hdc next 2 sts tog, 1 hdc in each of next 7 sts, sl st last hdc to first hdc—8 sts.

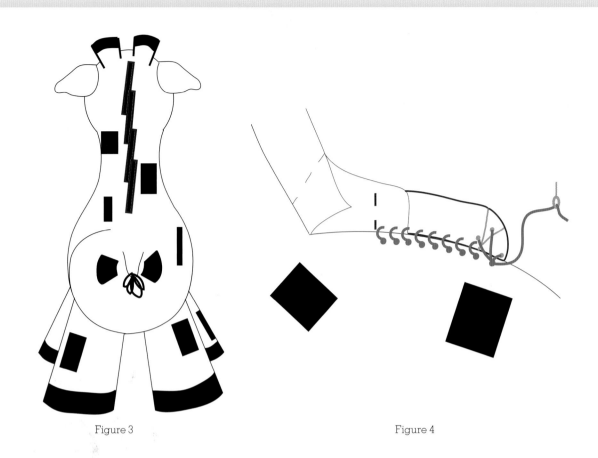

Rnd 6: Ch 2, TW, hdc next 2 sts tog, 1 hdc in each of next 6 sts, sl st last hdc to first hdc—7 sts.

Rnd 7: Ch 2, TW, hdc next 2 sts tog, 1 hdc in each of next 5 sts, sl st last hdc to first hdc—6 sts.

Rnd 8: Ch 2, TW, hdc next 2 sts tog, 1 hdc in each of next 4 sts, sl st last hdc to first hdc—5 sts.

Rnd 9: Ch 2, TW, hdc next 2 sts tog, 1 hdc in each of next 3 sts, sl st last hdc to first hdc—4 sts. Fasten off, leaving an 8" (20cm) tail. Whip stitch opening closed. Tie off and weave in ends. Sew base of tail to body (Figs. 1 and 3). Tie off and weave in ends.

Tail Hair

Make 1.

Rnd 1: With B, leaving a 6" (15cm) tail, ch 8, sl st last ch to first ch to make first loop.

Rnd 2: Ch 12, sl st last ch to first ch of first loop to make 2nd loop.

Rnd 3: Ch 16, sl st last ch to first ch of first loop to make 3rd loop.

Rnd 4: Ch 8, sl st last ch to first ch of first loop to make 4th loop. Fasten off, leaving a 6" (15cm) tail. Tie beg and ending tails tog. Thread both through darning needle and attach hair to tip of tail. Weave in ends.

Mane Hair

Make 4.

Row 1: With B, leaving a 12" (30cm) tail, ch 10, starting with 3rd ch from hook, 1 hdc in each ch to end of row—8 sts.

Rows 2–3: Ch 2, TW, 1 hdc in each st to end of row—8 sts. Fasten off. Using tail, whip stitch to neck and body (Figs. 1 and 3). On last section of hair (closest to hind end of body), whip stitch to create a downward curve as shown (Fig. 4). Tie off and weave in ends.

Hannah the Hippo

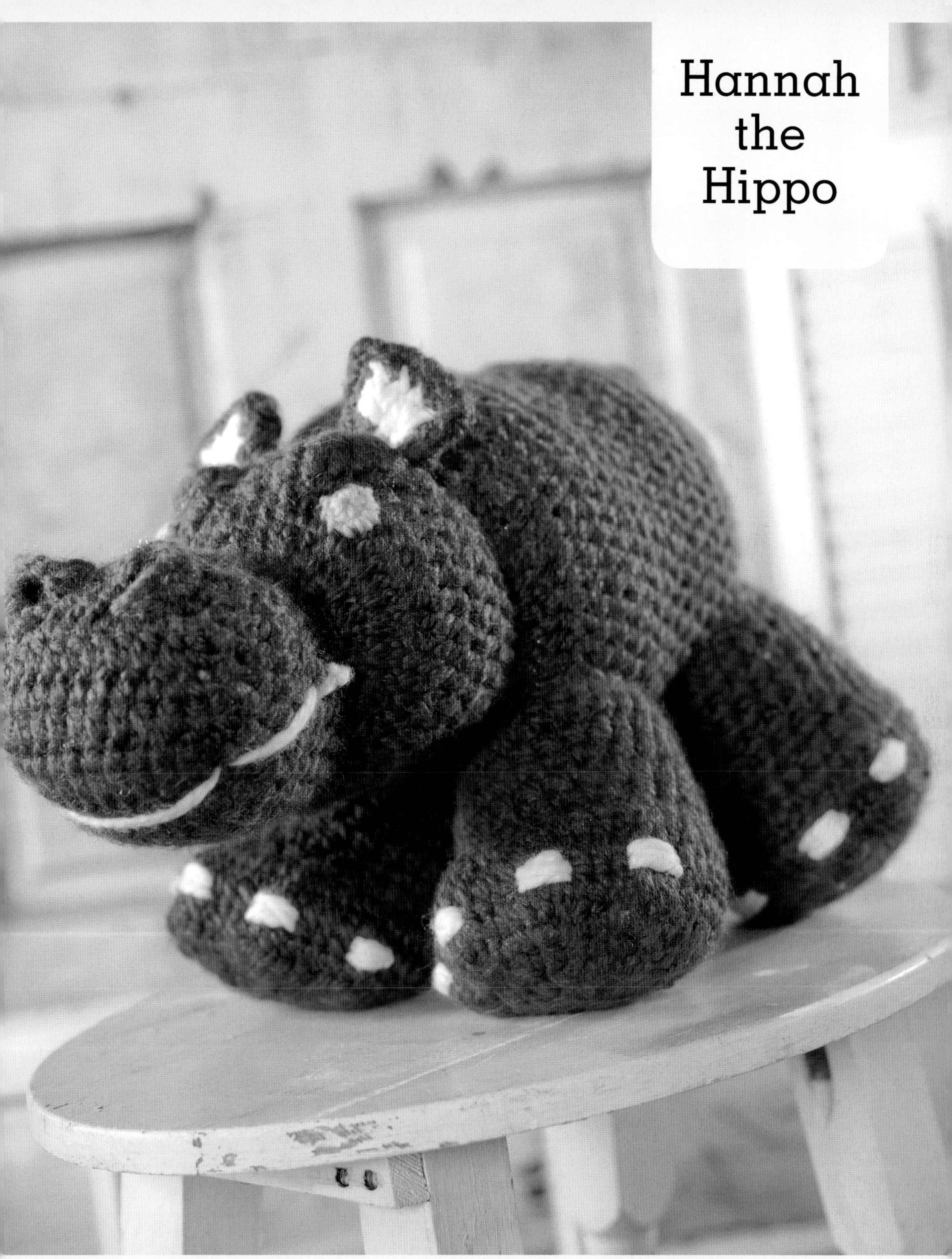

Hannah the Hippo

Hannah is the protector of the watering hole. She makes sure that there are no predators lying in wait below the surface when the other animals come to get a drink. It is also her job to break up any quarrels over who deserves the first sip. Sometimes she even plays lifeguard when baby animals walk too far into the deep end.

YARN

Super bulky (6) yarn in 2 colors; 424 yds (388m) of color **A** and 50 yds (46m) of color **B**

Medium (4) yarn in 1 color; 3 yds (3m) of color **C**

*The project shown on page 83 uses Lion Brand Wool-Ease Thick & Quick (80% acrylic/20% wool, 106 yds [97m], 6 oz [170g]) in Fig (**A**) and Fisherman (**B**) and Lion Brand Nature's Choice Organic Cotton (organically grown cotton, 103 yds [94m], 3 oz [85g]) in Macadamia (**C**).*

HOOKS AND NOTIONS

G/6 (4mm) and I/9 (5.5mm) crochet hooks • Size 13 darning needle • Polyester fiberfill • Stuffing stick

GAUGE

5 hdc and 4 rows = 2" (5cm) using size I/9 (5.5mm) hook

FINISHED SIZE

Approx 10" (25cm) tall, 15" (38cm) long

Head

Make 1.

Row 1 (first ch marks front top right corner of head): With I/9 (5.5mm) hook and A, ch 10, starting with 3rd ch from hook 1 hdc in each st to end of row—8 sts.

Row 2: Ch 2, TW, 1 hdc in each st to end of row—8 sts.

Row 3: Ch 1, TW, hdc next 2 sts tog, 1 hdc in each of next 4 sts, sc next 2 sts tog—6 sts.

Row 4: Ch 2, TW, 1 hdc in each st to end of row—6 sts.

Row 5: Ch 1, TW, hdc next 2 sts tog, 1 hdc in each of next 2 sts, sc next 2 sts tog—4 sts.

Row 6: Ch 2, TW, 1 hdc in each st to end of row—4 sts. Beg working in rnds, stuffing as work progresses.

Rnd 1: Ch 2, do not TW, work 1 hdc in the end of Rows 6–2, 2 hdc in the end of Row 1, 1 hdc in each of next 8 chs, 2 hdc in the end of Row 1, work 1 hdc each in the end of Rows 2–6, 1 hdc in each of next 4 sts, sl st last hdc to first hdc—26 sts.

Rnd 2: Ch 2, TW, 1 hdc in each of next 4 sts, hdc next 2 sts tog, hdc next 2 sts tog, * 2 hdc in next st; rep from * three more times, 1 hdc in each of next 6 sts, ** 2 hdc in next st; rep from ** three more times, *** hdc next 2 sts tog; rep from *** one more time, sl st last hdc to first hdc—30 sts.

Rnd 3: Ch 2, TW, hdc next 2 sts tog, hdc next 2 sts tog, 2 hdc in each of next 6 sts, 1 hdc in each of next 6 sts, 2 hdc in each of next 6 sts, hdc next 2 sts tog, hdc next 2 sts tog, 2 hdc in next st, 1 hdc in each of next 2 sts, 2 hdc in next st, sl st last hdc to first hdc—40 sts.

Rnd 4: Ch 1, do not TW, sc next 2 sts tog, sc next 2 sts tog, 2 hdc in each of next 8 sts, 1 hdc in each of next 10 sts, 2 hdc in each of next 8 sts, sc next 2 sts tog, sc next 2 sts tog, 1 hdc in each of next 2 sts, 2 hdc in each of next 2 sts, 1 hdc in each of next 2 sts, sl st last hdc to first sc—54 sts.

Rnd 5: Ch 2, TW, skip 1st, 1 hdc in each of next 26 sts, * hdc next 2 sts tog; rep from * four more times, skip 1 st, 1 hdc in each of next 16 sts, sl st last hdc to first hdc—47 sts.

Rnd 6: Ch 2, TW, skip 1 st, 1 hdc in next st, * hdc next 2 sts tog; rep from * one more time, 1 hdc in each of next 25 sts, **hdc next 2 sts tog; rep from ** one more time, 1 hdc in each of next 12 sts, sl st last hdc to first hdc—42 sts.

Rnd 7: Ch 2, TW, 1 hdc in each of next 11 sts, hdc next 2 sts tog, 1 hdc in each of next 26 sts, hdc next 2 sts tog, 1 hdc in next st, sl st last hdc to first hdc—40 sts.

Rnd 8: Ch 2, TW, 1 hdc in each st to end of rnd, sl st last hdc to first hdc—40 sts.

Rnd 9: Ch 2, TW, 1 hdc in each of next 10 sts, hdc next 2 sts tog, hdc next 2 sts tog, 1 hdc in each of next 22 sts, hdc next 2 sts tog, hdc next 2 sts tog, sl st last hdc to first hdc—36 sts.

Rnd 10: Ch 2, TW, 1 hdc in each st to end of rnd, sl st last hdc to first hdc—36 sts.

Rnd 11: Ch 2, TW, * 1 hdc in each of next 4 sts, hdc next 2 sts tog; rep from * five more times, sl st last hdc to first hdc—30 sts.

Rnd 12: Ch 2, TW, * 1 hdc in each of next 3 sts, hdc next 2 sts tog; rep from * five more times, sl st last hdc to first hdc—24 sts.

Rnd 13: Ch 2, TW, * hdc next 2 sts tog; rep from * to end of rnd, sl st last hdc to first hdc—12 sts.

Rnd 14 (back side of head): Ch 2, TW, * hdc next 2 sts tog; rep from * to end of rnd, sl st last hdc to first hdc—6 sts. Fasten off, leaving an 8" (20cm) tail. Whip stitch opening closed. Tie off and weave in ends.

Body

Make 1.

Rnd 1 (neck end): With I/9 (5.5mm) hook and A, leaving a 36" (91cm) tail and stuffing as work progresses, ch 40, sl st last ch to first ch to make a loop.

Rnd 2: Ch 2, * 2 hdc in next ch, 1 hdc in next ch; rep from * four more times, 1 hdc in each of next 20 chs, ** 1 hdc in next ch, 2 hdc in next ch; rep from ** four more times, sl st last hdc to first hdc—50 sts.

Rnds 3-8: Ch 2, TW, 1 hdc in each st to end of rnd, sl st last hdc to first hdc—50 sts.

Rnd 9: Ch 2, TW, 1 hdc in each of next 15 sts, * hdc next 2 sts tog, 1 hdc in each of next 2 sts; rep from * four more times, 1 hdc in each of next 15 sts, sl st last hdc to first hdc—45 sts.

Rnds 10-11: Ch 2, TW, 1 hdc in each st to end of rnd, sl st last hdc to first hdc—45 sts.

Rnd 12: Ch 2, TW, 1 hdc in each of next 15 sts, * 2 hdc in next st, 1 hdc in each of next 3 sts; rep from * two more times, 2 hdc in each of next 2 sts, 1 hdc in each of next 16 sts, sl st last hdc to first hdc—50 sts.

Rnd 13: Ch 2, TW, 1 hdc in each st to end of rnd, sl st last hdc to first hdc—50 sts.

Rnd 14: Ch 2, TW, 1 hdc in each of next 15 sts, * 2 hdc in next st, 1 hdc in each of next 3 sts; rep from * four more times, 1 hdc in each of next 15 sts, sl st last hdc to first hdc—55 sts.

Rnds 15-16: Ch 2, TW, 1 hdc in each st to end of rnd, sl st last hdc to first hdc—55 sts.

Rnd 17: Ch 2, TW, * 1 hdc in each of next 3 sts, hdc next 2 sts tog; rep from * ten more times, sl st last hdc to first hdc—44 sts.

Rnd 18: Ch 2, TW, * 1 hdc in each of next 2 sts, hdc next 2 sts tog; rep from * ten more times, sl st last hdc to first hdc—33 sts.

Rnd 19: Ch 2, TW, 1 hdc in each st to end of rnd, sl st last hdc to first hdc—33 sts.

Rnd 20: Ch 2, TW, * 1 hdc in each of next 9 sts, hdc next 2 sts tog; rep from * two more times, sl st last hdc to first hdc—30 sts.

Rnd 21: Ch 2, TW, * 1 hdc in each of next 3 sts, hdc next 2 sts tog; rep from * five more times, sl st last hdc to first hdc—24 sts.

Rnd 22: Ch 2, TW, * 1 hdc in each of next 2 sts, hdc next 2 sts tog; rep from * five more times, sl st last hdc to first hdc—18 sts.

Rnd 23: Ch 2, TW, * hdc next 2 sts tog; rep from * eight more times, sl st last hdc to first hdc—9 sts.

Rnd 24: Ch 2, TW, 1 hdc in next st, * hdc next 2 sts tog; rep from * three more times to end of rnd, sl st last hdc to first hdc—5 sts. Fasten off, leaving a 10" (25cm) tail. Whip stitch opening closed. Tie off and weave in ends. Turn body so seam is centered under belly. Using top right corner of head (marked in pattern) as reference point, position back of head in center of head end of body. Whip stitch head to body as shown (Fig. 1).

Nose

Make 1.

Row 1: With I/9 (5.5mm) hook and A, ch 12, TW, 1 hdc in each ch to end of row, starting with 3rd ch from hook—10 sts.

Row 2: Ch 2, TW, 2 hdc in first st, 1 hdc in each of next 8 sts, 2 hdc in next st—12 sts.

Row 3: Ch 2, TW, 2 hdc in first st, 1 hdc in each of next 10 sts, 2 hdc in next st—14 sts.

Row 4: Ch 2, TW, 1 hdc in each st to end of row—14 sts.

Row 5: Ch 2, TW, hdc next 2 sts tog, 1 hdc in each of next 10 sts, hdc next 2 sts tog—12 sts.

Row 6: Ch 2, TW, 1 hdc in each st to end of row—12 sts.

Row 7: Ch 2, TW, hdc next 2 sts tog, 1 hdc in each of next 8 sts, hdc next 2 sts tog—10 sts. Beg working in rnds.

Rnd 1: Ch 2, work 1 hdc each in the end of Rows 7-1, 1 hdc in each of next 10 chs, work 1 hdc each in the end of Rows 1-7, 2 hdc in next st, 1 hdc in each of next 8 sts, 2 hdc in next st, sl st last hdc to first hdc—36 sts.

Rnds 2-3: Ch 2, TW, 1 hdc in each st to end of rnd—36 sts.

Rnd 4: Ch 2, TW, hdc next 2 sts tog, 1 hdc in each of next 6 sts, * hdc next 2 sts tog; rep from * two more times, 1 hdc in each of next 18 sts, ** hdc next 2 sts tog; rep from ** one more time, sl st last hdc to first hdc—30 sts.

Rnd 5: Ch 2, TW, * hdc next 2 sts tog; rep from * one more time, 1 hdc in each of next 14 sts, **hdc next 2 sts tog; rep from ** one more time, 1 hdc in each of next 8 sts, sl st last hdc to first hdc—26 sts.

Rnds 6-7: Ch 2, TW, 1 hdc in each st to end of rnd, sl st last hdc to first hdc—26 sts. Fasten off, leaving a 32" (81cm) tail. Stuff. Align nose with bump on front of head (Fig. 1) and whip stitch in place. Weave in ends.

Figure 1 (front view)

Figure 1 (side view)

Leg

Make 4.

Rnd 1: With I/9 (5.5mm) hook and A, leaving a 36" (91cm) tail, ch 24, sl st last ch to first ch to make a loop.

Rnds 2–7: Ch 2, TW, 1 hdc in each ch/st to end of rnd, sl st last hdc to first hdc—24 sts.

Rnd 8: Ch 2, TW, 1 hdc in each of next 4 sts, * 2 hdc in next st, 1 hdc in next st; rep from * seven more times, 1 hdc in each of next 4 sts, sl st last hdc to first hdc—32 sts.

Rnd 9: Ch 2, TW, 1 hdc in each of next 6 sts, * 2 hdc in next st, 1 hdc in next st; rep from * nine more times, 1 hdc in each of next 6 sts, sl st last hdc to first hdc—42 sts.

Rnd 10 (end of leg): Ch 2, TW, 1 hdc in each st to end of rnd, sl st last hdc to first hdc—42 sts. Fasten off, weave in ends.

Bottom of Foot

Make 4.

Rnd 1: With I/9 (5.5mm) hook and A, ch 4, sl st last ch to first ch to make a loop.

Rnd 2: Ch 2, TW, work 10 hdc in the center of the loop, sl st last hdc to first hdc—10 sts.

Rnd 3: Ch 2, TW, * 1 hdc in next st, 2 hdc in next st; rep from * four more times, sl st last hdc to first hdc—15 sts.

Rnd 4: Ch 2, TW, * 1 hdc in next st, 2 hdc in next st; rep from * six more times, 1 hdc in next st, sl st last hdc to first hdc—22 sts.

Rnd 5: Ch 2, TW, 2 hdc in each of next 4 sts, sc in next st, 4 hdc in next st, sl st in next st, * sc in next st, 4 hdc in next st, sc in next st, sl st in next st; rep from * one more time, 4 hdc in next st, sc in next st, sl st in next st, 2 hdc in each of next 4 sts, sl st last hdc to first hdc—42 sts. Fasten off, leaving a 36" (91cm) tail. Whip stitch bottom of foot to end of leg, aligning bottom of foot so 4 rounded toes are on front of foot. Stuff.

Toenails

With darning needle and C (B for alternate version shown on page 93), embroider four toenails on each foot as shown (Fig. 2). Whip stitch legs to body (Fig. 1). Tie off and weave in ends.

Eye

Make 2.

Rnd 1: With G/6 (4mm) hook and C (B for alternate version shown on page 93), ch 3, sl st last ch to first ch to make a loop.

Rnd 2: Ch 1, TW, work 6 sc in center of loop, sl st last sc to first sc—6 sts. Fasten off, leaving a 12" (30cm) tail. Whip stitch eye to head (Fig. 1). Tie off and weave in ends.

Mouth

With darning needle and B, embroider mouth as shown (Fig. 1).

Eyelid

Make 2.

Row 1 (base): With I/9 (5.5mm) hook and A, leaving a 12" (30cm) tail, ch 7, TW, 1 sc in 2nd ch from hook, 1 hdc in each of next 4 chs, 1 sc in next ch—6 sts.

Row 2: Ch 1, TW, * hdc next 2 sts tog; rep from * two more times—3 sts. Fasten off. Align base end parallel to eye as shown (Fig. 1) and whip stitch around, stuffing as work progresses. Tie off and weave in ends.

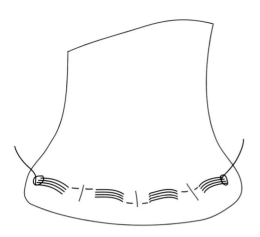

Figure 2

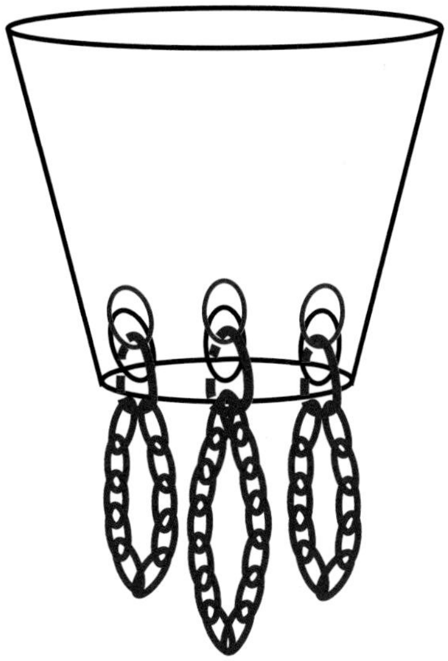

Figure 3

Nostril

Make 2.

Row 1: With I/9 (5.5mm) hook and A, leaving a 12" (30cm) tail, ch 8, TW, 1 sc in each ch to end of row, starting with 2nd ch from hook—7 sts. Fasten off, weave in ends. Pinch nostril tog in the shape of an upside-down U. Position on face as shown and whip stitch in place (Fig. 1), taking care not to stitch down the front edge of the nostril. Tie off and weave in ends.

Inner Ear

Make 2.

Row 1 (base): With I/9 (5.5mm) hook and B, ch 4, TW, starting with 3rd ch from hook, 1 hdc in each ch to end of row—2 sts.

Row 2: Ch 2, TW, 2 hdc in each of next 2 sts—4 sts. Fasten off. Weave in ends.

Inner Ear Edging

Row 1: With I/9 (5.5mm) hook, join A to first ch of Row 1 of inner ear, ch 1, work 1 sc in the end of Rows 1–2, 2 sc in next st, 1 sc in next 2 sts, 2 sc in next st, 1 sc in the end of Rows 2–1—10 sts. Fasten off. Weave in ends.

Outer Ear

Make 2.

Row 1 (base): With I/9 (5.5mm) hook and A, leaving a 36" (91cm) tail, ch 6, TW, starting with 3rd ch from hook, 1 hdc in each ch to end of row—4 sts.

Row 2: Ch 2, TW, 2 hdc in next st, 1 hdc in each of next 2 sts, 2 hdc in next st—6 sts.

Row 3: Ch 1, TW, 1 sc in each st to end of row—6 sts. Fasten off. Align inner and outer ear and whip stitch around, then whip stitch base of ear to top of head (Fig. 1). Tie off and weave in ends.

Tail

Make 1.

Rnd 1 (base): With I/9 (5.5mm) hook and A, leaving a 24" (61cm) tail, ch 10, sl st last ch to first ch to make loop.

Rnd 2: Ch 2, TW, 1 hdc in each ch to end of rnd, sl st last hdc to first hdc—10 sts.

Rnd 3: Ch 2, TW, * hdc next 2 sts tog, 1 hdc in each of next 3 sts; rep from * one more time, sl st last hdc to first hdc—8 sts.

Rnd 4: Ch 2, TW, * hdc next 2 sts tog, 1 hdc in each of next 2 sts; rep from * one more time, sl st last hdc to first hdc—6 sts.

Rnd 5: Ch 2, TW, 1 hdc in each st to end of rnd, sl st last hdc to first hdc—6 sts. Fasten off. Pinch base of tail tog to flatten and whip stitch to body (Fig. 1). Tie off and weave in ends.

Tail Hair

Make 1.

Pinch tip of tail so that 3 sts are on top and 3 are underneath (Fig. 3).

Rnd 1: With I/9 (5.5mm) hook, join B through both layers of the first st, ch 10, sl st last ch to first ch to make first loop.

Rnd 2: Work 1 sc through both layers of the 2nd st, ch 14, sl st last ch to first ch to make 2nd loop.

Rnd 3: Work 1 sc through both layers of the 3rd st, ch 10, sl st last ch to first ch to make 3rd loop. Fasten off. Weave in ends.

Ellie the Elephant

Ellie the Elephant

Ellie watches over all of the smaller creatures in the kingdom. She uses her large and intimidating body to scare or push away anyone or anything that might endanger her little friends. Her specialty is crowd control. When Ellie sees a stampede forming, she gathers together any small animals nearby and diverts the stampede around them. Once all danger has passed, she continues patrolling the plains.

YARN

Super bulky (6) yarn in 2 colors; 432 yds (395m) of color **A** and 54 yds (50m) of color **D**

Medium (4) yarn in 3 colors; 85 yds (78m) of color **B**, 5 yds (5m) of color **C** and 3 yds (3m) of color **E**

*The project shown on page 88 uses Lion Brand Wool-Ease Thick & Quick (80% acrylic/20% wool, 106 yds [97m], 6 oz [170g]) in Charcoal (**A**) and Fisherman (**D**) and Lion Brand Vanna's Choice (acrylic, 170 yds [155m], 3.5 oz [100g]) in White (**B**), Black (**C**) and Beige (**E**).*

HOOKS AND NOTIONS

F/5 (3.75mm), G/6 (4mm) and I/9 (5.5mm) crochet hooks • Size 13 darning needle • Polyester fiberfill • Stuffing stick

GAUGE

5 hdc and 4 rows = 2" (5cm) using size I/9 (5.5mm) hook

FINISHED SIZE

Approx 10" (25cm) tall, 11" (28cm) long

Head

Make 1.

Row 1 (chin): With I/9 (5.5mm) hook and A, ch 7, TW, starting with 3rd ch from hook, 1 hdc in each of next 5 chs—5 sts.

Row 2: Ch 2, TW, 2 hdc in first st, 1 hdc in each of next 3 sts, 2 hdc in last st—7 sts.

Row 3: Ch 2, TW, 2 hdc in first st, 1 hdc in each of next 5 sts, 2 hdc in last st—9 sts.

Row 4: Ch 2, TW, 3 hdc in first st, 1 hdc in each of next 7 sts, 3 hdc in last st—13 sts.

Rows 5-6: Ch 2, TW, 1 hdc in each st to end of row—13 sts.

Row 7: Ch 2, TW, hdc first 2 sts tog, 1 hdc in each of next 9 sts, hdc last 2 sts tog—11 sts.

Row 8: Ch 2, TW, hdc first 2 sts tog, 1 hdc in each of next 7 sts, hdc last 2 sts tog—9 sts.

Row 9 (top of head): Ch 2, TW, hdc first 2 sts tog, 1 hdc in each of next 5 sts, hdc last 2 sts tog—7 sts. Beg working in rnds (without turning work between rnds) as follows, stuffing as work progresses.

Rnd 1: Ch 2, work 2 hdc in the end of Row 9, work 1 hdc each in the end of Rows 8-2, work 2 hdc in the end of Row 1, work 1 hdc in each of next 5 chs, work 2 hdc in the end of Row 1, work 1 hdc each in the end of Rows 2-8, work 2 hdc in the end of Row 9, work 1 hdc in each of next 3 sts, 2 hdc in next st, 1 hdc in each of next 3 sts, sl st last hdc to first hdc—35 sts.

Rnds 2-3: Ch 2, 1 hdc in each st to end of rnd, sl st last hdc to first hdc—35 sts.

Rnd 4: Ch 2, * 1 hdc in each of next 5 sts, hdc next 2 sts tog; rep from * four more times to end of rnd, sl st last hdc to first hdc—30 sts.

Rnd 5: Ch 2, 1 hdc in each st to end of rnd, sl st last hdc to first hdc—30 sts.

Rnd 6: Ch 2, * 1 hdc in each of the next 4 sts, hdc next 2 sts tog; rep from * four more times to end of rnd, sl st last hdc to first hdc—25 sts.

Rnd 7: Ch 2, * 1 hdc in each of next 3 sts, hdc next 2 sts tog; rep from * four more times to end of rnd, sl st last hdc to first hdc—20 sts.

Rnd 8: Ch 2, * 1 hdc in each of next 2 sts, hdc next 2 sts tog; rep from * four more times to end of rnd, sl st last hdc to first hdc—15 sts.

Rnd 9: Ch 1, * sc next 2 sts tog; rep from * six more times, sc in last st, sl st last sc to first sc—8 sts.

Rnd 10 (back of head): Ch 1, * sc next 2 sts tog; rep from * three more times, sl st last sc to first sc—4 sts. Fasten off, leaving a 10" (25cm) tail. Whip stitch opening closed. Tie off and weave in ends.

Body

Make 1.

Rnd 1: With I/9 (5.5mm) hook and A, stuffing as work progresses, ch 4, st st last ch to first ch to make a loop—4 chs.

Rnd 2: Ch 2, work 8 hdc into the center of the loop, sl st last hdc to first hdc—8 sts.

Rnd 3: Ch 2, 2 hdc in each st to end of rnd, sl st last hdc to first hdc—16 sts.

Rnd 4: Ch 2, 2 hdc in each st to end of rnd, sl st last hdc to first hdc—32 sts.

Rnd 5: Ch 2, * 1 hdc in each of next 3 sts, 2 hdc in next st; rep from * seven more times to end of rnd, sl st last hdc to first hdc—40 sts.

Rnd 6: Ch 2, * 1 hdc in each of next 4 sts, 2 hdc in next st; rep from * seven more times, sl st last hdc to first hdc—48 sts.

Rnds 7–8: Ch 2, 1 hdc in each st to end of rnd, sl st last hdc to first hdc—48 sts.

Rnd 9: Ch 2, * 1 hdc in each of the next 7 sts, 2 hdc in next st; rep from * five more times to end of rnd, sl st last hdc to first hdc—54 sts.

Rnds 10–17: Ch 2, 1 hdc in each st to end of rnd, sl st last hdc to first hdc—54 sts.

Rnd 18: Ch 2, * 1 hdc in each of next 7 sts, hdc next 2 sts tog; rep from * five more times to end of rnd, sl st last hdc to first hdc—48 sts.

Rnd 19: Ch 2, * 1 hdc in each of next 6 sts, hdc next 2 sts tog; rep from * five more times to end of rnd, sl st last hdc to first hdc—42 sts.

Rnd 20: Ch 2, * 1 hdc in each of next 5 sts, hdc next 2 sts tog; rep from * five more times to end of rnd, sl st last hdc to first hdc—36 sts.

Rnd 21: Ch 2, * 1 hdc in each of next 4 sts, hdc next 2 sts tog; rep from * five more times to end of rnd, sl st last hdc to first hdc—30 sts.

Rnd 22: Ch 2, * 1 hdc in each of next 3 sts, hdc next 2 sts tog; rep from * five more times to end of rnd, sl st last hdc to first hdc—24 sts.

Rnd 23: Ch 2, * 1 hdc in each of next 2 sts, hdc next 2 sts tog; rep from * five more times to end of rnd, sl st last hdc to first hdc—18 sts.

Rnd 24: Ch 2, * hdc next 2 sts tog; rep from * eight more times to end of rnd, sl st last hdc to first hdc—9 sts.

Rnd 25 (neck end): Ch 1, * sc next 2 sts tog; rep from * three more times, sc in next st, sl st last sc to first sc—5 sts. Fasten off, leaving a 10" (25cm) tail. Whip stitch opening closed. Tie off and weave in ends. Whip stitch back side of head to neck end of body (Fig. 1). Tie off and weave in ends.

Leg

Make 4.

Rnd 1: With I/9 (5.5mm) hook and A, leaving a 24" (61cm) tail, ch 25, sl st last ch to first ch to make a loop.

Rnds 2–7: Ch 2, TW, 1 hdc in each ch or st to end of rnd, sl st last hdc to first hdc—25 sts.

Rnd 8: Ch 2, TW, * 1 hdc in next st, 2 hdc in next st; rep from * eleven more times, 2 hdc in last st, sl st last hdc to first hdc—38 sts.

Rnd 9 (foot end of leg): Ch 2, TW, * 1 hdc in each of next 3 sts, 2 hdc in next st; rep from * eight more times, 1 hdc in each of next 2 sts, sl st last hdc to first hdc—47 sts. Fasten off.

Bottom of Foot

Make 4.

Rnd 1: With I/9 (5.5mm) hook and A, ch 4, TW, sl st last ch to first ch to make a loop.

Rnd 2: Ch 2, TW, work 12 hdc in center of loop, sl st last hdc to first hdc—12 sts.

Rnd 3: Ch 2, TW, 3 hdc in each st to end of rnd, sl st last hdc to first hdc—36 sts.

Rnd 4: Ch 2, TW, * 1 hdc in each of next 2 sts, 2 hdc in next st; rep from * ten more times, 1 hdc in each of next 3 sts, sl st last hdc to first hdc—47 sts. Fasten off, leaving a 36" (91cm) tail. Whip stitch botto of foot to end of leg. Stuff.

Toenail

Make 12.

Row 1: With F/5 (3.75mm) hook and B, leaving a 10" (25cm) tail, ch 6, TW, starting with 2nd ch from hook, work 1 sc in each ch to end of row—5 sts.

Rows 2–3: Ch 1, TW, 1 sc in each st to end of row—5 sts.

Row 4: Ch 1, sc next 2 sts tog, 1 sc in next st, sc next 2 sts tog—3 sts.

Row 5: Ch 1, TW, sc next 2 sts tog, 1 sl st in next st—2 sts. Fasten off. Whip stitch 3 nails to each foot, spacing them ½" (13mm) apart. Sew legs to body (Fig. 1). Tie off and weave in ends.

Trunk

Make 1.

Row 1 (tip of trunk): With I/9 (5.5mm) hook and A, leaving a 12" (30cm) tail, ch 6, TW, starting with 3rd ch from hook, 1 hdc in each of next 4 chs—4 sts.

Row 2: Ch 2, TW, 2 hdc in next st, 1 hdc in each of next 2 sts, 2 hdc in next st—6 sts.

Row 3: Ch 2, TW, 2 hdc in next st, 1 hdc in each of next 4 sts, 2 hdc in next st—8 sts. Beg working in rnds.

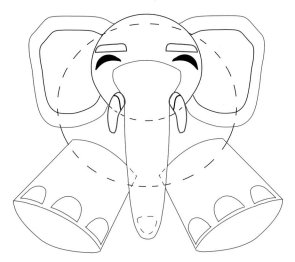

Figure 1 (front view)

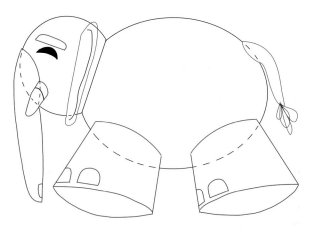

Figure 1 (side view)

Rnd 1: Ch 2, TW, 2 hdc in next st, 1 hdc in each of next 6 sts, 2 hdc in next st, sl st last hdc to first hdc—10 sts.

Rnd 2: Ch 2, TW, 1 hdc in each st to end of rnd, sl st last hdc to first hdc—10 sts.

Rnd 3: Ch 2, TW, 2 hdc in next st, 1 hdc in each of next 4 sts, 2 hdc in next st, 1 hdc in each of next 4 sts, sl st last hdc to first hdc—12 sts.

Rnds 4–9: Ch 2, TW, 1 hdc in each st to end of rnd, sl st last hdc to first hdc—12 sts.

Rnd 10: Ch 1, TW, 1 sl st in each of next 2 sts, 1 sc in next st, 1 hdc in next 6 sts, 1 sc in next st, 1 sl st in each of next 2 sts, sl st last st to first st—12 sts.

Rnd 11: Ch 1, 1 sl st in each of next 2 sts, 1 sc in next st, * 2 hdc in next st, 1 hdc in next st; rep from * two more times, sc in next st, 1 sl st in each of next 2 sts, sl st last st to first st to end rnd—15 sts. Beg working in rows.

Row 1: Ch 1, TW, 1 sl st in each of next 3 sts, 2 hdc in next 9 sts, 1 sl st in each of next 3 sts—24 sts. Fasten off, leaving a 20" (51cm) tail. Set aside.

Tip of Trunk Insert

Make 1.

Rnd 1: With I/9 (5.5mm) hook and D, ch 3, sl st last ch to first ch to make a loop.

Rnd 2: Ch 1, TW, work 8 sc in center of loop, sl st last sc to first sc—8 sts. Fasten off. Whip stitch tip of trunk insert to opening at tip of trunk (Fig. 1). Stuff trunk, whip stitch trunk to front of head (Fig. 1). Tie off and weave in ends.

Eye

Make 2.

Row 1 (lower edge): With G/6 (4mm) hook and E, leaving an 18" (46cm) tail, ch 5, TW, 1 sc in each of next 4 chs, starting with 2nd ch from hook—4 sts.

Row 2: Ch 2, TW, sc next 2 sts tog, sc next 2 sts tog—2 sts. Fasten off. Push up middle of the lower edge of the eye to curve, then whip stitch in place on face as shown (Fig. 1). Tie off and weave in ends.

Eyelid

Make 2.

Row 1 (base): With I/9 (5.5mm) hook and A, leaving a 12" (30cm) tail, ch 7, TW, 1 hdc in each of next 5 chs, starting with 3rd ch from hook—5 sts. Fasten off. Align base of eyelid on face, parallel to top of eye (Fig. 1), and whip stitch around, stuffing lightly. Tie off and weave in ends.

Inner Ear

Make 2.

Row 1 (base): With I/9 (5.5mm) hook and D, ch 10, TW, starting with 3rd ch from hook, 1 hdc in each of next 7 chs, 2 hdc in next ch—9 sts.

Row 2: Ch 2, TW, 2 hdc in first st, 1 hdc in each of next 7 sts, 2 hdc in next st—11 sts.

Row 3: Ch 2, TW, 1 hdc in each st to end of row—11 sts.

Row 4: Ch 2, TW, 2 hdc in first st, 1 hdc in each rem st to end of row—12 sts.

Row 5: Ch 2, TW, hdc first 2 sts tog, 1 hdc in each of next 8 sts, hdc last 2 sts tog—10 sts.

Row 6: Ch 2, TW, hdc first 2 sts tog, 1 hdc in each of next 4 sts, hdc next 2 sts tog, sc last 2 sts tog—7 sts.

Row 7: Ch 1, TW, sc first 2 sts tog, hdc next 2 sts tog, hdc next 2 sts tog, sc in last st—4 sts. Fasten off. Weave in ends.

Right Inner Ear Edging

With I/9 (5.5mm) hook, join A to first ch of Row 1 of one inner ear piece.

Row 1: Ch 2, TW, 1 hdc each in the end of Rows 1–4, 3 hdc in the end of Row 5, 1 hdc in the end of Row 6, 3 hdc in the end of Row 7, 1 hdc in each of next 4 sts, 1 hdc in the end of Row 7, 3 hdc in the end of Row 6, 1 hdc in the end of Row 5, 3 hdc in the end of Row 4, 1 hdc each in the end of Rows 3–1—26 sts. Fasten off, weave in ends.

Left Inner Ear Edging

With I/9 (5.5mm) hook, join A to last ch of Row 1 of other inner ear piece.

Row 1: Ch 2, 1 hdc each in the end of Rows 1–3, 3 hdc in the end of Row 4, 1 hdc in the end of Row 5, 3 hdc in the end of Row 6, 1 hdc in the end of Row 7, 1 hdc in each of the next 4 sts, 3 hdc in the end of Row 7, 1 hdc in the end of Row 6, 3 hdc in the end of Row 5, 1 hdc each in the end of Rows 4–1—26 sts. Fasten off, weave in ends.

Outer Ear

Make 2.

Row 1 (base): With I/9 (5.5mm) hook and A, leaving a 36" (91cm) tail, ch 12, TW, starting with 3rd ch from hook, 1 hdc in each of next 9 chs, 2 hdc in last ch—11 sts.

Row 2: Ch 2, TW, 2 hdc in first st, 1 hdc in each of next 9 sts, 2 hdc in last st—13 sts.

Rows 3–5: Ch 2, TW, 1 hdc in each st to end of row—13 sts.

Row 6: Ch 2, TW, 2 hdc in first st, 1 hdc in each rem st to end of row—14 sts.

Row 7: Ch 2, TW, hdc first 2 sts tog, 1 hdc in each of next 10 sts, hdc last 2 sts tog—12 sts.

Row 8: Ch 2, TW, hdc first 2 sts tog, 1 hdc in each of next 6 sts, hdc next 2 sts tog, sc last 2 sts tog—9 sts.

Row 9: Ch 1, TW, sc first 2 sts tog, hdc next 2 sts tog, hdc next 2 sts tog, 1 hdc in each of next 2 sts, sc in last st—6 sts. Fasten off. Align inner and outer ear and whip stitch around. Whip stitch ear to side of head (Fig. 1). Tie off and weave in ends.

Tusk

Make 2.

Rnd 1 (base): With I/9 (5.5mm) hook and A, leaving a 10" (25cm) tail, ch 4, sl st last ch to first ch to make a loop.

Rnd 2: Ch 1, 1 sc in each ch to end of rnd, sl st last sc to first sc—4 sts. Drop A, pick up B, tie off A and switch to F/5 (3.75mm) hook .

Rnd 3: Ch 1, 2 sc in each of next 4 sts, sl st last sc to first sc—8 sts.

Rnds 4–5: Ch 1, TW, 1 sc in each st to end of rnd, sl st last sc to first sc—8 sts.

Rnd 6: Ch 1, TW, * 1 sc in each of next 2 sts, sc next 2 sts tog; rep from * one more time to end of rnd, sl st last sc to first sc—6 sts.

Rnd 7: Ch 1, TW, 1 sc in each st to end of rnd, sl st last sc to first sc—6 sts.

Rnd 8: Ch 1, TW, * sc in next st, sc next 2 sts tog; rep from * one more time to end of rnd, sl st last sc to first sc—4 sts. Fasten off, leaving a 6" (15cm) tail. Whip stitch opening closed. Tie off and weave in ends. Lightly stuff tusk, whip stitch in place at base of trunk as shown (Fig. 1). Tie off and weave in ends.

Tail

Make 1.

Rnd 1 (base): With I/9 (5.5mm) hook and A, leaving a 12" (30cm) tail, ch 6, sl st last ch to first ch to make a loop.

Rnds 2–5: Ch 2, TW, 1 hdc in each ch/st to end of rnd, sl st last hdc to first hdc—6 sts.

Rnd 6: Ch 2, TW, * 1 hdc in next st, hdc next 2 sts tog; rep from * one more time to end of rnd, sl st last hdc to first hdc—4 sts.

Rnds 7–8: Ch 2, TW, 1 hdc in each st to end of rnd, sl st last hdc to first hdc—4 sts.

Rnd 9: Ch 1, TW, * hdc next 2 sts tog; rep from * one more time to end of rnd, sl st last hdc to first hdc—2 sts. Fasten off. Whip stitch base of tail to body (Fig. 1). Tie off and weave in ends.

Tail Hair

Make 1.

Rnd 1: With F/5 (3.75mm) hook and C, leaving a 6" (15cm) tail, ch 12, sl st last ch to first ch to make first loop.

Rnd 2: Ch 16, sl st last ch to first ch of first loop to make 2nd loop.

Rnd 3: Ch 22, sl st last ch to first ch of first loop to make 3rd loop.

Rnd 4: Ch 10, sl st last ch to first ch of first loop to make 4th loop.

Rnd 5: Ch 14, sl st last ch to first ch of first loop to make 5th loop. Fasten off, leaving a 6" (15cm) tail. Tie beg and ending tails tog. Thread both through darning needle and attach hair to tip of tail. Tie off and weave in ends.

See page 126 for the yarn colors used to make these versions.

CHAPTER 5

The Scientists:
Exotic Creatures

There are some animals that most of us will only see in real life if we visit our local zoo. However, because this particular foursome live in such remote locales, they have dedicated themselves to bringing the people of the world together through scientific research. The macaw strives to discover new ways of keeping us all healthier. The kangaroo tries to protect us from harm by keeping Mother Nature's wrath at bay. The panda and koala focus their efforts on exploring the unknowns of the paranormal and extraterrestrial worlds. But they all share a single purpose: to show us that what we thought we knew yesterday doesn't hold a candle to what we will know tomorrow.

Flora
the
Macaw

Flora the Macaw

Flora is a botanist who specializes in prehistoric plant life. There is legend of a life-giving singing flower, *Acapellae Purpura*, that once occupied the rainforests of South America. Known today as the "Purple Singer," the flower was believed to have great healing powers. You'd simply ask the flower to sing you a song, and within days of hearing its sacred tune, you would be cured of your illness. Flora believes that this flower still exists and has made it her life's work to find it!

YARN

Bulky (5) yarn in 3 colors; 185 yds (169m) of color **A**, 85 yds (78m) of color **D** and 85 yds (78m) of color **E**

Medium (4) yarn in 2 colors; 85 yds (78m) of color **B** and 85 yds (78m) of color **C**

*The project shown on page 95 uses Lion Brand Homespun (98% acrylic/2% polyester, 185 yds [169m], 6 oz [170g]) in Candy Apple (**A**), Sunshine State (**D**) and Montana Sky (**E**); and Lion Brand Vanna's Choice (acrylic, 170 yds [155m], 3.5 oz [100g]) in White (**B**) and Black (**C**)*

HOOKS AND NOTIONS

D/3 (3.25mm), E/4 (3.5mm) and I/9 (5.5mm) crochet hooks • Size 13 darning needle • Polyester fiberfill • Stuffing stick

GAUGE

5 hdc and 4 rows = 2" (5cm) using I/9 (5.5mm) hook and Color A

FINISHED SIZE

Approx 11" (28cm) tall

Head

Make 1.

Row 1 (face side): With I/9 (5.5mm) hook and A, ch 6, TW, starting with 3rd ch from hook, 1 hdc in each ch to end of row—4 sts. Beg working in rnds, stuffing as work progresses.

Rnd 1: Ch 2, TW, work 1 hdc in each of next 4 sts, work 2 hdc in the end of Row 1, work 1 hdc in each of the next 4 chs, work 2 hdc in the end of Row 1, sl st last hdc to first hdc—12 sts.

Rnd 2: Ch 2, TW, * 2 hdc in each of next 2 sts, 1 hdc in each of next 4 sts; rep from * one more time to end of rnd, sl st last hdc to first hdc—16 sts.

Rnd 3: Ch 2, TW, 1 hdc in each of next 5 sts, 2 hdc in each of next 2 sts, 1 hdc in each of next 6 sts, 2 hdc in each of next 2 sts, 1 hdc in next st, sl st last hdc to first hdc—20 sts.

Rnds 4–7: Ch 2, TW, 1 hdc in each st to end of rnd, sl st last hdc to first hdc—20 sts.

Rnd 8: Ch 2, TW, * 1 hdc in each of next 2 sts, hdc next 2 sts tog; rep from * four more times to end of rnd, sl st last hdc to first hdc—15 sts.

Rnd 9: Ch 2, TW, * 1 hdc in next st, hdc next 2 sts tog; rep from * four more times to end of rnd, sl st last hdc to first hdc—10 sts.

Rnd 10: Ch 2, TW, * hdc next 2 sts tog; rep from * four more times to end of rnd, sl st last hdc to first hdc—5 sts. Fasten off, leaving an 8" (20cm) tail. Whip stitch opening closed. Tie off and weave in ends.

Body

Make 1.

Rnd 1: With I/9 (5.5mm) hook and A, stuffing as work progresses, ch 4, sl st last ch to first ch to make a loop.

Rnd 2: Ch 2, TW, work 8 hdc in center of loop, sl st last hdc to first hdc—8 sts.

Rnd 3: Ch 2, TW, 2 hdc in each st to end of rnd, sl st last hdc to first hdc—16 sts.

Rnd 4: Ch 2, TW, * 1 hdc in next st, 2 hdc in next st; rep from * seven more times to end of rnd, sl st last hdc to first hdc—24 sts.

Rnd 5: Ch 2, TW, * 1 hdc in each of next 2 sts, 2 hdc in next st; rep from * seven more times to end of rnd, sl st last hdc to first hdc—32 sts.

Rnd 6: Ch 2, TW, * 1 hdc in each of next 7 sts, 2 hdc in next st; rep from * three more times to end of rnd, sl st last hdc to first hdc—36 sts.

Rnds 7–15: Ch 2, TW, 1 hdc in each st to end of rnd, sl st last hdc to first hdc—36 sts.

Rnd 16: Ch 2, TW, * 1 hdc in each of next 4 sts, hdc next 2 sts tog; rep from * five more times to end of rnd, sl st last hdc to first hdc—30 sts.

Figure 1 (front view)

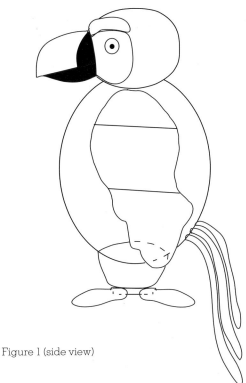

Figure 1 (side view)

Rnd 17: Ch 2, TW, * 1 hdc in each of next 3 sts, hdc next 2 sts tog; rep from * five more times to end of rnd, sl st last hdc to first hdc—24 sts.

Rnd 18: Ch 2, TW, * 1 hdc in each of next 2 sts, hdc next 2 sts tog; rep from * five more times to end of rnd, sl st last hdc to first hdc—18 sts.

Rnd 19: Ch 2, TW, * 1 hdc in next st, hdc next 2 sts tog; rep from * five more times to end of rnd, sl st last hdc to first hdc—12 sts.

Rnd 20 (head end): Ch 2, TW, * hdc next 2 sts tog; rep from * five more times to end of rnd, sl st last hdc to first hdc—6 sts. Fasten off, leaving an 8" (20cm) tail. Whip stitch opening closed. Tie off and weave in ends. Using a 36" (91cm) length of A, whip stitch head to body (Fig. 1). Tie off and weave in ends.

Eye Patch

Make 2.

Row 1: With E/4 (3.5mm) hook and B, leaving a 20" (51cm) tail, ch 6, TW, 2 hdc in 3rd ch from hook, 1 hdc in each of next 2 sts, 2 hdc in next st—6 sts.

Row 2: Ch 2, TW, 2 hdc in next st, 1 hdc in each of next 4 sts, 2 hdc in next st—8 sts.

Rows 3–6: Ch 2, TW, 1 hdc in each st to end of rnd—8 sts.

Row 7 (bottom edge): Ch 1, TW, hdc next 2 sts tog, 1 hdc in each of next 4 sts, hdc next 2 sts tog—6 sts. Fasten off. Whip stitch eye patch to side of face (Fig. 1). Tie off and weave in ends.

Eye

Make 2.

Rnd 1: With E/4 (3.5mm) hook and D, ch 3, sl st last ch to first ch to make a loop.

Rnd 2: Ch 1, TW, work 5 sc in center of loop, sl st last sc to first sc—5 sts. Fasten off, leaving a 15" (38cm) tail. With C, embroider a pupil in the center. Whip stitch eye to eye patch (Fig. 1). Tie off and weave in ends.

Eyelid

Make 2.

Row 1: With I/9 (5.5mm) hook and A, leaving a 15" (38cm) tail, ch 8, TW, starting with 3rd ch from hook, work 1 hdc in each st to end of row—6 sts. Fasten off. Whip stitch eyelid in place just above eye (Fig. 1), stuffing as work progresses. Tie off and weave in ends.

Side of Upper Beak

Make 2.

Row 1 (base): With E/4 (3.5mm) hook and C, ch 3, TW, 2 hdc in 3rd ch from hook—2 sts.

Row 2: Ch 2, TW, 2 hdc in each of next 2 sts—4 sts.

Row 3: Ch 2, TW, 2 hdc in each st to end of row—8 sts.

Rows 4–5: Cut C, join B, ch 2, TW, hdc next 2 sts tog, 1 hdc in each of next 5 sts, 2 hdc in next st—8 sts.

Row 6: Ch 2, TW, 2 hdc in next st, 1 hdc in each of next 3 sts, hdc next 2 sts tog, hdc next 2 sts tog—7 sts.

Row 7: Ch 2, TW, hdc next 2 sts tog, hdc next 2 sts tog, 1 hdc in each of next 2 sts, 2 hdc in next st—6 sts.

Row 8: Ch 2, TW, 2 hdc in each of next 2 sts, 1 hdc in each of next 2 sts, hdc next 2 sts tog—7 sts. Fasten off. Align pieces, whip stitch tog the upper curve (in B) only (Fig. 2). Tie off and weave in ends.

Lower Beak

Make 1.

Row 1 (tip): With E/4 (3.5mm) hook and C, ch 3, TW, 2 hdc in 3rd ch from hook—2 sts.

Row 2: Ch 2, TW, 2 hdc in each of next 2 sts—4 sts.

Row 3: Ch 2, TW, 2 hdc in each st to end of row—8 sts.

Row 4: Ch 2, TW, 2 hdc in next st, 1 hdc in each of next 6 sts, 2 hdc in next st—10 sts.

Rows 5–8 (base): Ch 2, TW, 1 hdc in each st to end of row—10 sts. Fasten off, leaving a 48" (122cm) tail. Whip stitch the bottom edges of the completed upper beak to the lower beak, lining up Row 1 of lower beak with tip of upper beak (Fig. 3) and leaving base unattached. Whip stitch open end of completed beak to head, stuffing as work progresses. Tie off and weave in ends.

Wing

Make 4.

Row 1 (base): With I/9 (5.5mm) hook and A, leaving a 12" (30cm) tail on 2 of the pieces, ch 5, TW, work 2 hdc in 3rd ch from hook, 1 hdc in next ch, 2 hdc in next ch—5 sts.

Row 2: Ch 2, TW, 2 hdc in next st, 1 hdc in each of next 3 sts, 2 hdc in next st—7 sts.

Row 3: Ch 2, TW, 2 hdc in next st, 1 hdc in each of next 5 sts, 2 hdc in next st—9 sts.

Row 4: Ch 2, TW, 1 hdc in each st to end of row—9 sts. Cut A, join D, leaving a 10" (25cm) tail.

Row 5: Ch 2, TW, 2 hdc in next st, 1 hdc in each of next 7 sts, 2 hdc in next st—11 sts.

Rows 6–8: Ch 2, TW, 1 hdc in each st to end of row—11 sts. At the end of Row 8, cut D, join E, leaving a 24" (61cm) tail of E.

Row 9: Ch 2, TW, 2 hdc in each of next 2 sts, 1 hdc in each of next 7 sts, hdc next 2 sts tog—12 sts.

Row 10: Ch 2, TW, hdc next 2 sts tog, 1 hdc in each of next 8 sts, 2 hdc in each of next 2 sts—13 sts.

Row 11: Ch 2, TW, 2 hdc in next st, 1 hdc in each of next 8 sts, hdc next 2 sts tog, hdc next 2 sts tog—12 sts.

Row 12: Ch 2, TW, hdc next 2 sts tog, 1 hdc in each of next 8 sts, hdc next 2 sts tog—10 sts.

Row 13: Ch 2, TW, hdc next 2 sts tog, 1 hdc in each of next 8 sts—9 sts.

Row 14: Ch 2, TW, hdc next 2 sts tog, 1 hdc in each of next 5 sts, hdc next 2 sts tog—7 sts.

Row 15: Ch 2, TW, 2 hdc in next st, 1 hdc in each of next 4 sts—6 sts.

Row 16: Ch 2, TW, * hdc next 2 sts tog; rep from * two more times to end of row—3 sts.

Row 17: Ch 2, TW, 1 hdc in next st, hdc next 2 sts tog—2 sts. Fasten off. Align one piece with a 12" (30cm) tail and one without and whip stitch around, using matching colors and joining new yarn where needed. Whip stitch base of completed wing in place on body (Fig. 1). Tie off and weave in ends.

Leg

Make 2.

Rnd 1: With I/9 (5.5mm) hook and A, leaving a 24" (61cm) tail, ch 18, sl st last ch to first ch to make a loop.

Rnds 2–3: Ch 2, TW, 1 hdc in each ch/st to end of rnd, sl st last hdc to first hdc—18 sts.

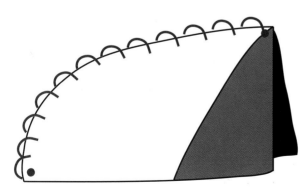

Figure 2 (upper beak)

Figure 3 (¾ bottom/back view of beak)

Rnd 4: Ch 2, TW, * 1 hdc in next st, hdc next 2 sts tog; rep from * five more times to end of rnd, sl st last hdc to first hdc—12 sts.

Rnd 5: Ch 2, TW, * hdc next 2 sts tog; rep from * five more times to end of rnd, sl st last hdc to first hdc—6 sts. Fasten off, leaving an 8" (20cm) tail. Whip stitch opening closed. Stuff. Whip stitch opening of leg to body (Fig. 1). Tie off and weave in ends.

Foot

Make 2.

Row 1: With D/3 (3.25mm) hook and C, ch 6, TW, work 2 hdc in 3rd ch from hook, 1 hdc in each of next 2 chs, 2 hdc in next ch—6 sts.

Row 2: Ch 2, TW, 2 hdc in next st, 1 hdc in each of next 4 sts, 2 hdc in next st—8 sts.

Rows 3-4: Ch 2, TW, 1 hdc in each st to end of row—8 sts.

Row 5: Ch 2, TW, hdc next 2 sts tog, 1 hdc in each of next 4 sts, hdc next 2 sts tog—6 sts.

Row 6: Ch 2, TW, hdc next 2 sts tog, 1 hdc in each of next 2 sts, hdc next 2 sts tog—4 sts. Fasten off, leaving a 20" (51cm) tail.

Claw

Make 8.

Rnd 1: With D/3 (3.25mm) hook and C, leaving a 12" (30cm) tail, ch 10, sl st last ch to first ch to make a loop.

Rnds 2-7: Ch 2, TW, 1 hdc in each ch/st to end of rnd, sl st last hdc to first hdc—10 sts.

Rnd 8: Ch 2, TW, * 1 hdc in each of next 3 sts, hdc next 2 sts tog; rep from * one more time, sl st last hdc to first hdc—8 sts.

Rnd 9: Ch 2, TW, * 1 hdc in each of next 2 sts, hdc next 2 sts tog; rep from * one more time, sl st last hdc to first hdc—6 sts. Fasten off, leaving a 5" (13cm) tail. Whip stitch opening closed. Tie off and weave in end. Stuff. Pinch open end closed and whip stitch to straight edge of foot (Fig. 4). Whip stitch foot to end of leg (Fig. 1). Tie off and weave in ends.

Upper Tail

Make 1.

Row 1: With I/9 (5.5mm) hook and E, leaving a 12" (30cm) tail, ch 6, TW, starting with 3rd ch from hook, 1 hdc in each of next 4 chs—4 sts.

Rows 2-12: Ch 2, TW, 1 hdc in each st to end of row—4 sts.

Row 13: Ch 1, TW, hdc next 2 sts tog, hdc next 2 sts tog—2 sts.

Row 14: Ch 1, TW, hdc next 2 sts tog—1 st. Fasten off. Whip stitch Row 1 to center of hind end (Fig. 1). Tie off and weave in ends.

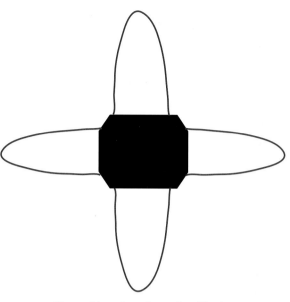

Figure 4 (top view of completed foot)

Middle Tail

Make 1.

Row 1: With I/9 (5.5mm) hook and A, leaving a 12" (30cm) tail, ch 8, TW, starting with 3rd ch from hook, 1 hdc in each of next 6 chs—6 sts.

Rows 2-14: Ch 2, TW, 1 hdc in each st to end of row—6 sts.

Row 15: Ch 1, TW, hdc next 2 sts tog, 1 hdc in each of next 2 sts, hdc next 2 sts tog—4 sts.

Row 16: Ch 1, TW, hdc next 2 sts tog, hdc next 2 sts tog—2 sts.

Row 17: Ch 1, TW, hdc next 2 sts tog—1 st. Fasten off. Whip stitch Row 1 to body centered just below upper tail (Fig. 1). Tie off and weave in ends.

Lower Tail

Make 1.

Row 1: With I/9 (5.5mm) hook and E, leaving a 12" (30cm) tail, ch 10, TW, starting with 3rd ch from hook, 1 hdc in each of next 8 chs—8 sts.

Rows 2-16: Ch 2, TW, 1 hdc in each st to end of row—8 sts.

Row 17: Ch 1, TW, hdc next 2 sts tog, 1 hdc in each of next 4 sts, hdc next 2 sts tog—6 sts.

Row 18: Ch 1, TW, hdc next 2 sts tog, 1 hdc in each of next 2 sts, hdc next 2 sts tog—4 sts.

Row 19: Ch 1, TW, hdc next 2 sts tog, hdc next 2 sts tog—2 sts.

Row 20: Ch 1, TW, hdc next 2 sts tog—1 st. Fasten off. Whip stitch Row 1 to body centered just below middle tail (Fig. 1). Tie off and weave in ends.

Kaya
the
Kangaroo

Kaya the Kangaroo

Kaya is one of the world's leading seismologists. Commissioned by the Dingo Senate to research ways to prevent earthquakes, she has traveled extensively and collaborated with countless scientists to try and achieve this goal. She recently teamed up with an extremely controversial volcanist based in Hawaii. Their work has largely been kept confidential, but insiders say it is groundbreaking. (No pun intended!)

YARN

Bulky (5) yarn in 3 colors; 370 yds (339m) of color **A**, 185 yds (170m) of color **B** and 93 yds (85m) of color **C**

Medium (4) yarn in 1 color; 2 yds (2m) of color **D**

The project shown on page 100 uses Lion Brand Homespun (98% acrylic/2% polyester, 185 yds [169m], 6 oz [170g]) in Nouveau (A), Deco (B) and Black (C); and Lion Brand Vanna's Choice (acrylic, 170 yds [155m], 3.5 oz [100g]) in Black (D).

HOOKS AND NOTIONS

H/8 (5mm) crochet hook • Size 13 darning needle • Polyester fiberfill • Stuffing stick

GAUGE

5 hdc and 4 rows = 2" (5cm) using size H/8 (5mm) hook

FINISHED SIZE

Approx 15" (38cm) tall

Head

Make 1.

Row 1: With A, ch 6, TW, starting with 3rd ch from hook, work 1 hdc in each of next 4 chs—4 sts.

Rows 2–4: Ch 2, TW, 1 hdc in each of next 4 sts—4 sts. Beg working in rnds, stuffing as work progresses.

Rnd 1: Ch 2, TW, 1 hdc in each of next 4 sts, work 1 hdc each in the end of Rows 4–1, 1 hdc in each of next 4 sts in Row 1, work 1 hdc each in the end of Rows 1–4, sl st last hdc to first hdc—16 sts.

Rnds 2–3: Ch 2, TW, 1 hdc in each st to end of rnd, sl st last hdc to first hdc—16 sts.

Rnd 4: Ch 2, TW, * 2 hdc in next st, 1 hdc in each of next 2 sts, 2 hdc in next st, ch 1; rep from * three more times to end of rnd, sl st last hdc to first hdc—24 sts.

Rnd 5: Ch 2, TW, * 1 hdc in each of next 6 sts, ch 1; rep from * three more times to end of rnd, sl st last hdc to first hdc—24 sts.

Rnd 6: Ch 2, TW, * 1 hdc in each of next 6 sts, ch 1; rep from * three more times to end of rnd, sl st last hdc to first hdc—24 sts.

Rnd 7: Ch 2, TW, * 1 hdc in each of next 3 sts, 2 hdc in next st, 1 hdc in each of next 2 sts, ch 1; rep from * three more times to end of rnd, sl st last hdc to first hdc—28 sts.

Rnd 8: Ch 2, TW, * 1 hdc in each of next 7 sts, ch 1; rep from *three more times to end of rnd, sl st last hdc to first hdc—28 sts.

Rnds 9–10: Ch 2, TW, 1 hdc in each st/ch to end of rnd, sl st last hdc to first hdc—28 sts.

Rnd 11: Ch 1, TW, * hdc next 2 sts tog, 1 hdc in each of next 2 sts; rep from * six more times to end of rnd, sl st last hdc to first hdc—21 sts.

Rnd 12: Ch 1, TW, * hdc next 2 sts tog, 1 hdc in next st; rep from * six more times to end of rnd, sl st last hdc to first hdc—14 sts.

Rnd 13: Ch 1, TW, * hdc next 2 sts tog; rep from * six more times to end of rnd, sl st last hdc to first hdc—7 sts. Fasten off, leaving an 8" (20cm) tail. Whip stitch opening closed. Tie off and weave in ends.

Body

Rnd 1 (head end): With A, leaving a 24" (61cm) tail and stuffing as work progresses, ch 25, sl st last ch to first ch.

Rnds 2–5: Ch 2, TW, 1 hdc in each ch/st to end of rnd, sl st last hdc to first hdc—25 sts.

Rnd 6: Ch 2, TW, * 1 hdc in each of next 4 sts, 2 hdc in next st; rep from * four more times to end of rnd, sl st last hdc to first hdc—30 sts.

Rnds 7–8: Ch 2, TW, 1 hdc in each st to end of rnd, sl st last hdc to first hdc—30 sts.

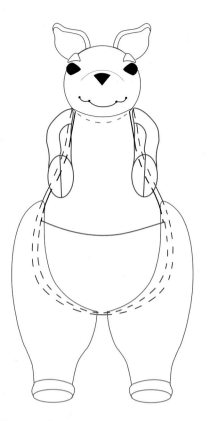

Figure 1 (front view)

Figure 1 (side view)

Rnd 9: Ch 2, TW, * 1 hdc in each of next 9 sts, 2 hdc in next st; rep from * two more times to end of rnd, sl st last hdc to first hdc—33 sts.

Rnd 10: Ch 2, TW, 1 hdc in each st to end of rnd, sl st last hdc to first hdc—33 sts.

Rnd 11: Ch 2, TW, * 1 hdc in each of next 10 sts, 2 hdc in next st; rep from * two more times to end of rnd, sl st last hdc to first hdc—36 sts.

Rnd 12: Ch 2, TW, 1 hdc in each st to end of rnd, sl st last hdc to first hdc—36 sts.

Rnd 13: Ch 2, TW, * 1 hdc in each of next 5 sts, 2 hdc in next st; rep from * five more times to end of rnd, sl st last hdc to first hdc—42 sts.

Rnd 14: Ch 2, TW, * 1 hdc in each of next 6 sts, 2 hdc in next st; rep from * five more times to end of rnd, sl st last hdc to first hdc—48 sts.

Rnd 15: Ch 2, TW, * 1 hdc in each of next 7 sts, 2 hdc in next st; rep from * five more times to end of rnd, sl st last hdc to first hdc—54 sts.

Rnds 16–22: Ch 2, TW, 1 hdc in each st to end of rnd, sl st last hdc to first hdc—54 sts.

Rnd 23: Ch 2, TW, * 1 hdc in each of next 7 sts, hdc next 2 sts tog; rep from * five more times to end of rnd, sl st last hdc to first hdc—48 sts.

Rnd 24: Ch 2, TW, * 1 hdc in each of next 6 sts, hdc next 2 sts tog; rep from * five more times to end of rnd, sl st last hdc to first hdc—42 sts.

Rnd 25: Ch 2, TW, * 1 hdc in each of next 5 sts, hdc next 2 sts tog; rep from * five more times to end of rnd, sl st last hdc to first hdc—36 sts.

Rnd 26: Ch 2, TW, * 1 hdc in each of next 4 sts, hdc next 2 sts tog; rep from * five more times to end of rnd, sl st last hdc to first hdc—30 sts.

Rnd 27: Ch 2, TW, * 1 hdc in each of next 3 sts, hdc next 2 sts tog; rep from * five more times to end of rnd, sl st last hdc to first hdc—24 sts.

Rnd 28: Ch 2, TW, * 1 hdc in each of next 2 sts, hdc next 2 sts tog; rep from * five more times to end of rnd, sl st last hdc to first hdc—18 sts.

Rnd 29: Ch 1, TW, * hdc next 2 sts tog; rep from * eight more times to end of rnd, sl st last hdc to first hdc—9 sts.

Rnd 30: Ch 1, TW, * hdc next 2 sts tog; rep from * three more times, 1 sc in next st, sl st last sc to first hdc—5 sts. Fasten off, leaving an 8" (20cm) tail. Whip stitch opening closed. Tie off and weave in ends. Whip stitch head to body (Fig. 1). Tie off and weave in ends.

Eyes, Nose and Mouth

With darning needle and D, embroider eyes, nose and mouth as shown (Fig. 1).

Eyelid

Make 2.

Row 1: With A, leaving a 12" (30cm) tail, ch 6, TW, starting with 3rd ch from hook, work 1 sc in each of next 4 chs—4 sts.

Row 2: Ch 1, TW, sc next 2 sts tog, sc next 2 sts tog—2 sts. Fasten off. Align Row 1 of eyelid parallel to eye and whip stitch around, stuffing lightly (Fig. 1). Tie off and weave in ends.

Inner Ear

Make 2.

Row 1 (base): With B, ch 6, TW, starting with 3rd ch from hook, 1 hdc in each of next 4 chs—4 sts.

Row 2: Ch 2, TW, 2 hdc in next st, 1 hdc in each of next 2 sts, 2 hdc in last st—6 sts.

Row 3: Ch 2, TW, 2 hdc in next st, 1 hdc in each of next 4 sts, 2 hdc in last st—8 sts.

Row 4: Ch 2, TW, 1 hdc in each of next 8 sts—8 sts.

Row 5: Ch 2, TW, hdc next 2 sts tog, 1 hdc in each of next 4 sts, hdc next 2 sts tog—6 sts.

Row 6: Ch 1, TW, hdc next 2 sts tog, 1 hdc in each of next 2 sts, hdc next 2 sts tog—4 sts.

Row 7: Ch 1, TW, [hdc next 2 sts tog] twice—2 sts.

Row 8: Ch 1, TW, hdc next 2 sts tog—1 st. Fasten off, weave in ends.

Outer Ear

Make 2.

Row 1 (base): With A, leaving a 20" (51cm) tail, ch 6, TW, starting with 3rd ch from hook, 1 hdc in each of next 4 chs—4 sts.

Row 2: Ch 2, TW, 2 hdc in next st, 1 hdc in each of next 2 sts, 2 hdc in last st—6 sts.

Row 3: Ch 2, TW, 2 hdc in next st, 1 hdc in each of next 4 sts, 2 hdc in last st—8 sts.

Row 4: Ch 2, TW, 1 hdc in each of next 8 sts—8 sts.

Row 5: Ch 2, TW, hdc next 2 sts tog, 1 hdc in each of next 4 sts, hdc next 2 sts tog—6 sts.

Row 6: Ch 1, TW, hdc next 2 sts tog, 1 hdc in each of next 2 sts, hdc next 2 sts tog—4 sts.

Row 7: Ch 1, TW, [hdc next 2 sts tog] twice—2 sts.

Row 8: Ch 2, TW, 1 hdc in each st to end of row—2 sts.

Row 9: Ch 1, TW, hdc next 2 sts tog—1 st. Fasten off. Align outer and inner ear, whip stitch around. Whip stitch base of completed ear in place on head (Fig. 1). Tie off and weave in ends.

Belly

Make 1.

Row 1 (neck end): With B, leaving a 48" (122cm) tail, ch 6, TW, starting with the 3rd ch from the hook, work 1 hdc in each of next 4 chs—4 sts.

Row 2: Ch 2, TW, 2 hdc in next st, 1 hdc in each of next 2 sts, 2 hdc in next st—6 sts.

Row 3: Ch 2, TW, 1 hdc in each st to end of row—6 sts.

Row 4: Ch 2, TW, 2 hdc in next st, 1 hdc in each of next 4 sts, 2 hdc in next st—8 sts.

Rows 5–7: Ch 2, TW, 1 hdc in each st to end of row—8 sts.

Row 8: Ch 2, TW, 2 hdc in next st, 1 hdc in each of next 6 sts, 2 hdc in next st—10 sts.

Row 9: Ch 2, TW, 1 hdc in each st to end of row—10 sts.

Row 10: Ch 2, TW, 2 hdc in next st, 1 hdc in each of next 8 sts, 2 hdc in next st—12 sts.

Row 11: Ch 2, TW, 2 hdc in next st, 1 hdc in each of next 10 sts, 2 hdc in next st—14 sts.

Rows 12–18: Ch 2, TW, 1 hdc in each st to end of row—14 sts.

Row 19: Ch 1, TW, hdc next 2 sts tog, 1 hdc in each of next 10 sts, hdc next 2 sts tog—12 sts.

Row 20: Ch 1, TW, hdc next 2 sts tog, 1 hdc in each of next 8 sts, hdc next 2 sts tog—10 sts.

Row 21: Ch 1, TW, hdc next 2 sts tog, 1 hdc in each of next 6 sts, hdc next 2 sts tog—8 sts. Fasten off. Place belly on body with neck end under chin and whip stitch in place (Fig. 1). Tie off and weave in ends.

Pouch

Make 1.

Row 1 (lower edge): With B, ch 8, TW, starting with 3rd ch from hook, work 2 hdc in next ch, 1 hdc in each of next 4 chs, 2 hdc in next ch—8 sts.

Row 2: Ch 2, TW, 2 hdc in next st, 1 hdc in each of next 6 sts, 2 hdc in next st—10 sts.

Row 3: Ch 2, TW, 2 hdc in next st, 1 hdc in each of next 8 sts, 2 hdc in next st—12 sts.

Row 4: Ch 2, TW, 2 hdc in next st, 1 hdc in each of next 10 sts, 2 hdc in next st—14 sts.

Rows 5–11: Ch 2, TW, 1 hdc in each st to end of row—14 sts. Fasten off, leaving a 24" (61cm) tail. Align pouch with lower half of belly and whip stitch in place, leaving top edge open (Fig. 1). Tie off and weave in ends.

Outer Arm

Make 2.

Row 1 (paw end): With A, leaving a 36" (91cm) tail, ch 6, TW, starting with 3rd ch from hook, work 2 hdc in next st, 1 hdc in each of next 2 sts, 2 hdc in next st—6 sts.

Rows 2–3: Ch 2, TW, 1 hdc in each st to end of row—6 sts.

Row 4: Ch 1, TW, hdc next 2 sts tog, 1 hdc in each of next 2 sts, hdc next 2 sts tog—4 sts.

Rows 5–9: Ch 2, TW, 1 hdc in each st to end of row—4 sts.

Row 10: Ch 1, TW, hdc next 2 sts tog, 1 hdc in next st, 2 hdc in next st—4 sts.

Row 11: Ch 2, TW, 2 hdc in next st, 1 hdc in next st, hdc next 2 sts tog—4 sts.

Row 12: Ch 1, TW, hdc next 2 sts tog, 1 hdc in next st, 3 hdc in next st—5 sts.

Row 13: Ch 2, TW, 3 hdc in next st, 1 hdc in each of next 2 sts, hdc next 2 sts tog—6 sts.

Row 14: Ch 2, TW, 2 hdc in next st, 1 hdc in each of next 4 sts, 2 hdc in next st—8 sts.

Rows 15–16: Ch 2, TW, 1 hdc in each st to end of row—8 sts.

Row 17: Ch 1, TW, hdc next 2 sts tog, 1 hdc in each of next 4 sts, hdc next 2 sts tog—6 sts.

Row 18: Ch 1, TW, hdc next 2 sts tog, 1 hdc in each of next 2 sts, hdc next 2 sts tog—4 sts. Fasten off.

Inner Arm

Make 2.

Row 1 (paw end): With C, ch 6, TW, starting with 3rd ch from hook, 2 hdc in next ch, 1 hdc in each of next 2 chs, 2 hdc in next ch—6 sts.

Rows 2–3: Ch 2, TW, 1 hdc in each st to end of row—6 sts.

Row 4: Ch 1, TW, hdc next 2 sts tog, 1 hdc in each of next 2 sts, hdc next 2 sts tog—4 sts.

Row 5: Cut C, join B, ch 2, TW, 1 hdc in each st to end of row—4 sts.

Rows 6–9: Ch 2, TW, 1 hdc in each st to end of row—4 sts.

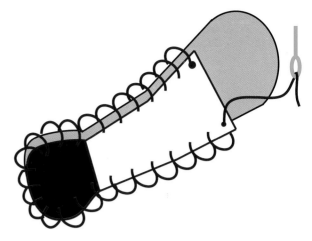

Figure 2

Row 10: Ch 1, TW, hdc next 2 sts tog, 1 hdc in next st, 2 hdc in next st—4 sts.

Row 11: Ch 2, TW, 2 hdc in next st, 1 hdc in next st, hdc next 2 sts tog—4 sts.

Row 12: Ch 1, TW, hdc next 2 sts tog, 1 hdc in next st, 3 hdc in next st—5 sts.

Row 13: Ch 2, TW, 3 hdc in next st, 1 hdc in each of next 2 sts, hdc next 2 sts tog—6 sts. Fasten off. Align outer and inner arm pieces so you clearly have one left and one right arm, and whip stitch around using A (Fig. 2). Stuff, adding extra stuffing to upper arm to define shoulder. Whip stitch shoulder opening in place on body (Fig. 1). Tie off and weave in ends.

Leg

Make 2.

Row 1 (hip end): With A, leaving a 48" (122cm) tail, ch 10, TW, starting with 3rd ch from hook, 2 hdc in next ch, 1 hdc in each of next 6 chs, 2 hdc in next ch—10 sts.

Row 2: Ch 2, TW, 2 hdc in next st, 1 hdc in each of next 8 sts, 2 hdc in next st—12 sts.

Row 3: Ch 2, TW, 2 hdc in next st, 1 hdc in each of next 10 sts, 2 hdc in next st—14 sts.

Row 4: Ch 2, TW, 2 hdc in next st, 1 hdc in each of next 12 sts, 2 hdc in next st—16 sts.

Rows 5–8: Ch 2, TW, 1 hdc in each st to end of row—16 sts.

Row 9: Ch 2, TW, 2 hdc in next st, 1 hdc in each of next 14 sts, 2 hdc in next st—18 sts.

Row 10: Ch 2, TW, 2 hdc in next st, 1 hdc in each of next 16 sts, 2 hdc in next st—20 sts.

Row 11: Ch 2, TW, 2 hdc in next st, 1 hdc in each of next 18 sts, 2 hdc in next st—22 sts. Beg working in rnds.

Rnd 1: Ch 14, sl st last ch to hdc at opposite end of Row 11 to make a rnd—36 sts.

Rnds 2–3: Ch 2, TW, 1 hdc in each ch/st to end of rnd, sl st last hdc to first hdc—36 sts.

Rnd 4: Ch 2, TW, * 1 hdc in each of next 4 sts, hdc next 2 sts tog; rep from * five more times to end of rnd, sl st last hdc to first hdc—30 sts.

Rnd 5: Ch 2, TW, * 1 hdc in each of next 3 sts, hdc next 2 sts tog; rep from * five more times to end of rnd, sl st last hdc to first hdc—24 sts.

Rnd 6: Ch 2, TW, * 1 hdc in each of next 2 sts, hdc next 2 sts tog; rep from * five more times to end of rnd, sl st last hdc to first hdc—18 sts.

Rnd 7: Ch 2, TW, * 1 hdc in each of next 4 sts, hdc next 2 sts tog; rep from * two more times to end of rnd, sl st last hdc to first hdc—15 sts.

Rnds 8–14: Ch 2, TW, 1 hdc in each st to end of rnd, sl st last hdc to first hdc—15 sts. Fasten off, leaving a 20" (51cm) tail. Stuff. Whip stitch hip opening of leg to body as shown (Fig. 1). (Note: If you happen to cover part of your pouch to get the correct alignment, just whip stitch right into the pouch if needed.) Tie off and weave in ends.

Top of Foot

Make 2.

Row 1 (heel end): With A, leaving a 36" (91cm) tail, ch 5, TW, starting with 3rd ch from hook, work 2 hdc in next st, 1 hdc in next st, 2 hdc in next st—5 sts.

Rows 2–16: Ch 2, TW, 1 hdc in each st to end of row—5 sts.

Row 17: Ch 1, TW, hdc next 2 sts tog, 1 hdc in next st, hdc next 2 sts tog—3 sts.

Rows 18–20: Ch 2, TW, 1 hdc in each st to end of row—3 sts. Fasten off.

Bottom of Foot

Make 2.

With C, work as for top of foot, omitting long tail at beg.

Align top and bottom of foot and whip stitch around, stuffing as work progresses. Whip stitch heel end of A side of foot to end of leg (Fig. 1). Tie off and weave in ends.

Tail

Make 1.

Rnd 1: With A, leaving a 36" (91cm) tail, ch 35, sl st last ch to first ch to make a loop.

Rnd 2: Ch 2, TW, 1 hdc in each ch to end of rnd, sl st last hdc to first hdc—35 sts.

Rnd 3: Ch 2, TW, 1 hdc in each st to end of rnd, sl st last hdc to first hdc—35 sts.

Rnd 4: Ch 2, TW, * 1 hdc in each of next 5 sts, hdc next 2 sts tog; rep from * four more times to end of rnd, sl st last hdc to first hdc—30 sts.

Rnds 5–8: Ch 2, TW, 1 hdc in each st to end of rnd, sl st last hdc to first hdc—30 sts.

Rnd 9: Ch 2, TW, * 1 hdc in each of next 4 sts, hdc next 2 sts tog; rep from * four more times to end of rnd, sl st last hdc to first hdc—25 sts.

Rnds 10–15: Ch 2, TW, 1 hdc in each st to end of rnd, sl st last hdc to first hdc—25 sts.

Rnd 16: Ch 2, TW, * 1 hdc in each of next 3 sts, hdc next 2 sts tog; rep from * four more times to end of rnd, sl st last hdc to first hdc—20 sts.

Rnds 17–22: Ch 2, TW, 1 hdc in each st to end of rnd, sl st last hdc to first hdc—20 sts.

Rnd 23: Ch 2, TW, * 1 hdc in each of next 2 sts, hdc next 2 sts tog; rep from * four more times to end of rnd, sl st last hdc to first hdc—15 sts.

Rnds 24–27: Ch 2, TW, 1 hdc in each st to end of rnd, sl st last hdc to first hdc—15 sts.

Rnd 28: Ch 2, TW, * 1 hdc in next st, hdc next 2 sts tog; rep from * four more times to end of rnd, sl st last hdc to first hdc—10 sts.

Rnds 29–31: Ch 2, TW, 1 hdc in each st to end of rnd, sl st last hdc to first hdc—10 sts.

Rnd 32: Ch 1, TW, * hdc next 2 sts tog; rep from * four more times to end of rnd, sl st last hdc to first hdc—5 sts.

Rnd 33: Ch 2, TW, 1 hdc in each st to end of rnd, sl st last hdc to first hdc—5 sts. Fasten off, leaving an 8" (20cm) tail. Whip stitch opening closed. Stuff. Whip stitch tail in place on body (Fig. 1). Tie off and weave in ends.

Spyro the Panda

Spyro the Panda

Spyro is the most highly sought-after paranormal researcher in all of China. His most recent case involved multiple sightings of a mist-like creature floating through a jungle. Many believed it was just an albino panda on a foggy day—until they moved in for a closer look, and it vanished into thin air! After Spyro was asked to investigate, he disappeared into the jungle for three days. When Spyro resurfaced, he left without saying a word. No one has reported seeing the mysterious jungle apparition since.

YARN

Bulky (5) yarn in 2 colors; 324 yds (297m) of color **A** and 324 yds (297m) of color **B**

*The project shown on page 106 uses Patons Shetland Chunky (75% Acrylic/25% Wool, 148 yds [136m], 3.5 oz [100g]) in Aran (**A**) and Black (**B**).*

HOOKS AND NOTIONS

H/8 (5mm) crochet hook • Size 13 darning needle • Polyester fiberfill • Stuffing stick

GAUGE

6 hdc and 5 rows = 2" (5cm) using size H/8 (5mm) hook

FINISHED SIZE

Approx 10" (25cm) tall

Head

Make 1.

Row 1: With A, ch 8, TW, starting with 3rd ch from hook, 2 hdc in next ch, 1 hdc in each of next 4 chs, 2 hdc in next ch—8 sts.

Row 2: Ch 2, TW, 2 hdc in next st, 1 hdc in each of next 6 sts, 2 hdc in next st—10 sts.

Row 3: Ch 2, TW, 2 hdc in next st, 1 hdc in each of next 8 sts, 2 hdc in next st—12 sts.

Row 4: Ch 2, TW, 1 hdc in each st to end of row—12 sts.

Row 5: Ch 2, TW, hdc next 2 sts tog, 1 hdc in each of next 8 sts, hdc next 2 sts tog—10 sts.

Row 6: Ch 2, TW, hdc next 2 sts tog, 1 hdc in each of next 6 sts, hdc next 2 sts tog—8 sts.

Row 7: Ch 2, TW, hdc next 2 sts tog, 1 hdc in each of next 4 sts, hdc next 2 sts tog—6 sts.

Row 8 (forehead end): Ch 2, TW, hdc next 2 sts tog, 1 hdc in each of next 2 sts, hdc next 2 sts tog—4 sts. Beg working in rnds, stuffing as work progresses.

Rnd 1: Ch 2, TW, 1 hdc in each of next 4 sts, 2 hdc in the end of Row 8, 1 hdc each in the end of Rows 7–2, 2 hdc in the end of Row 1, 1 hdc in each of the 8 sts of Row 1, 2 hdc in the end of Row 1, 1 hdc each in the end of Rows 2–7, 2 hdc in the end of Row 8, sl st last hdc to first hdc—32 sts.

Rnd 2: Ch 2, TW, * 1 hdc in each of next 3 sts, 2 hdc in next st; rep from * seven more times, sl st last hdc to first hdc—40 sts.

Rnd 3: Ch 2, TW, 1 hdc in each st to end of rnd, sl st last hdc to first hdc—40 sts.

Rnd 4: Ch 2, TW, * 1 hdc in each of next 8 sts, hdc next 2 sts tog; rep from * three more times to end of rnd, sl st last hdc to first hdc—36 sts.

Rnd 5: Ch 2, TW, * 1 hdc in each of next 4 sts, hdc next 2 sts tog; rep from * five more times to end of rnd, sl st last hdc to first hdc—30 sts.

Rnd 6: Ch 2, TW, * 1 hdc in each of next 3 sts, hdc next 2 sts tog; rep from * five more times to end of rnd, sl st last hdc to first hdc—24 sts.

Rnd 7: Ch 2, TW, * 1 hdc in each of next 2 sts, hdc next 2 sts tog; rep from * five more times to end of rnd, sl st last hdc to first hdc—18 sts.

Rnd 8: Ch 2, TW, * 1 hdc in next st, hdc next 2 sts tog; rep from * five more times to end of rnd, sl st last hdc to first hdc—12 sts.

Rnd 9: Ch 1, TW, * hdc next 2 sts tog; rep from * five more times to end of rnd, sl st last hdc to first hdc—6 sts. Fasten off, leaving an 8" (20cm) tail. Whip stitch opening closed. Tie off and weave in ends.

Figure 1 (front view)   Figure 1 (side view)

Snout

Make 1.

Row 1: With A, ch 4, TW, starting with 3rd ch from hook, 2 hdc in each of next 2 chs—4 sts.

Row 2: Ch 2, TW, 2 hdc in next st, 1 hdc in each of next 2 sts, 2 hdc in next st—6 sts.

Rows 3–5: Ch 2, TW, 1 hdc in each st to end of row—6 sts.

Row 6: Ch 2, TW, hdc next 2 sts tog, 1 hdc in each of next 2 sts, hdc next 2 sts tog—4 sts. Beg working in rnds.

Rnd 1: Ch 2, TW, 1 hdc in each of next 4 sts, 2 hdc in the end of Row 6, 1 hdc each in the end of Rows 5–2, 2 hdc in the end of Row 1, hdc next 2 sts of Row 1 tog, hdc next 2 sts tog, 2 hdc in the end of Row 1, 1 hdc each in the end of Rows 2–5, 2 hdc in the end of Row 6, sl st last hdc to first hdc—22 sts.

Rnds 2–7: Ch 2, TW, 1 hdc in each st to end of rnd, sl st last hdc to first hdc—22 sts. Fasten off, leaving a 20" (51cm) tail. Whip stitch snout to head (Fig. 1), stuffing as work progresses. Tie off and weave in ends.

Body

Make 1.

Row 1 (back of neck): With A, leaving a 36" (91cm) tail and stuffing as work progresses, ch 10, TW, starting with 3rd ch from hook, 2 hdc in next ch, 1 hdc in each of next 6 chs, 2 hdc in next ch—10 sts.

Row 2: Ch 2, TW, 2 hdc in next st, 1 hdc in each of next 8 sts, 2 hdc in next st—12 sts.

Row 3: Ch 2, TW, 2 hdc in next st, 1 hdc in each of next 10 sts, 2 hdc in next st—14 sts.

Row 4: Ch 2, TW, 2 hdc in next st, 1 hdc in each of next 12 sts, 2 hdc in next st—16 sts.

Row 5: Ch 2, TW, 2 hdc in next st, 1 hdc in each of next 14 sts, 2 hdc in next st—18 sts.

Row 6: Ch 2, TW, 2 hdc in next st, 1 hdc in each of next 16 sts, 2 hdc in next st—20 sts.

Row 7: Ch 2, TW, 2 hdc in next st, 1 hdc in each of next 18 sts, 2 hdc in next st—22 sts.

Row 8: Ch 2, TW, 2 hdc in next st, 1 hdc in each of next 20 sts, 2 hdc in next st—24 sts. Cut A, join B. Beg working in rnds.

Rnd 1: Ch 2, TW, 2 hdc in next st, 1 hdc in each of next 22 sts, 2 hdc in next st, ch 18, sl st last ch to first hdc—44 sts.

Rnd 2: Ch 2, TW, 1 hdc in each ch/st to end of rnd, sl st last hdc to first hdc—44 sts.

Rnd 3: Ch 2, TW, * 1 hdc in each of next 10 sts, 2 hdc in next st; rep from * three more times to end of rnd, sl st last hdc to first hdc—48 sts.

Rnd 4: Ch 2, TW, * 1 hdc in each of next 7 sts, 2 hdc in next st; rep from * five more times to end of rnd, sl st last hdc to first hdc—54 sts.

Rnds 5–7: Ch 2, TW, 1 hdc in each st to end of rnd, sl st last hdc to first hdc—54 sts.

Rnd 8: Cut B, join A, ch 2, TW, 1 hdc in each st to end of rnd, sl st last hdc to first hdc—54 sts.

Rnd 9: Ch 2, TW, * 1 hdc in each of next 17 sts, 2 hdc in next st; rep from * two more times to end of rnd, sl st last hdc to first hdc—57 sts.

Rnds 10–12: Ch 2, TW, 1 hdc in each st to end of rnd, sl st last hdc to first hdc—57 sts.

Rnd 13: Ch 2, TW, * 1 hdc in each of next 18 sts, 2 hdc in next st; rep from * two more times to end of rnd, sl st last hdc to first hdc—60 sts.

Rnds 14–19: Ch 2, TW, 1 hdc in each st to end of rnd, sl st last hdc to first hdc—60 sts.

Rnd 20: Ch 2, TW, * 1 hdc in each of next 8 sts, hdc next 2 sts tog; rep from * five more times to end of rnd, sl st last hdc to first hdc—54 sts.

Rnd 21: Ch 2, TW, * 1 hdc in each of next 7 sts, hdc next 2 sts tog; rep from * five more times to end of rnd, sl st last hdc to first hdc—48 sts.

Rnd 22: Ch 2, TW, * 1 hdc in each of next 6 sts, hdc next 2 sts tog; rep from * five more times to end of rnd, sl st last hdc to first hdc—42 sts.

Rnd 23: Ch 2, TW, * 1 hdc in each of next 4 sts, hdc next 2 sts tog; rep from * six more times to end of rnd, sl st last hdc to first hdc—35 sts.

Rnd 24: Ch 2, TW, * 1 hdc in each of next 3 sts, hdc next 2 sts tog; rep from * six more times to end of rnd, sl st last hdc to first hdc—28 sts.

Rnd 25: Ch 2, TW, * 1 hdc in each of next 5 sts, hdc next 2 sts tog; rep from * three more times to end of rnd, sl st last hdc to first hdc—24 sts.

Rnd 26: Ch 2, TW, * 1 hdc in each of next 4 sts, hdc next 2 sts tog; rep from * three more times to end of rnd, sl st last hdc to first hdc—20 sts.

Rnd 27: Ch 2, TW, * 1 hdc in each of next 3 sts, hdc next 2 sts tog; rep from * three more times to end of rnd, sl st last hdc to first hdc—16 sts.

Rnd 28: Ch 1, TW, * hdc next 2 sts tog; rep from * seven more times to end of rnd, sl st last hdc to first hdc—8 sts. Fasten off, leaving a 10" (25cm) tail. Whip stitch opening closed. Tie off and weave in ends. Whip stitch body to head, lining up Row 1 of body with the center of the top of the head to create a hunched back (Fig. 1). Tie off and weave in ends.

Eye Patch

Make 2.

Row 1 (top edge): With B, leaving a 15" (38cm) tail, ch 3, TW, starting with 2nd ch from hook, 2 sc in next ch, 1 sc in next ch—3 sts.

Row 2: Ch 1, TW, 1 sc in each of next 2 sts, 2 sc in next st—4 sts.

Row 3: Ch 1, TW, 2 sc in next st, 2 sc in next st, sc next 2 sts tog—5 sts.

Row 4: Ch 1, TW, sc next 2 sts tog, 1 sc in next st, 2 sc in each of next 2 sts—6 sts.

Row 5: Ch 1, TW, 1 sc in each st to end of row—6 sts.

Row 6: Ch 1, TW, 1 sc in each of next 4 sts, sc next 2 sts tog—5 sts.

Row 7: Ch 1, TW, sc next 2 sts tog, 1 sc in each of next 3 sts—4 sts.

Row 8: Ch 1, TW, 1 sc in each of next 2 sts, sc next 2 sts tog—3 sts.

Row 9: Ch 1, TW, sc next 2 sts tog, 1 sc in next st—2 sts. Fasten off. Whip stitch eye patch in place (Fig. 1). Tie off and weave in ends. With darning needle and A, embroider eye as shown.

Nose and Mouth

With darning needle and B, embroider nose and mouth as shown (Fig. 1).

Ear

Make 4.

Row 1 (base): With B, leaving a 20" (51cm) tail, ch 6, TW, starting with 3rd ch from hook, 2 hdc in next ch, 1 hdc in each of next 2 chs, 2 hdc in next ch—6 sts.

Rows 2–3: Ch 2, TW, 1 hdc in each st to end of row—6 sts.

Row 4: Ch 2, TW, hdc next 2 sts tog, 1 hdc in each of next 2 sts, hdc next 2 sts tog—4 sts.

Row 5: Ch 2, TW, hdc next 2 sts tog, hdc next 2 sts tog—2 sts. Fasten off. Align two ear pieces and whip stitch tog, then whip stitch base of completed ear to head (Fig. 1). Tie off and weave in ends.

Outer Arm

Make 2.

Row 1: With B, leaving a 24" (61cm) tail, ch 6, TW, 2 hdc in 3rd ch from hook, 1 hdc in each of next 2 chs, 2 hdc in next ch—6 sts.

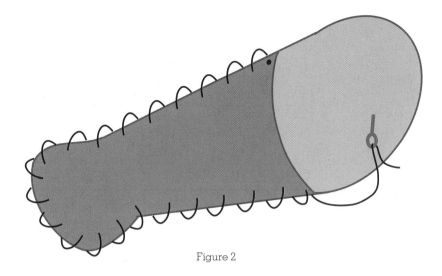

Figure 2

Row 2: Ch 2, TW, 2 hdc in next st, 1 hdc in each of next 4 sts, 2 hdc in next st—8 sts.

Row 3: Ch 2, TW, 2 hdc in next st, 1 hdc in each of next 6 sts, 2 hdc in next st—10 sts.

Rows 4–8: Ch 2, TW, 1 hdc in each st to end of row—10 sts.

Row 9: Ch 2, TW, hdc next 2 sts tog, 1 hdc in each of next 6 sts, hdc next 2 sts tog—8 sts.

Rows 10–13: Ch 2, TW, 1 hdc in each st to end of row—8 sts.

Row 14: Ch 2, TW, hdc next 2 sts tog, 1 hdc in each of next 4 sts, hdc next 2 sts tog—6 sts.

Rows 15–17: Ch 2, TW, 1 hdc in each st to end of row—6 sts.

Row 18: Ch 2, TW, 1 hdc in each of next 3 sts, 2 hdc in next st, 1 hdc in each of next 2 sts—7 sts.

Row 19: Ch 2, TW, 1 hdc in each of next 4 sts, 2 hdc in next st, 1 hdc in each of next 2 sts—8 sts.

Row 20: Ch 2, TW, 1 hdc in each st to end of row—8 sts.

Row 21 (paw end): Ch 2, TW, hdc next 2 sts tog, 1 hdc in each of next 4 sts, hdc next 2 sts tog—6 sts. Fasten off.

Inner Arm

Make 2.

Row 1: With B, leaving a 36" (91cm) tail, ch 12, TW, starting with 3rd ch from hook, 1 hdc in each ch to end of row—10 sts.

Row 2: Ch 2, TW, 1 hdc in each st to end of row—10 sts.

Row 3: Ch 2, TW, hdc next 2 sts tog, 1 hdc in each of next 6 sts, hdc next 2 sts tog—8 sts.

Rows 4–7: Ch 2, TW, 1 hdc in each st to end of row—8 sts.

Row 8: Ch 2, TW, hdc next 2 sts tog, 1 hdc in each of next 4 sts, hdc next 2 sts tog—6 sts.

Rows 9–11: Ch 2, TW, 1 hdc in each st to end of row—6 sts.

Row 12: Ch 2, TW, 1 hdc in each of next 3 sts, 2 hdc in next st, 1 hdc in each of next 2 sts—7 sts.

Row 13: Ch 2, TW, 1 hdc in each of next 4 sts, 2 hdc in next st, 1 hdc in each of next 2 sts—8 sts.

Row 14: Ch 2, TW, 1 hdc in each st to end of row—8 sts.

Row 15 (paw end): Ch 2, TW, hdc next 2 sts tog, 1 hdc in each of next 4 sts, hdc next 2 sts tog—6 sts. Fasten off. Align inner and outer arm pieces so you clearly have one left and one right arm and whip stitch each around (Fig. 2). Turn completed arm right side out. Stuff. Whip stitch shoulder opening of arm in place on body (Fig. 1). Tie off and weave in ends.

Outer Leg

Make 2.

Row 1: With B, leaving a 24" (61cm) tail, ch 6, TW, 2 hdc in 3rd ch from hook, 1 hdc in each of next 2 chs, 2 hdc in next ch—6 sts.

Row 2: Ch 2, TW, 2 hdc in next st, 1 hdc in each of next 4 sts, 2 hdc in next st—8 sts.

Row 3: Ch 2, TW, 2 hdc in next st, 1 hdc in each of next 6 sts, 2 hdc in next st—10 sts.

Row 4: Ch 2, TW, 2 hdc in next st, 1 hdc in each of next 8 sts, 2 hdc in next st—12 sts.

Rows 5–16: Ch 2, TW, 1 hdc in each st to end of row—12 sts.

Row 17: Ch 2, TW, hdc next 2 sts tog, 1 hdc in each of next 8 sts, hdc next 2 sts tog—10 sts.

Rows 18–21 (ankle end): Ch 2, TW, 1 hdc in each st to end of row—10 sts. Fasten off.

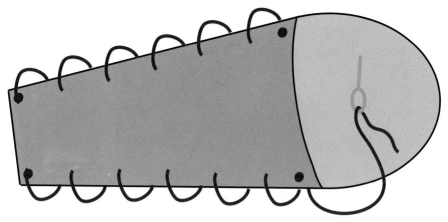

Figure 3

Inner Leg

Make 2.

Row 1: With B, leaving a 24" (61cm) tail, ch 14, TW, starting with 3rd ch from hook, 1 hdc in each ch to end of row—12 sts.

Rows 2–8: Ch 2, TW, 1 hdc in each st to end of row—12 sts.

Row 9: Ch 2, TW, hdc next 2 sts tog, 1 hdc in each of next 8 sts, hdc next 2 sts tog—10 sts.

Rows 10–13 (ankle end): Ch 2, TW, 1 hdc in each st to end of row—10 sts. Fasten off. Align ankle end of inner and outer leg and whip stitch sides tog, leaving ankle and hip ends open (Fig. 3). Turn completed leg right side out. Stuff. Whip stitch hip end of leg in place on body (Fig. 1). Tie off and weave in ends.

Foot

Make 4.

Row 1 (heel end): With B, leaving a 24" (61cm) tail, ch 6, TW, 2 hdc in 3rd ch from hook, 1 hdc in each of next 2 chs, 2 hdc in last ch—6 sts.

Row 2: Ch 2, TW, 2 hdc in next st, 1 hdc in each of next 4 sts, 2 hdc in next st—8 sts.

Rows 3–5: Ch 2, TW, 1 hdc in each st to end of row—8 sts.

Row 6: Ch 2, TW, 1 hdc in each of next 4 sts, 2 hdc in next st, 1 hdc in each of next 3 sts—9 sts.

Row 7: Ch 2, TW, 1 hdc in each st to end of row—9 sts.

Row 8: Ch 2, TW, 1 hdc in each of next 4 sts, 2 hdc in next st, 1 hdc in each of next 4 sts—10 sts.

Row 9: Ch 2, TW, 1 hdc in each st to end of row—10 sts.

Row 10: Ch 2, TW, hdc next 2 sts tog, 1 hdc in each of next 6 sts, hdc next 2 sts tog—8 sts.

Row 11: Ch 2, TW, hdc next 2 sts tog, 1 hdc in each of next 4 sts, hdc next 2 sts tog—6 sts. Fasten off. Align two foot pieces and whip stitch tog, stuffing as work progresses. Tie off and weave in ends. Whip stitch top layer of ankle end of foot to ankle end of leg (Fig. 1). Tie off and weave in ends.

Tail

Make 2.

Row 1 (base end): With A, leaving a 20" (51cm) tail, ch 10, TW, starting with 3rd ch from hook, 1 hdc in each ch to end of row—8 sts.

Rows 2–3: Ch 2, TW, 1 hdc in each st to end of row—8 sts.

Row 4: Ch 2, TW, hdc next 2 sts tog, 1 hdc in each of next 4 sts, hdc next 2 sts tog—6 sts.

Row 5: Ch 2, TW, hdc next 2 sts tog, 1 hdc in each of next 2 sts, hdc next 2 sts tog—4 sts. Fasten off. Align tail pieces and whip stitch tog, stuffing as work progresses. Whip stitch base end of tail to body (Fig. 1). Tie off and weave in ends.

Jaxson
the
Koala

Jaxson the Koala

Jaxson was once the top researcher for Australia's aerospace program. He theorized that stars were actually miniature planets. So, he sent eight wombat astronauts to the most stable star he could find. They beamed back beautiful camera images of a new world. Unfortunately, Jaxson lost the footage on his way to a symposium, and the wombats decided to stay on the star. Without evidence or witnesses, he was deemed "mad," shunned and is now trying to finance his own expedition to the star.

YARN

Super bulky (6) yarn in 2 colors; 330 yds (302m) of color **A** and 106 yds (97m) of color **B**

Bulky (5) novelty yarn in 1 color; 128 yds (117m) of color **C**

*The project shown on page 112 uses Lion Brand Wool-Ease Thick & Quick (80% acrylic/20% wool, 106 yds [97m], 6 oz [170g]) in Denim (**A**) and Black (**B**); and Lion Brand Fun Fur (polyester, 64 yds [59m], 1.75 oz [50g]) in White (**C**).*

HOOKS AND NOTIONS

I/9 (5.5mm) crochet hook • Size 13 darning needle • Polyester fiberfill • Stuffing stick

Note: For alternate version (shown on page 117), you will also use G/6 (4mm), with Color C only.

GAUGE

5 hdc and 4 rows = 2" (5cm) using size I/9 hook

FINISHED SIZE

Approx 12" (30cm) tall

Body

Make 1.

Rnd 1: With I/9 (5.5mm) hook and A, stuffing as work progresses, ch 3, sl st last ch to first ch to make a loop.

Rnd 2: Ch 2, TW, work 8 hdc in center of loop, sl st last hdc to first hdc—8 sts.

Rnd 3: Ch 2, TW, 2 hdc in each st to end of rnd, sl st last hdc to first hdc—16 sts.

Rnd 4: Ch 2, TW, 2 hdc in each st to end of rnd, sl st last hdc to first hdc—32 sts.

Rnd 5: Ch 2, TW, * 1 hdc in each of next 3 sts, 2 hdc in next st; rep from * seven more times to end of rnd, sl st last hdc to first hdc—40 sts.

Rnd 6: Ch 2, TW, 1 hdc in each st to end of rnd, sl st last hdc to first hdc—40 sts.

Rnd 7: Ch 2, TW, * 1 hdc in each of next 3 sts, 2 hdc in next st; rep from * nine more times to end of rnd, sl st last hdc to first hdc—50 sts.

Rnds 8-16: Ch 2, TW, 1 hdc in each st to end of rnd, sl st last hdc to first hdc—50 sts.

Rnd 17: Ch 2, TW, * 1 hdc in each of next 8 sts, hdc next 2 sts tog; rep from * four more times to end of rnd, sl st last hdc to first hdc—45 sts.

Rnds 18-19: Ch 2, TW, 1 hdc in each st to end of rnd, sl st last hdc to first hdc—45 sts.

Rnd 20: Ch 2, TW, * 1 hdc in each of next 7 sts, hdc next 2 sts tog; rep from * four more times to end of rnd, sl st last hdc to first hdc—40 sts.

Rnds 21-22: Ch 2, TW, 1 hdc in each st to end of rnd, sl st last hdc to first hdc—40 sts.

Rnd 23: Ch 2, TW, * 1 hdc in each of next 6 sts, hdc next 2 sts tog; rep from * four more times to end of rnd, sl st last hdc to first hdc—35 sts.

Rnd 24: Ch 2, TW, 1 hdc in each st to end of rnd, sl st last hdc to first hdc—35 sts.

Rnd 25: Ch 2, TW, * 1 hdc in each of next 5 sts, hdc next 2 sts tog; rep from * four more times to end of rnd, sl st last hdc to first hdc—30 sts.

Rnd 26: Ch 2, TW, * hdc next 2 sts tog; rep from * fourteen more times to end of rnd, sl st last hdc to first hdc—15 sts.

Rnd 27: Ch 2, TW, * hdc next 2 sts tog; rep from * six more times, 1 hdc in next st, sl st last hdc to first hdc—8 sts.

Rnd 28 (neck end): Ch 2, TW, * hdc next 2 sts tog; rep from * three more times to end of rnd, sl st last hdc to first hdc—4 sts. Fasten off, leaving an 8" (20cm) tail. Whip stitch opening closed. Tie off and weave in ends.

Head

Row 1 (face side): With I/9 (5.5mm) hook and A, ch 5, TW, starting with 3rd ch from hook, 1 hdc in each ch to end of row—3 sts.

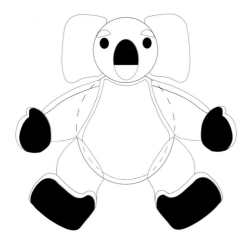

Figure 1 (front view)

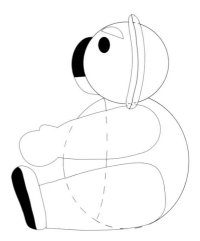

Figure 1 (side view)

Rows 2–3: Ch 2, TW, 1 hdc in each st to end of row—3 sts. Beg working in rnds, stuffing as work progresses.

Rnd 1: Ch 2, TW, 1 hdc in next st, 2 hdc in next st, 1 hdc in next st, work 1 hdc each in the end of Rows 3–1, 1 hdc in next ch, 2 hdc in next ch, 1 hdc in next ch, work 1 hdc each in the end of Rows 1–3, sl st last hdc to first hdc—14 sts.

Rnd 2: Ch 2, TW, 1 hdc in each st to end of rnd, sl st last hdc to first hdc—14 sts.

Rnd 3: Ch 2, TW, 2 hdc in next st, 1 hdc in next st, 2 hdc in next st, 1 hdc in next st, 2 hdc in each of next 2 sts, 1 hdc in next st, 2 hdc in next st, 1 hdc in next st, 2 hdc in next st, 1 hdc in next st, 2 hdc in each of next 2 sts, 1 hdc in next st, sl st last hdc to first hdc—22 sts.

Rnd 4: Ch 2, TW, * 2 hdc in next st, 1 hdc in each of next 4 sts, 2 hdc in each of next 2 sts, 1 hdc in each of next 3 sts, 2 hdc in next st; rep from * one more time to end of rnd, sl st last hdc to first hdc—30 sts.

Rnd 5: Ch 2, TW, 1 hdc in each st to end of rnd, sl st last hdc to first hdc—30 sts.

Rnd 6: Ch 2, TW, * 2 hdc in next st, 1 hdc in each of next 6 sts, 2 hdc in next st, 1 hdc in each of next 7 sts; rep from * one more time to end of rnd, sl st last hdc to first hdc—34 sts.

Rnds 7–10: Ch 2, TW, 1 hdc in each st to end of rnd, sl st last hdc to first hdc—34 sts.

Rnd 11: Ch 2, TW, 1 hdc in next st, * 1 hdc in each of next 6 sts, hdc next 2 sts tog; rep from * three more times, 1 hdc in next st, sl st last hdc to first hdc—30 sts.

Rnd 12: Ch 2, TW, * 1 hdc in next st, hdc next 2 sts tog; rep from * nine more times to end of rnd, sl st last hdc to first hdc—20 sts.

Rnd 13: Ch 2, TW, * 1 hdc in each of next 2 sts, hdc next 2 sts tog; rep from * four more times to end of rnd, sl st last hdc to first hdc—15 sts.

Rnd 14: Ch 2, TW, * 1 hdc in next st, hdc next 2 sts tog; rep from * four more times to end of rnd, sl st last hdc to first hdc—10 sts.

Rnd 15: Ch 1, TW, * hdc next 2 sts tog; rep from * four more times to end of rnd, sl st last hdc to first hdc—5 sts. Fasten off, leaving an 8" (20cm) tail. Whip stitch opening closed. Tie off and weave in ends. Position head on body so seam runs down bottom right side as you look at face, and whip stitch in place (Fig. 1). Tie off and weave in ends.

Nose

With darning needle and B, embroider an oblong nose covering approx two-thirds of the bump on front of head (Fig. 1).

Chin

Make 1.

Row 1: With I/9 (5.5mm) hook (G/6 [4mm] hook for alternate version on page 117) and C, leaving a 20" (51cm) tail, ch 10, TW, starting with 3rd ch from hook, 1 hdc in each ch to end of row—8 sts.

Row 2: Ch 2, TW, hdc next 2 sts tog, 1 hdc in each of next 4 sts, hdc next 2 sts tog—6 sts.

Row 3: Ch 2, TW, hdc next 2 sts tog, 1 hdc in each of next 2 sts, hdc next 2 sts tog—4 sts.

Row 4: Ch 2, TW, hdc next 2 sts tog, hdc next 2 sts tog—2 sts. Fasten off. Align Row 1 with bottom edge of nose and whip stitch in place as shown (Fig. 1). Tie off and weave in ends. If using novelty yarn, trim as desired.

Outer Ear

Make 2.

Row 1 (base): With I/9 (5.5mm) hook and A, leaving a 48" (122cm) tail, ch 10, TW, starting with 3rd ch from hook, 2 hdc in next st, 1 hdc in each of next 6 sts, 2 hdc in next st—10 sts.

Row 2: Ch 2, TW, 1 hdc in each of next 9 sts, 2 hdc in next st—11 sts.

Row 3: Ch 2, TW, 1 hdc in each st to end of row—11 sts.

Row 4: Ch 2, TW, 2 hdc in next st, 1 hdc in each of next 10 sts—12 sts.

Row 5: Ch 2, TW, hdc next 2 sts tog, 1 hdc in each of next 9 sts, 2 hdc in next st—12 sts.

Row 6: Ch 2, TW, 1 hdc in each of next 10 sts, hdc next 2 sts tog—11 sts.

Row 7: Ch 2, TW, hdc next 2 sts tog, 1 hdc in each of next 9 sts—10 sts. Fasten off. Weave in ends.

Inner Ear

Make 2.

Row 1 (base): With I/9 (5.5mm) hook (G/6 [4mm] hook for alternate version on page 117) and C, ch 12, TW, starting with 3rd ch from hook, 2 hdc in next st, 1 hdc in each of next 8 sts, 2 hdc in next st—12 sts.

Row 2: Ch 2, TW, 2 hdc in next st, 1 hdc in each of next 10 sts, 2 hdc in next st—14 sts.

Row 3: Ch 2, TW, 2 hdc in next st, 1 hdc in each of next 12 sts, 2 hdc in next st—16 sts.

Rows 4–7: Ch 2, TW, 1 hdc in each st to end of row—16 sts.

Row 8: Ch 2, TW, 1 hdc in each of next 15 sts, 2 hdc in next st—17 sts.

Row 9: Ch 2, TW, 1 hdc in each of next 15 sts, hdc next 2 sts tog—16 sts.

Row 10: Ch 2, TW, hdc next 2 sts tog, 1 hdc in each of next 13 sts, 2 hdc in next st—16 sts.

Row 11: Ch 2, TW, 1 hdc in each st to end of row—16 sts. Fasten off. Align inner and outer ear pieces so you clearly have one right and one left ear and whip stitch each around. Whip stitch base of completed ear to head (Fig. 1). Tie off and weave in ends.

Belly

Make 1.

Row 1 (neck end): With I/9 (5.5mm) hook (G/6 [4mm] hook for alternate version on page 117) and C, leaving a 48" (122cm) tail, ch 12, TW, starting with 3rd ch from hook, 2 hdc in next ch, 1 hdc in each of next 8 chs, 2 hdc in next ch—12 sts.

Row 2: Ch 2, TW, 1 hdc in each st to end of row—12 sts.

Row 3: Ch 2, TW, 2 hdc in next st, 1 hdc in each of next 10 sts, 2 hdc in next st—14 sts.

Row 4: Ch 2, TW, 1 hdc in each st to end of row—14 sts.

Row 5: Ch 2, TW, 2 hdc in next st, 1 hdc in each of next 12 sts, 2 hdc in next st—16 sts.

Row 6: Ch 2, TW, 1 hdc in each st to end of row—16 sts.

Row 7: Ch 2, TW, 2 hdc in next st, 1 hdc in each of next 14 sts, 2 hdc in next st—18 sts.

Rows 8–23: Ch 2, TW, 1 hdc in each st to end of row—18 sts.

Row 24: Ch 2, TW, hdc next 2 sts tog, 1 hdc in each of next 14 sts, hdc next 2 sts tog—16 sts.

Row 25: Ch 2, TW, 1 hdc in each st to end of row—16 sts.

Row 26: Ch 2, TW, hdc next 2 sts tog, 1 hdc in each of next 12 sts, hdc next 2 sts tog—14 sts.

Rows 27–28: Ch 2, TW, 1 hdc in each st to end of row—14 sts. Fasten off. Position belly on body and whip stitch in place (Fig. 1). If desired, stuff belly before finishing seam. Tie off and weave in ends. If using novelty yarn, trim as desired.

Eye

Make 2.

Rnd 1: With I/9 (5.5mm) hook and B, ch 3, TW, sl st last ch to first ch to make a loop.

Rnd 2: Ch 1, TW, work 5 sc in center of loop, sl st last sc to first sc—5 sts. Fasten off, leaving a 12" (30cm) tail. Whip stitch eye to head (Fig. 1). Tie off and weave in ends.

Eyelid

Make 2.

Row 1: With I/9 (5.5mm) hook and A, leaving a 15" (38cm) tail, ch 6, TW, starting with 3rd ch from hook, 1 hdc in each ch to end of row—4 sts. Fasten off. Place eyelid parallel to eye and whip stitch around, stuffing as work progresses (Fig. 1). Tie off and weave in ends.

Outer Arm

Make 2.

Row 1 (shoulder end): With I/9 (5.5mm) hook and A, ch 6, TW, starting with 3rd ch from hook, 2 hdc in next ch, 1 hdc in each of next 2 chs, 2 hdc in next ch—6 sts.

Row 2: Ch 2, TW, 2 hdc in next st, 1 hdc in each of next 4 sts, 2 hdc in next st—8 sts.

Row 3: Ch 2, TW, 2 hdc in next st, 1 hdc in each of next 6 sts, 2 hdc in next st—10 sts.

Rows 4–11: Ch 2, TW, 1 hdc in each st to end of row—10 sts.

Row 12: Ch 2, TW, hdc next 2 sts tog, 1 hdc in each of next 6 sts, hdc next 2 sts tog—8 sts.

Row 13: Ch 2, TW, 1 hdc in each st to end of row—8 sts.

Row 14: Ch 2, TW, hdc next 2 sts tog, 1 hdc in each of next 4 sts, hdc next 2 sts tog—6 sts.

Row 15: Ch 2, TW, 1 hdc in each st to end of row—6 sts.

Row 16: Ch 2, TW, hdc next 2 sts tog, 1 hdc in each of next 2 sts, hdc next 2 sts tog—4 sts.

Row 17: Ch 2, TW, 2 hdc in next st, 1 hdc in each of next 2 sts, 2 hdc in next st—6 sts.

Row 18: Ch 2, TW, 2 hdc in next st, 1 hdc in each of next 4 sts, 2 hdc in next st—8 sts.

Row 19: Ch 2, TW, 2 hdc in next st, 1 hdc in each of next 7 sts—9 sts.

Row 20: Ch 2, TW, 1 hdc in each of next 7 sts—7 sts.

Row 21: Ch 2, TW, 1 hdc in each of next 5 sts, hdc next 2 sts tog—6 sts.

Row 22 (paw end): Ch 1, TW, hdc next 2 sts tog, 1 hdc in each of next 2 sts, hdc next 2 sts tog—4 sts. Fasten off, weave in ends.

Inner Arm

Make 2.

Row 1 (shoulder end): With I/9 (5.5mm) hook (G/6 [4mm] hook for alternate version on page 117) and C, ch 16, TW, starting with 3rd ch from hook, 1 hdc in each st to end of row—14 sts.

Rows 2–10: Ch 2, TW, 1 hdc in each st to end of row—14 sts.

Row 11: Ch 2, TW, hdc next 2 sts tog, 1 hdc in next 10 sts, hdc next 2 sts tog—12 sts.

Row 12: Ch 2, TW, 1 hdc in each st to end of row—12 sts.

Row 13: Ch 2, TW, hdc next 2 sts tog, 1 hdc in next 8 sts, hdc next 2 sts tog—10 sts.

Row 14: Ch 2, TW, 1 hdc in each st to end of row—10 sts.

Row 15: Ch 2, TW, hdc next 2 sts tog, 1 hdc in each of next 6 sts, hdc next 2 sts tog—8 sts.

Row 16: Ch 2, TW, 1 hdc in each st to end of row—8 sts.

Row 17: Ch 2, TW, hdc next 2 sts tog, 1 hdc in next 4 sts, hdc next 2 sts tog—6 sts. Cut C, join B (change to I/9 [5.5mm] hook for alternate version on page 117).

Row 18: Ch 2, TW, 1 hdc in next 6 sts—6 sts.

Row 19: Ch 2, TW, 2 hdc in next st, 1 hdc in each of next 4 sts, 2 hdc in next st—8 sts.

Row 20: Ch 2, TW, 2 hdc in next st, 1 hdc in each of next 7 sts—9 sts.

Row 21: Ch 2, TW, 1 hdc in each of next 7 sts—7 sts.

Row 22: Ch 2, TW, 1 hdc in each of next 5 sts, hdc next 2 sts tog—6 sts.

Row 23 (paw end): Ch 1, TW, hdc next 2 sts tog, 1 hdc in each of next 2 sts, hdc next 2 sts tog—4 sts. Fasten off, weave in ends. Align inner and outer arm pieces so you clearly have one right and one left arm and whip stitch around using A, stuffing as work progresses (Fig. 2). Whip stitch shoulder opening of arm to body (Fig. 1). Tie off and weave in ends.

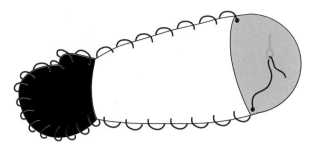

Figure 2

Leg

Make 2.

Row 1 (hip end): With I/9 (5.5mm) hook and A, leaving a 36" (91cm) tail, ch 6, TW, starting with 3rd ch from hook, 2 hdc in next st, 1 hdc in each of next 2 sts, 2 hdc in next st—6 sts.

Row 2: Ch 2, TW, 2 hdc in next st, 1 hdc in next 4 sts, 2 hdc in next st—8 sts.

Row 3: Ch 2, TW, 2 hdc in next st, 1 hdc in next 6 sts, 2 hdc in next st—10 sts.

Rows 4–8: Ch 2, TW, 1 hdc in each st to end of row—10 sts. Beg working in rnds.

Rnd 1: Ch 2, TW, 1 hdc in next 10 sts, ch 10, sl st last ch to first hdc to make a loop—20 sts.

Rnds 2–10 (ankle end): Ch 2, TW, 1 hdc in each st/ch to end of rnd, sl st last hdc to first hdc—20 sts. Fasten off, leaving a 24" (61cm) tail. Stuff. Whip stitch opening of hip end of leg in place on body (Fig. 1). Tie off and weave in ends.

Foot

Make 2 in A and 2 in B.

Row 1 (heel end): With I/9 (5.5mm) hook, leaving a 32" (81cm) tail on A pieces, ch 6, TW, 2 hdc in 3rd ch from hook, 1 hdc in each of next 2 chs, 2 hdc in next ch—6 sts.

Row 2: Ch 2, TW, 2 hdc in next st, 1 hdc in each of next 4 sts, 3 hdc in next st—9 sts.

Row 3: Ch 2, TW, 2 hdc in next st, 1 hdc in each of next 8 sts—10 sts.

Rows 4–9: Ch 2, TW, 1 hdc in each of next 7 sts—7 sts.

Row 10: Ch 1, TW, hdc next 2 sts tog, 1 hdc in each of next 3 sts, hdc next 2 sts tog—5 sts. Fasten off. Align A and B pieces so you clearly have one right and one left foot and whip stitch around using A, stuffing as work progresses. Whip stitch heel end of A side of foot to ankle end of leg as shown (Fig. 1). Tie off and weave in ends.

See page 126 for the yarn colors used to make these versions.

Yarn and Supplies

Yarn

All of the yarns used in this book are made by Lion Brand Yarn or Patons, and are available at most large chain craft stores in the U.S. If you can't find the color or yarn that you're looking for, you can order directly from the suggested vendor's website (see Yarn Resources on page 119).

If you would like your animal to be a little fluffier, hairier or smoother than the ones you see in this book, there is a whole world of different yarns to choose from. I like to go to my local craft store and feel the yarns and see the colors in person. Things are always a little different in person than they seem on the Internet or in a catalog.

If you don't like the texture of one of the yarns suggested here, you can switch it for a similarly weighted yarn. However, just because two yarns are labeled as being the same weight doesn't mean that they will make equally sized swatches. So, be sure to use the gauging guidelines to make a swatch. This will help you to keep the size of the animal as close to the suggested size as possible.

If you are making one of the animals as a gift for someone with sensitive skin, try substituting the suggested yarns with natural fiber yarns or even a chenille for an extra-plush snuggle buddy.

Crochet Hooks

I use whatever aluminum crochet hook I can find in my local craft stores. I have found that Boye is the most readily available brand.

Darning Needles

I have seen these referred to as many different things, including tapestry needles and yarn needles. You can find these in craft or chain department stores. I recommend buying four to six darning needles, as you may need them to hold body parts in place while you're whip stitching them together. If you don't need them for this purpose, two needles will do. It's always good to have a backup in case you lose the first one.

Stuffing and Stuffing Stick

Polyester fiberfill is available in most craft stores and a few chain department stores. If you're going to make more than one animal, I suggest getting the biggest bag you can find. It'll save you money in the long run and it will keep you from running out of a smaller bag when you're in the middle of a project.

I have noticed that a lot of bags of fiberfill that I buy come with a free stuffing stick inside. If the fiberfill that you buy doesn't include this, you can make your own—it's essentially just a $1/8$" (3mm) dowel cut down to about 10" (25cm) long. But, you don't even need to get that fancy. You can just use the eraser end of a pencil!

Animal Care

I don't suggest washing your completed animals by submersing them in water. Every yarn is different, and not all yarns are washable. Be sure to read the labels on each skein carefully for individual washing and care instructions. For washable yarns, I suggest spot cleaning with a damp washcloth, using the temperature of water suggested on the label.

Substituting Yarns

If you substitute yarn, be sure to select a yarn of the same weight as the yarn recommended for the project. Even after checking that the recommended gauge on the yarn you plan to substitute is the same as for the yarn listed in the pattern, be sure to crochet a swatch to ensure that the yarn and hook you are using will produce the correct gauge.

Weight	Lace (0)	Super Fine (1)	Fine (2)	Light (3)	Medium (4)	Bulky (5)	Super Bulky (6)
	0 LACE	**1** SUPER FINE	**2** FINE	**3** LIGHT	**4** MEDIUM	**5** BULKY	**6** SUPER BULKY
Weight	fingering, 10-count crochet thread	sock, fingering, 2ply, 3ply	sport, baby, 4ply	light worsted, DK	worsted, afghan, aran	chunky, craft, rug	super-chunky, bulky, roving
Crochet Gauge Range*	32–42 sts	21–32 sts	16–20 sts	12–17 sts	11–14 sts	8–11 sts	5–9 sts
Recommended Hook Range**	Steel*** 6, 7, 8 Regular hook B/1 (1.4mm–2.25mm)	B/1 to E/4 (2.25mm–3.5mm)	E/4 to 7 (3.5mm–4.5mm)	7 to I/9 (4.5mm–5.5mm)	I/9 to K/10½ (5.5mm–6.5mm)	K/10½ to M/13 (6.5mm–9mm)	M/13 and larger (9mm and larger)

Yarn Weight Guidelines

Since the names given to different weights of yarn can vary widely depending on the country of origin or the yarn manufacturer's preference, the Craft Yarn Council of America has put together a standard yarn weight system to impose a bit of order on the sometimes unruly yarn labels. Look for a picture of a skein of yarn with a number 0–6 on most kinds of yarn to figure out its "official" weight. The information in the chart above is taken from www.yarnstandards.com.

CROCHET HOOK CONVERSIONS

U.S. size	diameter (mm)
B/1	2.25
C/2	2.75
D/3	3.25
E/4	3.5
F/5	3.75
G/6	4
7	4.5
H/8	5
I/9	5.5
J/10	6
K/10½	6.5
L/11	8
M/13, N/13	9
N/15, P/15	10
P/Q	15
Q	16
S	19

Notes: * Gauge (what U.K. crocheters call "tension") is measured over 4" (10cm) in single crochet (except for Lace [0], which is worked in double crochet).

** US hook sizes are given first, with UK equivalents in parentheses.

*** Steel crochet hooks are sized differently from regular hooks—the higher the number, the smaller the hook, which is the reverse of regular hook sizing.

Yarn Resources

Lion Brand Yarn:
www.lionbrand.com

Patons:
www.patonsyarns.com

Stitches and Techniques

In this section we'll review the stitches and other techniques you need to know to complete the projects in this book.

Slip Knot

Before you can make anything, you have to get the yarn onto the hook, using a slip knot. Then you're ready to create!

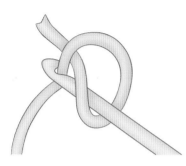

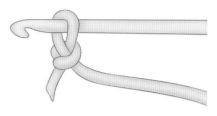

1 Grab the yarn at least 5" (13cm) away from the end. Make a loop, crossing the length of yarn that leads to the skein over the 5" (13cm) length. Insert your hook into the loop, wrap the yarn over the hook, and pull it back through.

2 Pull to tighten, so that the loop is pulled close, but not too tightly, around your hook.

Stitches Used in This Book

If you are a U.K. crocheter, please note the U.K. conversions for some of the U.S. crochet terms used in the book.

U.S. crochet term	U.K. crochet term
chain (ch)	chain (ch)
slip stitch (sl st)	single crochet (sc)
single crochet (sc)	double crochet (dc)
half double crochet (hdc)	half treble (htr)
double crochet (dc)	treble (tr)
popcorn stitch	popcorn stitch
running stitch	running stitch
whip stitch	whip stitch

Abbreviations

[ ] - work instructions within brackets as many times as directed
approx - approximately
beg - beginning
ch(s) - chain(s)
dc - double crochet
hdc - half double crochet
rem - remain(ing)
rnd(s) - round(s)
sc - single crochet
sl st - slip stitch
st(s) - stitch(es)
tog - together
TW - turn work

Chain (ch)

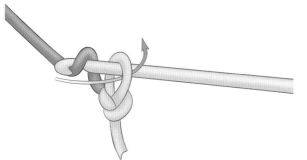

Wrap the yarn over your hook from back to front and pull it through the loop on your hook.

Slip Stitch (sl st)

Insert your hook into the indicated stitch/chain, wrap the yarn over your hook and pull it through the stitch/chain and the loop on the hook.

Single Crochet (sc)

1 Insert your hook into the indicated stitch/chain, wrap the yarn over the hook and pull it back through the stitch/chain (two loops remain on the hook).

2 Wrap the yarn over your hook again and pull it through these two loops to complete the stitch.

Single Crochet Decrease (sc next 2 sts tog)

Begin by working as for Step 1 of Single Crochet (two loops on the hook). Then, insert your hook into the following stitch/chain, wrap the yarn over your hook, and pull it through the stitch/chain only (three loops on the hook). Finally, wrap the yarn over the hook again and pull it through all three loops on the hook to complete the stitch.

Double Crochet (dc)

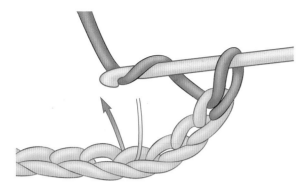

1 Wrap the yarn over your hook from back to front.

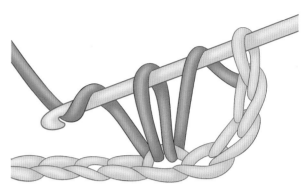

2 Insert your hook into the indicated stitch/chain, wrap the yarn over the hook and pull it through the first loop on the hook (three loops remain on the hook).

3 Wrap the yarn over your hook and pull it through the first two loops on the hook (two loops remain on the hook). Wrap the yarn over the hook once more and pull it through both loops on the hook to complete the stitch.

Double Crochet Decrease (dc next 2 sts tog)

Follow Steps 1–2 of Double Crochet. Wrap the yarn over the hook and pull it through two loops on the hook (half of the decrease is now made—two loops remain on the hook). Wrap the yarn over your hook and insert it into the next stitch or chain. Wrap the yarn over the hook and pull it through the first loop on the hook (four loops remain on the hook). Wrap the yarn over the hook and pull it through two loops on the hook. Wrap the yarn around the hook once more and pull through all three loops on the hook. Two double crochet stitches have been worked together and the stitch count is decreased by one stitch.

Half Double Crochet (hdc)

Wrap the yarn over your hook from back to front. Insert the hook into the indicated stitch/chain, wrap the yarn over the hook and pull it through the first loop on the hook (three loops remain on the hook). Wrap the yarn over your hook and pull it through all three loops on the hook.

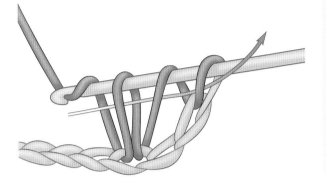

Half Double Crochet Decrease (hdc next 2 sts tog)

Wrap the yarn over your hook from back to front. Insert the hook into the indicated stitch/chain, wrap the yarn over the hook, and pull it through the first loop on the hook (three loops remain on the hook). Keeping these three loops on hook, wrap the yarn over your hook from back to front and insert the hook into the next stitch (five loops now on hook), wrap the yarn around the hook and draw through all five loops on the hook.

Changing Colors

Work the stitch to the last step (with two loops remaining on your hook).

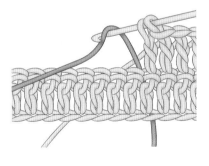

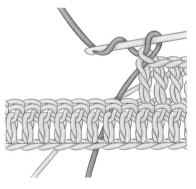

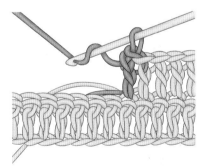

1 Drop the first color and pick up the second, being careful to leave enough of an end to weave in later.

2 With the new color, complete the stitch. If the first color is no longer needed, cut it, leaving a long enough end to tie off and weave in.

3 Continue in the new color.

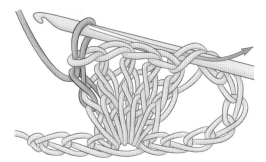

Popcorn Stitch (popcorn)

Work 5 hdc into indicated stitch/chain. Remove loop from hook, keeping loop intact. Insert hook in first hdc, place last loop back on hook and pull through first hdc. Pop stitch out with finger to finish. Take care to keep all stitches "popped" out to the same side.

Popcorn Stitch Decrease (1 popcorn decrease over next 2 sts)

Work Half Double Crochet Decrease over the first 2 stitches, then work the remaining 4 hdc in the second stitch—5 hdc worked over a total of 2 stitches. Complete as for popcorn.

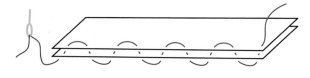

Running Stitch

Thread your yarn on a darning needle. Insert the needle down through both layers to be joined, then come back up approximately 1/2" (13mm) farther down the seam line. Move down another 1/2" (13mm) and insert the needle back through. Continue moving the needle up and down through the layers until the seam is complete.

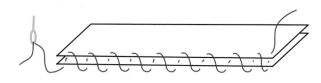

Whip Stitch

Thread your yarn on a darning needle. Holding the edges to be joined together, insert the needle down through both layers approximately 1/8" (3mm) in from the edges. Bring the needle back to the top and insert it down through again to create the next stitch, moving a bit down the seam line each time. Continue in this looping fashion for the rest of the seam.

Gauging Yarn Lengths

Lengths are given for yarn tails whenever they are needed for sewing pieces together later. Exact measuring of tails is not necessary, but take the suggestions as a guide. Where not given, be sure to leave a few inches (or several centimeters) when cutting yarn for weaving in the end. A helpful hint for estimating yarn amounts for seams: Wrap yarn around the distance to be seamed three times; it will almost always be enough.

Whip Stitching Pieces Together

There's no exact science to attaching body parts to the body. But, by using the photographs and illustrations throughout the book, you can see where the individual pieces go. Use pins or extra darning needles to hold pieces in place while sewing. Whip stitch the pieces together as described on page 124, then secure with a double knot before weaving in the end (or just drawing the end through the stuffed portion of the body to trap it).

Embroidering a Facial or Body Feature

Eyes, noses, mouths and even toenails can be created with simple embroidery. Thread your yarn on a darning needle and, using the photos and diagrams as a guide, make straight satin and back stitches to form the features. Secure the ends with a knot and draw ends into the center of the body to weave them in.

For example, with a nose, begin in the corner of the nose and work closely spaced satin stitches in progressively shorter lengths until a triangular nose is made. For eyes, do the same type of stitch in the shape desired. Finish the ends as described above.

For mouths, use a back stitch. Insert the needle at the top corner of the mouth. Pass the needle under the fabric for approximately one-third of the total desired length, then up through the fabric and back down at the starting point. Repeat this step once more. Bring the needle back up through the end of the first segment, over the fabric and down through the end of the second segment (two-thirds across). Bring the needle back up through the end of the first segment, across the fabric and insert it into the end of the second segment again. Complete the last segment as for the first segment. Finish the ends as described above.

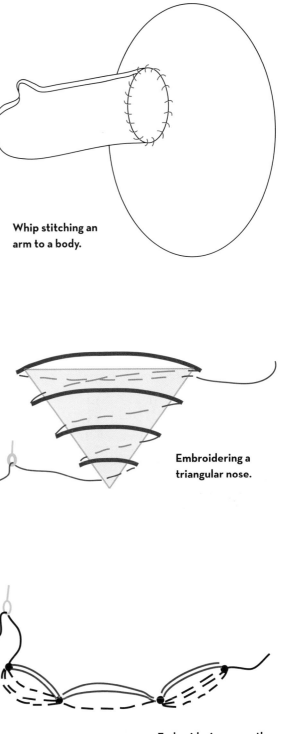

Whip stitching an arm to a body.

Embroidering a triangular nose.

Embroidering a mouth.

About the Author

Christine Lucas is a graduate of the Art Institute of Philadelphia with a degree in Industrial Design. She learned everything she knows about crochet from her mother, starting at the age of eight. She has built upon that foundation and has been designing her own blankets, purses, scarves and hats for more than twenty years. For more helpful hints on basic crochet and to see what Christine is currently creating, visit www.scarecroworiginals.com.

Yarns for Alternate Color Versions

To make the alternate versions that end each chapter, replace each project's yarn with the following colors in the same amounts and brands, unless otherwise noted. Or, try creating your own unique versions with comparable yarns in colors of your choice.

Snake: Sky Blue (**A**), Fisherman (**B**), Lemongrass (**C**), Black (**D**)
Squirrel: Apple Green (**A**), Sunshine State* (**B**), Black (**C**), Apple Green* (**D**), Colonial* (**E**)
Raccoon: Mustard** (**A**), Rust** (**B**), White** (**C**), Black (**D**), Black (**E**)
Snail: Apple Green (**A**), Colonial (**B**), Sunshine State (**C**), Grape (**D**), White (**E**)
Cow: Fisherman (**A**), Taupe (**B**), Magenta (**C**), Deep Earth (**D**)
Sheep: Dusty Blue (**A**), Sea Ice Tweeds (**B**), Black (**C**), Black (**D**)
Pig: Colonial Blue (**A**), Purple Mist (**B**), Black (**C**)
Horse: Fisherman (**A**), Sky Blue (**B**)
Penguin: Currant*** (**A**), White (**B**), Water Chestnut*** (**C**), Dusty Purple (**D**)
Octopus: Lemon (**A**), Regency (**B**), White (**C**), White (**D**)
Dolphin: Apricot‡ (**A**), Fisherman‡ (**B**), Beige (**C**)
Lion: Pumpkin‡ (**A**), Fisherman‡ (**B**), Fig‡ (**C**), Cranberry‡ (**D**), Black (**E**)
Giraffe: Windsor (**A**), Apple Green (**B**), Baroque (**C**), Black (**D**)
Hippo: Raspberry (**A**), Lemongrass (**B**) (NOTE: No Color C in this version.)
Elephant: Lemongrass (**A**), White (**B**), Black (**C**), Fisherman (**D**), Beige (**E**)
Macaw: Baroque (**A**), White (**B**), Black (**C**), Deco (**D**), Sierra (**E**)
Kangaroo: Colonial (**A**), Regency (**B**), Black (**C**), Apple Green* (**D**)
Panda: Aran (**A**), Deep Red Tweedsß (**B**)
Koala: Raspberry (**A**), Apricot (**B**), Sunshine State* (**C**)

* Lion Brand Homespun	‡ Lion Brand Wool-Ease Thick & Quick
** Lion Brand Vanna's Choice	ß Patons Shetland Chunky Tweeds
*** Patons Classic Wool	

Index

These and other fine F+W Media, Inc. titles are available at your local craft retailer, bookstore or online supplier, or visit our website at www.mycraftivitystore.com.

Crochet Now!
29 Projects for Baby, Home, Gifts and More
Candi Jensen

This companion book to the PBS show *Knit and Crochet Now!* features 29 crochet projects from designers including Drew Emborsky, Kriston Nicholas, Mary Jane Hall and Ellen Gormley. The included DVD features television segments for 12 crochet afghan squares.

paperback; 8.25" × 10.875"; 128 pages

Knitted Toy Tales
Irresistable Characters for All Ages
Laura Long

From bunnies and bears to Russian dolls and robots, readers will discover a unique range of over 20 adorable little knitted characters, each packed with personality and charm.

paperback; 8.25" × 10.875"; 128 pages

Crochet The Complete Guide
Jane Davis

The perfect reference guide for every crochet enthusiast, with over 200 stitch patterns and the basics for all types of crochet—from thread and bead crochet to cables. Includes customizable projects.

hardcover with concealed spiral; 5.625" × 7.625"; 256 pages

Why not add Shelldon the Sea Turtle to your underwater collection? Find this free bonus project online at

www.mycraftivitystore.com/Huggable_Crochet_patterns
(Please note: this link is case sensitive.)